A CENSUS OF BRITISH NEWSPAPERS
AND PERIODICALS, 1620-1800

A CENSUS OF
BRITISH NEWSPAPERS AND PERIODICALS
1620-1800

BY

R. S. CRANE AND F. B. KAYE

WITH THE ASSISTANCE OF

M. E. PRIOR

CHAPEL HILL, N. C., U. S. A.
THE UNIVERSITY OF NORTH CAROLINA PRESS
Agent for Great Britain and the Continent:
Cambridge University Press, Fetter Lane, London, E. C. 4.

1927

COPYRIGHT, 1927, BY
THE UNIVERSITY OF NORTH CAROLINA PRESS

PRINTED BY J. H. FURST COMPANY
BALTIMORE, MARYLAND

CONTENTS

	PAGE
INTRODUCTION	1
List of Libraries, with their Symbols	9
Other Abbreviations and Symbols	11
I. BRITISH PERIODICALS, 1620-1800, ACCESSIBLE IN AMERICAN LIBRARIES	13
II. BRITISH PERIODICALS, 1620-1800, NOT FOUND IN AMERICAN LIBRARIES	116
III. CHRONOLOGICAL INDEX	179
IV. GEOGRAPHICAL INDEX OF PERIODICALS PUBLISHED OUTSIDE OF LONDON	202

A CENSUS OF BRITISH NEWSPAPERS AND PERIODICALS, 1620-1800

Gratis quando datur equus, os non inspiciatur.

HE student of the intellectual and social history of England during the seventeenth and eighteenth centuries who wishes to study the periodical literature of the time can turn to a number of bibliographical guides. But even the most valuable of these—the *Tercentenary Handlist* and the *Union List of Serials,* now approaching completion in its provisional edition—still leave certain needs of the scholar uncared for. The *Union List,* because of its vast scope and its lack of any chronological arrangement, is not very convenient for the student of a special period; and the *Tercentenary Handlist,* which omits Scotch and Irish periodicals and limits itself to holdings in certain British libraries, does not, naturally, attempt completeness. It has seemed to us, therefore, that this present work would be of service to scholars.

We have tried, first, to give a two-fold bibliography, containing both a detailed finding-list of the precise holdings of the leading American libraries and a list of British periodicals apparently not found in these libraries. In these lists we have attempted to include all recognized types of periodicals—newspapers, magazines, reviews, essay sheets in the *Spectator* tradition, annuals, etc.[1]—from 1620 to 1800, and Scotch, Irish, and Welsh, as well as English publications. In the second place, we have supplied two indexes, the first chronological, so that the student may know just what periodicals were published during any particular year, and the second

---

[1] With the exception of almanacs, though a few of these may have been inadvertently included.

geographical, so that he may easily discover the output of periodicals for any particular place outside of London.

The finding-list of periodicals in American libraries has been compiled in the main from the reports of thirty-seven libraries.[2] It attempts to record not merely the possession of a periodical, but, wherever possible, the precise "run" possessed. In the case of rare periodicals, therefore, the student can often piece out a file of the journal from the scattered holdings.

In making this census we have had to rely chiefly on reports made to us by the various librarians and by certain friends of ours who have had access to these libraries: naturally, we have seen only a small proportion of the periodicals.[3] In spite, therefore, of the extraordinary amiability and conscientiousness of the librarians, there are inevitable errors and omissions in this list against which the user should be warned. (1) Since it is almost impossible for large libraries to single out all their periodicals, it is certain that our list of holdings is incomplete. (2) A few of the items reported are probably not periodicals. (3) As some of the periodicals had a complicated and obscure history, which the existing bibliographies do not untangle, and as the reports of holdings were not all equally full, there are certainly errors in description. Thus many changes in title may well have escaped us; in some instances continuations under a different title may be separated from the original periodical; and in some cases we may have joined what the publishers put asunder. Sometimes, again, we may have failed to discover that a periodical was published outside of London. There are also, no doubt, errors in dates, especially in periodicals of the seventeenth century, because of the difficulty of discriminating between Old and New Style in the reports. Finally, it has sometimes not been possible to be sure of the initial and terminal dates of periodicals,

---

[2] For a list of these libraries see below, pp. 9-11.

[3] We have also used the provisional edition of the *Union List of Serials* (A-O), from which we have taken a few titles, indicated on our list by the symbol U. L., as well as a few holdings of libraries not included in our original list. The *Checklist of Newspapers and Official Gazettes in the New York Public Library* (New York, 1915), the *List of Newspapers in the Yale University Library* (New Haven, 1916), and J. T. Gerould's *Sources of English History of the Seventeenth Century, 1603-1689, in the University of Minnesota Library* (Minneapolis, 1921) have likewise been consulted with profit.

especially of newspapers—to know when a run is complete; and in some cases our terminal dates are simply those of the longest run reported.

After all, however, this part of the census is fundamentally a convenience for the locating of periodicals, and anyone using it for that purpose will necessarily, in the periodicals themselves, have a check against its errors. To safeguard the user, however, we have indicated a query whenever we had specific cause for doubt. And we have, moreover, taken great pains to reduce error to a minimum. Queries have been sent again and again to libraries, and a good many of the more perplexing periodicals have been personally examined.[4] As a result, the finding-list, for all its undoubted faultiness, is more complete than any hitherto published for the period.

We did not at first intend to publish the supplementary list of periodicals not found in America. In the course of preparing the finding-list, however, it began to come into being, and we presently realized that it might be expanded into a bibliographical convenience and made a part of the chronological and geographical indexes. We therefore set ourselves to pillage bibliographies [5] and to secure

[4] This fact will explain some of our deviations from the usual bibliographical descriptions (*e. g.*, in the terminal dates of John Houghton's two *Collections*). We felt, in those cases, that we had more trustworthy data.

[5] The works which we have utilized in this way are:

Aitken, G. A. *Life of Richard Steele.* London, 1889. 2 vols.

Allnutt, W. H. "English Provincial Presses, Part III." *Bibliographica,* II (1896), 276-308.

Andrews, A. *The History of British Journalism, from the Foundation of the Newspaper Press in England to the Repeal of the Stamp Act in 1855.* London, 1859. 2 vols.

Austin, Roland. "Gloucester Journal." *Notes and Queries,* 12th series, X (1922), 261-64, 283-85.

Austin, Roland. "Robert Raikes, the Elder, & the 'Gloucester Journal.'" *The Library,* 3rd series, VI (1915), 1-24.

Barwick, G. F. "A List of Magazines of the Eighteenth Century." *Transactions of the Bibliographical Society,* X (1908-09), 109-40.

Bibliotheca Lindesiana. Catalogue of the Printed Books preserved at Haigh Hall, Wigan, Co. Pal. Lancast. Aberdeen, 1910. 4 vols.

Bourne, H. R. Fox. *English Newspapers. Chapters in the History of Journalism.* London, 1887. 2 vols.

Bowes, Robert. *A Catalogue of Books printed at or relating to the University Town and County of Cambridge from 1521 to 1893.* Cambridge, 1894.

4   *A Census of British Newspapers and Periodicals, 1620-1800*

information in the British Museum, including the Hendon Repository, and in the Bodleian Library. And the list grew and grew. Soon, as the difficulties accumulated, we felt like Frankensteins. For, from the nature of the case, this list could not be made as trustworthy as the finding-list. The finding-list contained only

British Museum. *Catalogue of Printed Books: Periodical Publications.* London, 1899-1900.
Brushfield, T. N. " Andrew Brice, and the Early Exeter Newspaper Press." *Report and Transactions of the Devonshire Association for the Advancement of Science, Literature, and Art,* XX (1888), 163-214.
Burn, J. H. *Catalogue of a Collection of Early English Newspapers and Essayists formed by the Late John Thomas Hope, Esq.* Oxford, 1865.
Catalogue of Periodicals contained in the Bodleian Library. Oxford, 1878-80. 2 vols.
Chalmers, George. *The Life of Thomas Ruddiman.* London, 1794.
Ch[isholm], H. "Newspapers: Sect. 2. British Newspapers." *Encyclopædia Britannica,* 11th ed., XIX (1911), 552-66.
Corns, A. R. *Bibliotheca Lincolniensis.* Lincoln, 1904.
Couper, W. J. *The Edinburgh Periodical Press.* Stirling, 1908. 2 vols.
Crossley, J. "'Works of the Learned.'" *Notes and Queries,* 1st series, VI (1852), 435-37.
Davidson, James. *Bibliotheca Devoniensis: A Catalogue of the Printed Books relating to the County of Devon.* Exeter, 1852.
Davies, Robert. *A Memoir of the York Press.* Westminster, 1868.
Dix, E. R. McC. *List of Books and Pamphlets printed in Strabane, Co. Tyrone, in the Eighteenth Century.* 2nd ed. Dundrum, 1908. ("Irish Bibliographical Pamphlets," No. 1.)
Dix, E. R. McC. *List of Books Newspapers and Pamphlets printed in Ennis, Co. Clare, in the Eighteenth Century.* Dublin, 1912. ("Irish Bibliographical Pamphlets," No. 8.)
Dix, E. R. McC. *List of Books, Pamphlets and Newspapers printed in Drogheda, Co. Louth, in the Eighteenth Century.* Dundalk, 1904. ("Irish Bibliographical Pamphlets," No. 3.)
Dix, E. R. McC. *List of Books, Pamphlets and Newspapers printed in Limerick from the Earliest Period to 1800.* Limerick, 1907. ("Irish Bibliographical Pamphlets," No. 5.)
Dix, E. R. McC. *List of Books, Pamphlets and Newspapers printed in Monaghan, in the Eighteenth Century.* Dundalk, 1906. ("Irish Bibliographical Pamphlets," No. 4.)
Dix, E. R. McC. *List of Books, Pamphlets, Newspapers, &c. printed in Londonderry, prior to 1801.* Dundalk, 1911. ("Irish Bibliographical Pamphlets," No. 7.)
Dix, E. R. McC. "Rare Ephemeral Magazines of the Eighteenth Century." *Irish Book Lover,* I (1910), 71-73.

items really in existence and could be checked by the reports of the libraries; but four-fifths of this list is, perforce, based on previous bibliographies of periodicals.

Only one who has worked with these bibliographies can realize the rich possibilities of confusion. Often it is impossible to tell whether two similar items in two bibliographies are the same or

Dix, E. R. McC. "The Earliest Periodicals published in Dublin." *Proceedings of the Royal Irish Academy*, 3rd series, VI (1900-02), 33-35.
Drake, Nathan. *Essays, Biographical, Critical, and Historical, illustrative of the Rambler, Adventurer, & Idler*. London, 1809-10. 2 vols.
Gilbert, H. M., and G. N. Godwin. *Bibliotheca Hantoniensis: A List of Books relating to Hampshire . . . with An Additional List of Hampshire Newspapers by F. E. Edwards*. Southampton, [1891.]
Graham, Walter. "Some Predecessors of the *Tatler*." *Journal of English and Germanic Philology*, XXIV (1925), 548-54.
Graham, Walter. *The Beginnings of English Literary Periodicals: A Study of Periodical Literature, 1665-1715*. New York, 1926.
Green, Emanuel. *Bibliotheca Somersetiensis*. Taunton, 1902. 3 vols.
Hyett, Francis A., and William Bazeley. *The Bibliographer's Manual of Gloucestershire Literature*. Gloucester, 1895-97. 3 vols.
Lee, William. "Forgotten Periodical Publications." *Notes and Queries*, 3rd series, IX (1866), 53-64.
Lee, William. "Periodical Publications during the Twenty Years 1712 to 1732." *Notes and Queries*, 3rd series, IX (1866), 72-75 and 92-95. Cf. also 3rd series, IX, 164, 268, and X, 134.
Madden, Richard Robert. *The History of Irish Periodical Literature, from the End of the 17th to the Middle of the 19th Century*. London, 1867. 2 vols.
Marr, G. S. *The Periodical Essayists of the Eighteenth Century, with Illustrative Extracts from the Rarer Periodicals*. London, 1923.
Mayo, Charles H. *Bibliotheca Dorsetiensis*. London, 1885.
McCutcheon, R. P. "The Beginnings of Book-reviewing in English Periodicals." *Publications of the Modern Language Association*, XXXVII (1922), 691-706.
Muddiman, J. G. *The King's Journalist, 1659-1689: Studies in the Reign of Charles II*. London, [1923.]
Nichols, John. *Literary Anecdotes of the Eighteenth Century*. London, 1812-16. Vols. I, IV, VIII, IX.
Norris, Herbert E. "St. Ives Mercury." *Notes and Queries*, 11th series, II (1910), 481-82.
"Old Newspapers." [Notes by various correspondents.] *Notes and Queries*, 12th series, XI (1922), 108, 157, 177.
Pierpoint, Robert. "Newcastle and Durham Papers." *Notes and Queries*, 12th series, XII (1923), 254.

not; some give dates Old Style, some New—and fail to tell you which; some standardize titles one way, some another; and in some bibliographies of periodicals—for example, the *Catalogue of Periodicals contained in the Bodleian Library*—many of the entries are not periodicals at all.[5a] As we realized on what authorities our list had sometimes to be based and tried to judge between two sources of information each of which might be thoroughly untrustworthy, we have often felt anxiety lest our efforts to resolve the confusion might not be adding "fat pollutions of our own."

There are two special difficulties in a list such as this. First, there are the "ghosts"—periodicals which get recorded, but which do not exist. A confusion of dates, a miswriting of a title, an error as to editors or printers—and a "ghost" walks. For exorcism many careful monographs are needed; and some of the wraiths

Plomer, H. R. *A Dictionary of the Booksellers and Printers who were at Work in England, Scotland and Ireland from 1641 to 1667*. London, 1907.

Plomer, H. R. *A Dictionary of the Printers and Booksellers who were at Work in England, Scotland and Ireland from 1668 to 1725*. Oxford, 1922.

Roberts, William. "The 'Gentleman's Magazine' and its Rivals." *Athenæum*, Oct. 26, 1889, p. 560.

Stevens, D. H. *Party Politics and English Journalism, 1702-1742*. Chicago, 1916.

Tercentenary Handlist of English & Welsh Newspapers, Magazines & Reviews. London, 1920.

"Tercentenary Handlist of Newspapers." [Additions and corrections by various correspondents.] *Notes and Queries*, 12th series, VIII (1921), 91-93, 118, 173-75, 252-53; X (1922), 191-94, 213-14.

Term Catalogues. Ed. Edward Arber. London, 1903-06. 3 vols.

Timperley, C. H. *Encyclopædia of Literary and Typographical Anecdote*. 2nd ed., London, 1842.

Wallis, Alfred. 'A Sketch of the Early History of the Printing Press in Derbyshire.' Reprinted from the *Journal of the Derbyshire Archæological and Natural History Society*, III (1881).

Welford, Richard. "Early Newcastle Typography, 1639-1800." *Archaeologia Aeliana*, 3rd series, III (1907), 1-134.

Williams, J. B. *A History of English Journalism to the Foundation of the "Gazette."* London, 1908.

[5a] Certain honorable exceptions, besides the two mentioned in our first paragraph, should be noted; for instance, Couper's *Edinburgh Periodical Press* and Madden's *History of Irish Periodical Literature*.

can never be laid. The second difficulty is incompleteness. Our list can of course be expanded by a further search in bibliographies and libraries, for the field is immense. In fact, as we saw how much was left, we put off publication and went on garnering material. That material is now included — and a new mass of information accumulating. At no matter what stage, indeed, we obligated ourselves to print, there would always be more that we could do. And meanwhile a useful tool would rust.

We have, however, a consolation in knowing that this list, as supplemented by the finding-list, is more nearly complete than any earlier one we have examined, and that, in addition, it contains a considerable number of periodicals not mentioned, so far as we know, in any other bibliographies.

In both lists certain information is always given—the title of the periodical, its place of publication, and its initial and terminal dates when these are available or calculable with some security. In addition, the names of editors, publishers, or printers are given (after the title) when these were known and thought to be of sufficient importance; and the frequency of publication is indicated when definitely known. In both lists, also, periodicals which changed their titles are placed under their initial title and a cross-reference given under the subsequent title or titles.

Two other matters should be understood. First, no effort is made to give information about that part of the run of a journal which extends beyond 1800; the mere indication of this fact by means of the symbol + is all that will be found. Secondly, when there is no statement of the provenience, London is to be presumed.

Entries have been standardized as much as possible. The capitalization of titles has been conformed to the A. L. A. rules. Articles at the beginning of titles have been omitted. Dates have, to the best of our knowledge, been uniformly expressed in New Style. Issues dated for a period of time instead of with a single date (e. g., Monday, Jan. 3 to Wednesday, Jan. 5) are, except in a few special instances, given only the latter date e. g., Jan. 5).

In the list of periodicals found in America, the descriptions of library holdings, unless it be otherwise specified, record the original issues (see, for example, the entries under the *Tatler* and Goldsmith's *Bee*).[6] When no entry follows the library symbol, the run is supposed to be complete.

In both lists, a question mark after a date means either that the date is inferential or that the authority for it is suspect. The user should remember, too, that the terminal date given is often merely that of the last number which we have found recorded.

In the two indexes, periodicals or parts of runs of periodicals not found in America are expressed by *italicized* numbers. We have also sought to facilitate reference by beginning the numbering in the second list with 1001. Transactions of societies are, with a few exceptions (e. g., the *Philosophical Transactions of the Royal Society*), indexed only under the date of their first appearance because of the frequently irregular appearance of these publications. Finally, it should be remembered that the periodicals in our second list cannot be so completely represented in the chronological index as those in the first list because the length of their runs is so often unknown.

We have been fortunate in the help which we have received in making this census. The librarians to whom we have applied have been more than generous of aid, and we have had the good luck to enlist the unselfish help of many friends. Professor A. E. Case, Professor R. H. Griffith, Professor George Sherburn, Mr. T. W. Koch, Mr. Andrew Keogh, Mr. A. T. Dorf, Mr. Stephen F. Crocker, Miss Emily H. Hall, and Miss Fannie Ratchford have verified entries and reported new ones to us or otherwise given us aid and comfort. Miss Bernice Ford, Mrs. R. S. Crane, and Mrs. G. R. Osler have spent laborious and effective hours on the lists and indexes. Professor R. P. McCutcheon, Mr. Aubrey L. Hawkins, and Mr. R. H. Thornton have, at much expenditure of time, sent us many entries which we should not otherwise have had. Miss Mary E. Craig has given us notes on Scottish periodicals more full than could be found in any bibliography.

One final note. This bibliography is to be looked upon as a first draft. No work such as this can possibly reach completion in

[6] Certain facts should be noted concerning our descriptions of library holdings. (1) Reprints in the collected works of an author or in the essay-collections of Chalmers and Harrison are not recorded. (2) Because of variations of method in the reports of the libraries, details of holdings

its first edition. We hope to be able in time to perfect it, and, to this end, we invite all users of these lists to send us corrections and additions, for, in cases like this, as Dr. Johnson said, " those who can add any thing . . . communicate their discoveries, and time produces what had eluded diligence."

University of Chicago.
Northwestern University.

LIST OF LIBRARIES, WITH THEIR SYMBOLS [7]

CSH	The Henry E. Huntington Library, San Marino, California
CSt	Leland Stanford University Library, Stanford University, California
CU	University of California Library, Berkeley, California
CtHT	*Trinity College Library, Hartford, Connecticut*
CtY	Yale University Library, New Haven, Connecticut
DA	*Library of U. S. Department of Agriculture, Washington, D. C.*
DCU	*Library of the Catholic University of America, Washington, D. C.*
DGS	*Library of the U. S. Geological Survey, Washington, D. C.*
DGU	*Library of Georgetown University, D. C.*
DLC	Library of Congress, Washington, D. C.
DNM	*U. S. National Museum, Washington, D. C.*

could not always be given with equal fullness. (3) When no comma appears before such terms as " rep.", " inc.", or " 2nd ed.", they apply only to the issue or volume immediately preceding (as in no. 840); when a comma appears before these terms, they apply to all the preceding issues or volumes back to the nearest semicolon or, in the absence of a semicolon, to the beginning of the holding (as in nos. 733, 101, and 199).

[7] In this list are included three groups of libraries. The first consists of those libraries whose detailed reports of holdings constitute the basis of our finding-list. The second group comprises a small number of private libraries the contents of which happened to be known to us; from these we have recorded certain rare periodicals for the possible convenience of scholars. The third group includes a number of libraries, mainly of a specialized character, occasional holdings of which have been inserted on the authority either of the *Union List of Serials* or of cards in the Union

DP   Library of the U. S. Patent Office, Washington, D. C.
DSG   Library of U. S. Surgeon General's Office, Washington, D. C.
ICJ   John Crerar Library, Chicago, Illinois
ICN   Newberry Library, Chicago, Illinois
ICS   Private Library of Professor George Sherburn, University of Chicago, Chicago, Illinois
ICU   University of Chicago Libraries, Chicago, Illinois
IEK   Private Library of Professor F. B. Kaye, Northwestern University, Evanston, Illinois
IEN   Northwestern University Library, Evanston, Illinois
IU   University of Illinois Library, Urbana, Illinois
IWS   Private library of Mr. A. W. Shaw, Winnetka, Illinois
Ia   *Iowa State Library, Des Moines, Iowa*
IaU   *Library of the University of Iowa, Iowa City, Iowa*
MAA   *Library of the Massachusetts Agricultural College, Amherst, Massachusetts*
MB   Boston Public Library
MBB   Library of the Boston Athenaeum
MBC   *Congregational Library, Boston, Massachusetts*
MBM   *Boston Medical Library, Boston, Massachusetts*
MH   Harvard College Library, Cambridge, Massachusetts
MH-A   *Library of the Arnold Arboretum, Cambridge, Massachusetts*
MH-L   *Library of the Harvard Law School, Cambridge, Massachusetts*
MHi   Massachusetts Historical Society, Boston, Massachusetts
MdBJ   Johns Hopkins University Library, Baltimore, Maryland
MdBM   *Library of the Medical and Chirurgical Faculty of the State of Maryland, Baltimore, Maryland*
MdBP   Peabody Institute, Baltimore, Maryland
MeB   *Bowdoin College Library, Brunswick, Maine*
MiD-B   *Burton Historical Collection, Detroit, Michigan*
MiU   University of Michigan Library, Ann Arbor, Michigan
MiUC   William L. Clements Library, University of Michigan, Ann Arbor, Michigan

Catalogue at the University of Chicago; these libraries are distinguished by italics in the above list. The symbols used are, with a few additions, those employed in the *Union List*. For permission to use them we are indebted to the publishers, the H. W. Wilson Company, New York.

MnU	University of Minnesota Library, Minneapolis, Minnesota
N	New York State Library, Albany, New York
NIC	Cornell University Library, Ithaca, New York
NN	New York Public Library, New York City
NNC	Columbia University Library, New York City
NNE	Engineering Societies Library, New York City
NNG	Library of the General Theological Seminary, New York City
NNU	Library of Union Theological Seminary, New York City
NcU	Library of the University of North Carolina, Chapel Hill, North Carolina
NjP	Princeton University Library, Princeton, New Jersey
NjPT	Library of Princeton Theological Seminary, Princeton, New Jersey
O	State Library, Columbus, Ohio
OO	Oberlin College Library, Oberlin, Ohio
PPL	Library Company, Philadelphia, Pennsylvania
PPAP	Library of the American Philosophical Society, Philadelphia, Pennsylvania
PPH	Historical Society of Pennsylvania, Philadelphia, Pennsylvania
PU	University of Pennsylvania Library, Philadelphia, Pennsylvania
RPB	Brown University Library, Providence, Rhode Island
TxAG	Private Library of Professor R. H. Griffith, University of Texas, Austin, Texas
TxU	University of Texas Library, Austin, Texas
VaU	Library of the University of Virginia, Charlottesville, Virginia
WH	Wisconsin Historical Society, Madison, Wisconsin
WU	University of Wisconsin Library, Madison, Wisconsin

OTHER ABBREVIATIONS AND SYMBOLS

a. = published annually
app. = appendix
d. = published daily

Ed. = edited by
f. = published fortnightly
impr. = imprint on titlepage bound with original sheets when these were collected into a volume
inc. = incomplete
ir. = published at irregular intervals
m. = published monthly
n. s. = new series
q. = published quarterly
rep. = reprint *or* reprinted
ser. = series
s. m. = published semi-monthly
suppl. = supplement
s. w. = published semi-weekly
t. w. = published tri-weekly
U. L. = *Union List of Serials*
w. = published weekly
+ = published until after 1800

I. BRITISH PERIODICALS, 1620-1800, ACCESSIBLE IN AMERICAN LIBRARIES

1. Aberdeen magazine. Aberdeen, 1761. m.
   NN (v. 1, July, 1761, inc.), **ICU**.

1a. Abstract of some speciall forreigne occurrences. Nathaniel Butter and Nicholas Bourne. 1638.
   MnU.

1b. Account of the proceedings of the meeting of the Estates in Scotland. *Continued as* Continuation of the proceedings of the Convention of the Estates in Scotland (from no. ?). *Printed for* R. Chiswell. 1689-90.
   CSH (nos. 82-147, 1690).

2. Account of the publick transactions in Christendom. *Continued as* Historical account of the publick transactions in Christendom (from no. 2, Aug. 18, 1694); *discontinued,* Sept. 8, 1694–May 4, 1695; *continued as* Holland pacquet-boat; or, An historical account of the publick transactions of Christendom (from no. 15, June 17, 1695); *amalgamated with* Post boy, and historical account, &c., with foreign and domestick news (nos. 16-71, June 19–Oct. 22, 1695); *continued as* Post man, and the historical account . . . (from no. 72, Oct. 24, 1695); *as* Œdipus; or, The postman remounted (from Feb. 24, 1729/30, with new numbering). Abel Boyer, John de Fonvive, Abel Roper, etc. 1694-1730(?). t. w.
   CSH (nos. 442-48, 446 [*sic*], 451-69, 471-78, 482-87, 491-92, 495-520, 522-31, 533-37, Mar. 26–Nov. 10, 1698; 537-61, Nov. 12, 1698–Jan. 12, 1699; 563-600, 602-11, 613-36, 638-46, 648-62, 664-68, Jan. 14–Oct. 26, 1699; 670-714, Oct. 28, 1699–Feb. 20, 1700; 710, 718-29, Feb. 24–Mar. 26, 1700), **CtY** (nos. 11050-10542, Jan. 4, 1715–Dec. 31, 1717), **IWS** (nos. 929, 947, 997-98, 1002-05, Feb. 3–Aug. 18, 1702), **NN** (Dec. 11, 1703), **TxU** (nos. 1158-1967, July 8, 1703–Oct. 23, 1708; 1847, Feb. 16, 1710; 2061, June 28, 1711; 11050, Sept. 4, 1714; 11050 [*sic*], Nov. 1, 1714), **WH** (nos. 869, Feb. 15, 1701; 919, Jan. 8, 1702; 1011, Sept. 5, 1702; 1078, Jan. 5, 1703; 1229, Jan. 20, 1704; 1363, Jan. 6, 1705; 1572, Jan. 26, 1706; 1803, July 8, 1707).

3. Adams's weekly courant. Chester, no. 241, June 29, 1737+. w.
   NN (Apr. 7, 1747).

4. Adventurer. *Ed.* J. Hawkesworth. Nos. 1-140, Nov. 7, 1752–Mar. 9, 1754. s. w.
   CSH (v. 1-2, 1752-53), **CtY** (also rep. 1756), **ICU, IU** (1753-54), **MB, NN, NNC** (nos. 71-140), **TxU** (lacking no. 71), **WH.**

   Advice from Parnassus. *See* News from Parnassus.

5. Adviser, by Abraham Briarcliff. Edinburgh, 1797. w.
   CtY (nos. 1-16, Feb. 11–May 27, 1797).

6. Advocate; or, A vindication of the Christian religion, and the Church of England in particular, against the vile and blasphemous writers of the age. 1720-21. w.
   MH (nos. 1-18, Nov. 9, 1720–Mar. 8, 1721).

7. Alter et idem, a new review. *Ed.* Robert Deverell. Reading, 1794.
   DLC (no. 1).

8. American gazette; being a collection of all the . . . addresses, memorials, letters, etc. which relate to the present disputes between Great Britain and her colonies. 1768-70. w.
   CSH, CtY (1768-70, inc.), **DLC** (nos. 1-5, 1768-69, 3rd ed.), **ICN** (nos. 1-2, 2nd ed., 1768), **MB** (nos. 1-3, 1768), **MiUC** (nos. 1-3), **NN** (no. 2, inc.).

9. American gazette, by several gentlemen from America. 1776. (From U. L.).
   DLC (nos. 2-4, Feb.–Mar. 1776).

9a. American repository; or, Lottery magazine of literature, politics, and pleasure . . . by Philanthropos. 1777.
   ICN, MB.

10. Analytical review; or, History of literature, domestic and foreign. 1788-99. m.
    CtY (v. 1-28, May 1788–Dec. 1798), **DLC, ICN** (v. 1-17, May 1788–Dec. 1793; 19-28, May 1794–Dec. 1798; n. s., v. 1, Jan.–June 1799), **IU** (v. 1-14, May 1788–Dec. 1792), **MB** (v. 1-22, 1788-96), **MBB, MH** (v. 1-17; 18-28, inc.), **N** (v. 1-17, May 1788–Dec. 1793; 19-28, May 1794–Dec. 1798), **NjP, NN, NNC** (v. 1-9, May 1788–Apr. 1791), **PPL, VaU** (v. 1-16, 1788-93).

11. Annals of agriculture and other useful arts. *Ed.* Arthur Young. London, 1784-89; Bury St. Edmunds, 1790+. q.
    CtY, CU, DLC (v. 1-17), **ICJ, ICU, IU** (v. 1-33, 1784-99), **MB, MnU, NIC, NNC** (inc.), **PU.**

12. Annals of Europe. 1739-44. a.
    CtY, TxAG (1743), **WH.**

13. Annals of Europe; or, Regal register shewing the succession of sovereigns. 1779. a.
    MB.
14. Annals of King George. 1716-21. a.
    CtY, DLC, ICU (v. 2-3), **RPB** (1716).

    Annals of medicine. *See* Medical and philosophical commentaries.
14a. Annotations on the Tatler, by W. Wagstaff. W. Oldisworth. 1710.
    CtY.
15. Annual advertiser. 1739-40. a.
    PPAP.
16. Annual register. *Founded by* R. Dodsley. 1759 (for the year 1758)+. a.
    CSH, CSt, CtY, CU, DLC, ICJ, ICN, ICU, IEN, IU, MB, MBB, MdBJ, MdBP, MH, MHi, MiU, MiUC, MnU, N, NIC, NjP, NN, NNC, NcU, PPH, PPL, PU, RPB, TxU, VaU (inc.), **WH.**
17. Anthologia Hibernica; or, Monthly collections of science, belles lettres, and history. Dublin, 1793-94. m.
    CtY, DLC, ICN, ICU, MB, MBB, MdBP, MH, MiU, NN, PPL (1793), **RPB, WH.**
18. Antidote against the malignant influence of Mercurius (surnamed) Aulicus. 1642.
    TxU (no. 1, Sept. 2, 1642).
19. Anti-Jacobin; or, Weekly examiner. *Ed.* W. Gifford. Nos. 1-36, Nov. 20, 1797–July 9, 1798. w.
    CtY (also 4th ed., 1799), **DLC, ICN, ICU, MB, MBB, MH** (4th ed.), **NIC** (4th ed.), **NN, NNC** (4th ed.), **PPL** (4th ed.), **RPB, TxU.**
20. Anti-Jacobin review and magazine. 1798+. m.
    CSt, CtY, DLC, ICN, ICU, IU (v. 1-3, July 1798-Aug. 1799), **MB, MBB, MdBJ** (v. 1), **MH, MiU, MnU, N, NIC, NjP, NN, NNC, PPL, WH.**

    Anti-Roman pacquet. *See* Pacquet of advice from Rome. . . .
21. Anti-theatre. Nos. 1-15, Feb. 15–Apr. 4, 1720. s. w.
    CtY (rep. 1791), **DLC** (nos. 2-15), **TxU** (no. 9).
22. Anti-union. Dublin, nos. 1-32, 1798-99. t. w.
    CtY, DLC (nos. 1-13, 15-19, Dec. 27, 1798-Feb. 7, 1799), **NN, NNC.**

    Applebee's original weekly journal. *See* Original weekly journal.

24. Archaeologia; or, Miscellaneous tracts relating to antiquity. 1770+.
    CSt, CtY, CU, DLC, ICN, ICU, IU, MB, MdBP, MH (lacking v. 3), N, NIC, NcU, NNC, WH.

25. Archaeologia Scotica; or, Transactions of the society of antiquaries of Scotland. Edinburgh, 1792+. a.
    CtY, MB, MdBP, NIC, NN, NNC, WH.

26. Argus. 1789-96(?). w.
    CtY (Oct. 29, 1795–May 18, 1796).

27. Aris's Birmingham gazette; or, The general correspondent. Birmingham, 1741+.
    NN (Dec. 22, 1755).

28. Arminian magazine. *Continued as* Methodist magazine (from Jan. 1798). *Ed.* John Wesley and others. 1778+. m.
    CtY, DLC, ICN (v. 1-20, Jan. 1778–Dec. 1797), ICU (v. 1-20), MB, NIC, NN (v. 19, 20 inc.), NNC, WH (v. 16, Jan.–Dec. 1793).

29. Artists' repository and drawing magazine. F. Fitzgerald. 1785-94. m.
    DLC (v. 1-4, 1785-88).

30. Asiatic annual register; or, A view of the history of Hindustan, and of the politics, commerce and literature of Asia. 1799+. a.
    CtY, DLC, MB, MdBP, MH, MiU, NNC, WH.

31. Asiatic miscellany. Calcutta and London, 1785-86.
    MH.

    Astrologer's magazine and philosophical miscellany. *See* Conjurer's magazine. . . .

    Asylum; or, Weekly miscellany. *See* Weekly miscellany of instruction and entertainment.

32. Athenian gazette; or, Casuistical mercury. *Continued as* Athenian mercury (from no. 2). John Dunton, assisted by Richard Sault, John Norris, Samuel Wesley, Sr., etc. V. 1-19, March 17, 1690/91–Feb. 8, 1696, thirty nos. in a volume; v. 20, May 14–June 14, 1697, ten nos. s. w. Five supplements.
    CtY (also suppl. 1-5), ICN (also suppl. 1-4), ICU (v. 1-8, Mar. 17, 1691–July 26, 1692; v. 9, nos. 2, 5-6, 13-14), IU (v. 1-11, 1691-93), MB, MH (v. 1-19, lacking v. 1, nos. 1-3, 7-8, 11, 15-16; v. 3, nos. 6, 13, 15; v. 4, nos. 3, 5, 6, 8, 9, and part of 4th suppl.), NN, NNC (v. 10-20, Mar. 28, 1693–June 14, 1697), PPL (v. 8, nos. 1, 23), TxU, WH (v. 3, nos. 4, 6; v. 10, nos. 22, 25, 28;

v. 11, nos. 7, 10, 11, 20, 21, 23, 25; v. 12, nos. 1, 4, 12, 13, 16, 18, 28; v. 13, nos. 6, 10).

Athenian mercury. *See* Athenian gazette; or, Casuistical mercury.

33. Attic miscellany; or, Characteristic mirror of men and things. Oct. 1789–Aug. 1792. m.
    DLC (v. 1, Oct. 1789–Sept. 1790, 2nd ed.), MBB (1789-91), MH.

34. Auditor. 1733-34. s. w.; w.
    CtY (Jan. 9-23, May 8, Dec. 5, 1733), DLC (nos. 1-45, Jan. 9, 1733–Jan. 30, 1734).

35. Auditor. Arthur Murphy. 1762-63. w.
    CtY (July 15, 1762–May 16, 1763, rep. in Political controversy, 1762-63), RPB (rep. in Political controversy).

"Bagweel" papers. *See* Occasional paper, 1716-19.

37. Baldwin's London journal; or, British chronicle. 1762-92(?). w.
    CtY (nos. 1-35, Jan. 2–Aug. 28, 1762).

Banks' currant intelligence. *See* Currant intelligence; or, An impartial account of transactions . . . (Banks).

38. Baptist annual register. 1790+. a.
    CtY, DLC (1794-97), ICN, ICU, MB, MiU, N (1790-93), NjP, NN, RPB.

Bath journal. *See* Boddely's Bath journal.

40. Beauties of all the magazines selected. 1762-64.
    CtY (v. 1-2, 1762-63), ICN (v. 1-2), MB (v. 1).

41. Bee. Oliver Goldsmith. Nos. 1-8, Oct. 6–Nov. 24, 1759. w.
    ICS, MH (rep. 1759).

42. Bee; or, Literary weekly intelligencer. *Ed.* James Anderson. Edinburgh, Dec. 22, 1790–Jan. 21, 1794. w.
    CSH, CtY, DLC, ICN, ICU, IU, MB (v. 1, Dec. 22, 1790–Mar. 2, 1791), MH, MHi, NjP (v. 3, May 11–July 6, 1791), NN, NNC, PPL, WH.

43. Bee; or, Universal weekly pamphlet. *Continued as* Bee; or, Universal weekly pamphlet revived (from v. 2, no. 1); *as* Bee revived; or, The universal weekly pamphlet (from v. 2, no. 4). E. Budgell. Feb. 3, 1733–June 14, 1735. w.
    CtY, DLC (no. 8, Mar. 1733), ICU (nos. 1-8, Feb. 3–Mar. 31, 1733), MB (nos. 1-77, Feb. 3, 1733–Aug. 24, 1734), MH, MHi (v. 6, no. 75, 1734), NN (v. 2, nos. 14-26, May 30–Aug. 22, 1733), NNC (nos. 2, Feb. 1733; 12, Apr. 1733), TxAG (v. 1-4, 6-9, 1733-35).

44. Bee revived; or, The prisoner's magazine. 1750.
    MH (prospectus, and v. 1, no. 1, 1750).
    Bee revived; or, The universal weekly pamphlet. *See* Bee; or, Universal weekly pamphlet.
45. Belfast news-letter, and general advertiser. *Continued as* Belfast news-letter (from ?). Belfast, 1737(?)+. s. w.
    NN (July 3, Dec. 14, 1795).
46. Bellamy's picturesque magazine and literary museum. 1793.
    MH (v. 1).
47. Bell's weekly messenger. 1796+. w.
    CtY (May 1, 1796–Dec. 31, 1797; Apr. 15-29, May 27, July 1, 1798; Jan. 20, Mar. 10, 31, Apr. 21, 1799), ICU (nos. 4-10, 12-15, 18-20, 22-28, 30-31, 33-38, 40-41, 43-48, 50, 52, 54-56, 59-61, 67-68, 71, 74-76, 78-87, 89-100, 102-06, 108-10, 113-18, 120-23, 125-26, May 22, 1796–Sept. 23, 1798), IU (1796+), MdBP.
47a. B. Berington's evening post. 1732(?)-33(?). t. w.
    TxU (Apr. 10, 1733).
48. Berkshire repository. Maidenhead, 1797.
    CtY (v. 1).
    Berrow's Worcester journal. *See* Worcester postman.
48a. Berwick museum; or, Monthly literary intelligencer. Berwick-on-Tweed, 1785-87. m.
    NN (Feb., Mar., May 1786).
49. Bibliotheca literaria, being a collection of inscriptions, medals, dissertations. *Ed.* S. Webb. 1722-24.
    CSH, CtY (nos. 1-10, 1722-24), DLC, ICS, ICU, IU, MH, N.
50. Biographical and imperial magazine. 1789-92. Monthly parts entitled The imperial magazine.
    CtY (v. 1-3, Jan. 1789–June 1790), IU (Jan. 1789).
51. Biographical magazine. 1773-76.
    DLC (4 v. in one, 1773-76), ICU.
52. Biographical magazine, containing portraits & characters of eminent and ingenious persons of every age & nation. 1794.
    CtY, MB, NN.
53. Biographical magazine; or, Complete historical library. *Printed for* F. Newbery. 1776-(?).
    DLC (v. 1-4, 1776), NN (v. 1, 1776), WH (v. 1-4).
53a. Boddely's Bath journal. *Continued as* Bath journal (from Mar. 8, 1773). Bath, 1744+. w.
    TxU (v. 2-5, Mar. 25, 1745–Mar. 20, 1749).

54. Botanical magazine; or, The flower garden displayed. *Continued as* Curtis' botanical magazine (from 1801). W. Curtis. 1787+.
    CSt (v. 1, impr. 1793; v. 14, impr. 1800), CtY, DLC, ICU (v. 1-3, 1787-92; 7-12, 1794-98), IU (v. 1-14), MB, MdBP, MnU, NIC, NN, NNC, VaU.

55. Botanical review. 1790-(?). (From U. L.)
    MH-A (v. 1, 1790).

56. Briefe relation of some affaires and transactions, civill and military, both forraigne and domestique. Walter Frost. Oct. 2, 1649–Oct. 22, 1650. w.
    MnU (no. 35, Apr. 23, 1650).

57. Bristol gazette and public advertiser. Bristol, 1767(?)+.
    NN (Aug. 20, 1772).

58. Britain. 1713.
    TxU (nos. 11, 13, 15, 16, Feb. 11, 18, 25, 28, 1713).

59. Britannic magazine; or, Entertaining repository of heroic adventures and memorable exploits. 1793+. m.
    CtY, DLC (v. 1-6, 1793-98), ICU (v. 1-7), MBB (1793-96).

60. British Apollo; or, Curious amusements for the ingenious. 1708-11. s. w. (to no. 79) ; t. w.
    CtY, DLC (v. 1-3, Feb. 13, 1708–Mar. 26, 1711), ICN (v. 1-2, Feb. 13, 1708–Mar. 24, 1710), ICU (4th ed., abridged, 1740), IU (2nd, 3rd eds.), MB (rep. 1740), MBB, MH (v. 1-3, Feb. 13, 1708–Mar. 26, 1711; v. 4, nos. 1-20, Mar. 28–May 11, 1711, lacking v. 2, no. 13, and v. 3, no. 113; also v. 1-3, 3rd ed., 1726; v. 1-2, 4th ed., 1740), NIC (v. 1-3, rep. 1726), NN (v. 1-3), NNC (rep. 1726), TxU, WH (v. 2, 1709-10).

60a. British antidote to Caledonian poison. *Continued as* Scots scourge: being a compleat supplement to the British antidote to Caledonian poison (from v. 3, 1763) ; *as* British antidote (from v. 5, 1766). 1762-66.
    DLC.

British champion; or, The impartial advertiser. *See* Champion; or, British mercury.

61. British critic, and quarterly theological review. *Ed.* W. Beloe and R. Nares. 1793+. m.
    CSt, CtY, CU, DLC, ICN, ICU, IU, MB, MBB, MdBP (v. 4, July-Dec. 1794), MH, MiU, N, NIC, NN, NNC, VaU (v. 1-3, 6-15, 21-23).

British gazette and Sunday monitor. *See* Johnson's British gazette and Sunday monitor.

62. British journal. *Continued as* British journal; or, The censor (from Jan. 20, 1728); *as* British journal; or, The traveller (from Nov. 30, 1730). 1722-31(?). w.
    CtY (Jan. 5, Feb. 16, Mar. 14-30, Apr. 13, 27-Dec. 7, 21, 1723; May 23, 30, Aug. 15, 29, Sept. 19, 26, Oct. 17, 31, Nov. 7-21, 1724; Feb. 20, 1725; Feb. 11-Dec. 30, 1727; Jan. 3, Feb. 14, 21, Apr. 25-Dec. 26, 1730), **MH** (nos. 2-136, Sept. 29, 1722-Apr. 24, 1725, lacking nos. 9, 12, 35, 51, 80, 99), **TxU** (nos. 4-13, Oct. 13-Dec. 15, 1722, lacking nos. 11-12; Mar. 23, 1723), **WH** (nos. 1-58, Sept. 22, 1722-Oct. 26, 1723; 60-75, Nov. 9, 1723-Feb. 22, 1724; 77-105, Mar. 7-Sept. 19, 1724).

63. British librarian. William Oldys. Nos. 1-6, Jan.–June, 1737. m.
    CtY, ICJ, ICS, ICU, IU, MB, MBB, MH, N, NcU, NIC, NN, NNC (rep. 1738), **RPB**.

64. British lyre; or, Muses repertory. 1793. a.
    MH.

65. British magazine. *Ed.* John Hill. 1746-50. m.
    CtY (July-Nov. 1747, July inc.), **DLC** (v. 4, 1749), **IU**.

66. British magazine. 1800+. m.
    DLC, ICN (v. 2, nos. 7-9, July-Sept. 1800), **PPL**.

67. British magazine and general review of the literature, employment and amusements of the times. 1772. m.
    DLC (v. 1, Mar.–June 1772; v. 2, July-Nov. 1772, lacking Aug.-Oct., Dec.), **ICU**.

68. British magazine and review; or, Universal miscellany of arts, sciences, etc. July 1782-Dec. 1783. m.
    CtY, IU, MB.

69. British magazine; or, Monthly repository for gentlemen and ladies. *Ed.* T. G. Smollett. Jan. 1760-Dec. 1767. m.
    CtY, ICU (v. 3-6, 8, 1762-67, lacking Sept. 1763, Mar. 1764, Jan. 1765, and Oct. 1767), **MB** (1760-61), **MHi** (Oct. 1761), **NN** (v. 2, 1761), **NNC** (v. 3-4, 1762-63), **WH** (v. 2-3, 1761-62).

70. British magazine; or, The London and Edinburgh intelligencer. Edinburgh, 1747-48.
    DLC.

71. British melody; or, The musical magazine. 1739.
    MH.

72. British merchant; or, Commerce preserv'd; in answer to [Defoe's] Mercator. . . . *Ed.* Charles King. Nos. 1-103, Aug. 7, 1713-July 30, 1714. s. w.
    CtY (nos. 16, 18-87, 89-101, 103, Sept. 29, 1713-July 30, 1714;

also 2nd ed., 1743; 3rd ed. 1748), **DLC** (rep. 1721), **ICU** (3rd ed., 1748), **IU** (rep. 1721), **MB** (rep. 1721), **NIC** (rep. 1721), **TxU**.

73. British mercury, published by the Company of London-insurers. *Continued as* British weekly mercury (from no. 498, Jan. 15, 1715). Nos. 1-566, 1710-16. s. w.
    WH (nos. 396-518, Feb. 4, 1713–June 4, 1715).

74. British mercury; or, Annals of history, politics, manners, literature, etc. 1787-90. w.
    NjP (v. 1-13, Apr. 4, 1787–June 26, 1790; v. 15, Oct. 2–Dec. 25, 1790).

75. British mercury; or, Historical and critical views of the events of the present time. *Ed.* J. Mallet de Pan. 1798-1800. s. m.
    CtY (v. 1-3, 1798-99; v. 1, 2nd ed.), **NN** (v. 1-5, 1798-1800), **PU** (v. 1-4).

76. British mercury; or, The Welch diurnall. 1643.
    TxU (no. 6, Dec. 3, 1643).

77. British military library, or journal. 1798+. m.
    DLC (v. 1, Oct. 1798–Sept. 1799), **MB, MH, NN** (v. 1-2), **WH**.

    British palladium. *See* Gentleman and lady's palladium.

78. British poetical miscellany. Huddersfield, 1799(?). w.
    CtY (nos. 1-30), **ICN** (4th ed., 1818).

79. British public characters. *Published by* R. Phillips. 1798+. a.
    CtY, DLC, ICN, IU, MB, MH, MnU, NcU, NIC, NN, NNC (ed. 1801-09), **PPL**.

79a. British telescope. 1724-49. a.
    DLC, NNC (v. 25, 1748), **PPAP** (1724-25, 1728-36, 1738-49), **WH**.

    British weekly mercury. *See* British mercury, 1710-16.

80. Briton. 1723-24. w.
    NN, TxU (nos. 1-30, Aug. 7, 1723–Feb. 19, 1724).

81. Briton. *Ed.* T. G. Smollett. Nos. 1-38, May 29, 1762–Feb. 12, 1763. w.
    CtY (rep. in Political controversy, 1762-63), **NN** (nos. 1-18, 20-24, 26-38), **WH** (nos. 1-23, May 29–Oct. 30, 1762).

82. Builder's magazine; or, Monthly companion for architects, carpenters, masons, etc. (by a society of architects). 1774.
    NNC.

83. Bulletins of the campaigns (from the London gazette). 1793+.

DLC (1793-96, 1798+), NNC (1793+), WH (Mar. 2, 1793-Dec. 14, 1799).

84. Bystander; or, Universal weekly expositor. Charles Dibdin. Aug. 15, 1789-Feb. 6, 1790. w.
    CtY, MH, NNC.

85. Cabinet, by a society of gentlemen. Norwich, 1794-95. m.
    CtY (v. 1-3, 1794-95), NjP (v. 1-3), RPB (v. 1-2).

86. Caledonian mercury. Edinburgh, 1720+. t. w.; d. (June 27-Sept. 2, 1776); t. w.
    CtY (nos. 8493-9099, Apr. 8, 1776-Dec. 29, 1779), IU (nos. 5255-5774, Aug. 16, 1755-Dec. 30, 1758), WH (nos. 1051-52, Jan. 9-10, 1727; 1078-80, Mar. 13-16, 1727).

87. Caledonian weekly magazine. Edinburgh, 1773-(?). w.
    CtY (v. 1, nos. for June 30, July 21-July 28, 1773).

88. Cambrian register. *Ed.* W. O. Pughe. 1795+.
    DLC, ICN, IU, MH, MnU, PPL (1795), RPB.

89. Cambridge intelligencer. Cambridge, 1793-1800. w.
    CtY (July 20, 1793-Dec. 26, 1795).

90. Candid review and literary repository. 1765. m.
    CtY (Jan.-June, 1765).

    Canterbury journal. *See* Kentish weekly post; or, Canterbury journal.

91. Carlton house magazine: or, Annals of taste, fashion, and politeness. Jan. 1792-Feb. 1796. m.
    CtY (Oct.-Dec. 1792), DLC (v. 1-2), MBB, MH (Jan. 1792-June 1793).

92. Cassandra (But I hope not). Charles Leslie. 1704.
    ICU (v. 1-2).

93. Catalogue of books printed and published at London. *Ed.* Robert Clavell. 1670-1709, 1711. q. Reprinted in Arber's Term catalogues, 1903-06.
    CSH (nos. 1-18, 1670-74; 2-21, 1675-79; Michaelmas term, 1680; Hilary term, 1681; nos. 18-23, 1686), ICN (nos. 1-10, 1674-76; 12-18, 1677-79; 1-6, 1680-82), NIC.

94. Catholick intelligence; or, Infallible news, both domestick and foreign. 1680. w.
    NN (Mar. 8-29, 1680), TxU (nos. 1-5, Mar. 1-29, 1680).

95. Censor. L. Theobald and others. Nos. 1-96, April 11-June 17, 1715; Jan. 1-June 1, 1717. t. w.
    CtY (v. 1-3, 1717; v. 1, 2nd ed.), DLC, PPL (nos. 64-96, Mar. 19-June 1, 1717), PU (v. 1-3).

Censor; or, Covent Garden journal. *See* Covent Garden journal; or, The censor.

96. Censura temporum, the good or ill tendencies of books, sermons, pamphlets, etc. impartially considered. Samuel Parker. 1708-10. m.
    DLC, IEK (v. 1, 1708), **IU** (v. 1, nos. 1-4, 1708), **MBB** (Oct. 1708; July 1709), **NNC.**

97. Centinel. 1757. w.; s. w.; d.
    TxU (nos. 1-22, Jan. 6–June 2, 1757).

98. Certaine informations from severall parts of the kingdom. William Ingler. 1643-44. w.
    CtY (nos. 16-17, May 8-15, 1643), **TxU** (nos. 3, 6, 8, 10, 12, 13, 14, 15, 16, 19, 21, 35, Feb. 6–Sept. 11, 1643).

    Certain passages of every dayes intelligence. *See* Perfect passages of every daies intelligence.

99. Certain speciall and remarkable passages from both Houses of Parliament. Samuel Pecke. 1642.
    TxU (Aug. 23).

100. Champion. 1763. w.
    CtY (rep. in Political controversy, 1763).

101. Champion; or, British mercury. *Continued as* Champion; or, Evening advertiser (from ?); *as* British champion; or, The impartial advertiser (1743). Henry Fielding (to June 1741), James Ralph, etc. Nov. 15, 1739-1743. t. w.
    CtY (nos. 1-94, Nov. 15, 1739–June 19, 1740, reps. 1741, 1743), **DLC** (rep. 1741), **IU** (nos. 1-94, rep. 1743), **MH** (nos. 1-94, rep. 1741), **NN** (June 10, 12, Oct. 11, 1740; May 7, 1741; Nov. 11, 1742; Aug. 4, 18, Sept. 10, 15, 1743), **TxU** (rep. 1741, 2 v.), **WH** (no. 125, Aug. 30, 1740).

102. Chelmsford and Colchester chronicle. *Continued as* Chelmsford chronicle (from April 5, 1771). Chelmsford, no. 179, Jan. 1, 1768+.
    CtY (Apr. 5–May 17, 1771; May 24, 1771–Mar. 27, 1772; Aug. 15, 1783–Dec. 30, 1785).

103. Children's magazine; or, Monthly repository of instruction and delight. Jan. 1799–Dec. 1800. m.
    DLC.

104. Christian magazine; or, Evangelical repository. Edinburgh, 1797+. m. (From U. L.)
    NNU (1797).

105. Christian miscellany; or, Religious and moral magazine. 1792.
    PPL (Jan.–May 1792).

106. Christian monthly history: or, An account of the revival and progress of religion, abroad, and at home. *Ed.* James Robe. Edinburgh, Nov. 1743–Jan. 1746. m.
    DLC, IU (nos. 1, 4, Nov. 1743, Feb. 1744), **MB** (nos. 1-2, Nov.–Dec. 1743), **MBC** (1743-45), **NjP** (1745).

107. Christian's gazette. *Ed.* John Dunton. 1713.
    CtY (Jan.–Apr., 2nd ed.).

108. Christian's magazine; or, A treasury of divine knowledge. V. 1-8, 1760-67.
    CtHT (v. 1-7), **CtY** (v. 2-4, 6-8, inc., 1761-67), **NNU** (v. 3, 5), **PPL** (v. 1-7, 1760-66).

    Churchman; or, Loyalist's weekly journal. *See* Churchman's last shift. . . .

109. Churchman's last shift; or, Loyalist's weekly journal. *Continued as* Churchman; or, Loyalist's weekly journal (from no. 23, Nov. 5, 1720). 1720-21. w.
    CtY (nos. 1-20, May 14–Oct. 15, 1720).

    City and countrey mercury. *See* True character of Mercurius urbanicus & rusticus.

110. City watchman. Dublin, 1754.
    CtY (nos. 1-2, May 31–June 7, 1754).

111. Collection for the improvement of husbandry and trade. John Houghton. Nos. 1-583, Mar. 30, 1692–Sept. 24, 1703; rep., with some omissions, in Husbandry and trade improv'd . . . , v. 1-3, 1727. w.
    CtY (nos. 1-320, Mar. 30, 1692–Sept. 9, 1698), **CU** (rep. 1727), **DLC** (v. 5, no. 107, Aug. 17, 1694; also rep. 1727), **ICJ** (rep. 1727), **NNC** (rep. 1727), **WU** (rep. 1727).

112. Collection of letters for the improvement of husbandry and trade. John Houghton. Sept. 8, 1681–June 16, 1683 [*i. e.* 1684]; partially rep. in Husbandry and trade improv'd, v. 4, 1728. ir.
    CtY, CU (rep. 1728), **DA, DLC** (rep. 1728), **MnU, NN** (no. 9, Oct. 19, 1682), **NNC** (rep. 1728), **WU** (rep. 1728).

112a. Comedian; or, Philosophical enquirer. *Ed.* Thomas Cooke. Nos. 1-9, Apr.–Nov. 1732; Apr. 1733. m.
    CtY.

113. Commercial and agricultural magazine. 1799+. m.
    MAA, MBB (v. 1, 3-5, 1799-1800), **NN** (v. 1, 3, 5), **PPL**.

114. Common sense; or, The Englishman's journal. Chesterfield, Lyttleton, etc. 1737-43. w. A separate series, with parallel date and numeration, entitled Old common

sense; or, The Englishman's journal, was issued between Nov. 26, 1737 and June 16, 1739 (nos. 43-123).
CtY (nos. 19, June 11, 1737; 34-48, Sept. 24–Dec. 31, 1737; 49-254, Jan. 7, 1738–Dec. 26, 1741; also rep. 1738-39, 2 v.), ICU (rep. 1738-39), IU (Feb. 5, 1737–Jan. 27, 1739), NN (Apr. 9, Aug. 13, Dec. 10, 1737; Sept. 23, 30, 1738; Jan. 27, July 14, Oct. 6, 13, 1739; Oct. 4, 1740; May 9, 1741; Nov. 13, 20, 1742; Aug. 6, 20, 1743), NNC (1737-39), RPB (1737-39), WH (no. 147, Nov. 24, 1739).

115. Compleat intelligencer and resolver. George Smith(?). 1643.
CtY (no. 3, Nov. 14, 1643).

116. Compleat library; or, News for the ingenious. *Ed.* Richard Wolley for John Dunton. May 1692–Apr. 1694. m.
DLC, ICN, IWS (May 1692–Dec. 1693), MH (May 1692–Dec. 1693), NcU (Dec. 1692–Dec. 1693), NNC (May–Nov. 1692).

117. Compleat mercury; or, The Haerlem courant truly rendered into English. Haarlem and London, 1682.
TxU (nos. 2, 4, Jan. 21-21, Jan. 30-28, 1682).

118. Conjuror's magazine; or, Magical and physiognomical mirror. *Continued as* Astrologer's magazine and philosophical miscellany (from Aug. 1793). 1791-94. m.
DLC (v. 1-2, Aug. 1791–July 1793), MB, NN (v. 1-2).

119. Connoisseur. George Colman, Bonnell Thornton, and others. Nos. 1-140, Jan. 31, 1754–Sept. 30, 1756. w.
CSt (also rep. 1793), CtY, ICU (rep. 1757, v. 1-2, and 1793), IU (rep. 1757-60), MH, NN (nos. 105-40), TxU (nos. 1-5).

120. Constitution. 1757. (From U. L.)
CtY, NN (nos. 1-3).

121. Con-test. Owen Ruffhead. Nos. 1-38, Nov. 23, 1756–Aug. 6, 1757. w.
CtY, DLC (nos. 7, 25), ICU, MnU (nos. 1-2, 4-5, 7-34), NN, TxU (no. 16), WH.

122. Continuation of a journall of passages of the Parliament, and other papers from the Scotts quarters. Samuel Pecke. *Printed for* F. L. 1646. w.
CtY (nos. 3-6, Nov. 5-26, 1646).

123. Continuation of certaine speciall and remarkable passages. *Printed for* Walt Cook and Robert Wood. 1642-43. w.
CtY (nos. 26-27, 35, 40, 43, 50-51, Jan. 12–June 8, 1643), TxU (nos. 31, 38).

124. Continuation of certain speciall and remarkable passages.

Samuel Pecke. *Printed for* Francis Leach and Francis Coles. Aug. 1642–Feb. 1646. w.
>CtY (nos. 21, 23-24, 27, 29-31, 33-34, 37-38, 40-42, 44, 46, 52, Dec. 1, 1642–Aug. 25, 1643), TxU (no. 38).

125. Continuation of certain speciall and remarkable passages informed to both Houses of Parliament. Samuel Pecke. 1642-43.
>TxU (nos. 33, 39, 40, 41, 42, 44, Feb. 23–May 11, 1643).

Continuation of the actions, passages, and occurrences. *See* Principall passages of Germany, Italy, France, etc.

126. Continuation of the forraine avisoes for two weekes last past. N. Butter and N. Bourne. (?)-1640(?).
>ICN (no. 49, Jan. 23, 1640).

Continuation of the proceedings of the Convention of the Estates in Scotland. *See* Account of the proceedings of the meeting of the Estates in Scotland.

Continuation of the true diurnall of passages in Parliament. *See* True diurnall of the last weeks passages in Parliament.

126a. Continuation of the true diurnall of the passages in Parliament. 1642. Distinct from no. 888.
>ICN (no. 6, Feb. 14-21, 1641/2).

127. Continuation of the intelligence from the . . . Earl of Manchester's army [slight variations in title]. S. Ash and W. Good. June–Aug. 1644.
>CtY (no. 4, June 17, 1644), TxU (no. 7, Aug. 16, 1644).

128. Contrast. Nos. 1-24, June 29–Dec. 14, 1763.
>CtY (nos. 1-10, rep. in Political controversy, July 4–Sept. 6, 1763).

129. Conventicle courant. John Hilton. 1682-83. w.
>CSH, TxU (nos. 1, 3, 5-30, [July 24?], 1682–Feb. 14, 1683).

130. Copper plate magazine; or, Monthly cabinet of picturesque prints, consisting of views in Great Britain and Ireland. 1792+. m.
>CSH, DLC, MH, NNC (v. 1-3), RPB (v. 1-3).

131. Copper plate magazine; or, Monthly treasure, for the admirers of the imitative arts. Nos. 1-42, Aug. 1774–Jan. 1778. m.
>DLC, DNM, MB (1778), NN, WH.

132. Coranto from beyond the sea. No. 1, June 9, 1643.
>ICU (no. 1).

133. Corant; or, Weekly newes from Italy, Germany, Hungaria, Polonia, Bohemia, France and the Low-countries. 1621.
NN (Aug. 6, 1621, photostat).

134. [Corantos of various titles.] Nathaniel Butter, Nicholas Bourne, etc. 1622-32. *See also* Abstract of some speciall forreigne occurrences, Continuation of the forraine avisoes, Newes of this present weeke, Ordinary weekly curranto, Principall passages of Germany, Italy, France, etc., *and* Swedish intelligencer. Note: These corantos are notoriously perplexing. As this is a finding-list and not an effort at bibliographical description, we have simply grouped the corantos in what seemed to us a sufficiently convenient manner. Certain corantos may appear on both this and our second list, but we have not dared attempt the discrimination.
MnU (no. 22, Mar. 7, 1623, beginning: The sentence and execution done upon the bodies of certaine persons . . .).

135. Cork evening post. *Printed by* G. and J. Knight. Cork, 1754-96. s. w.
NN (June 26, July 3, 7, 14-21, 28, 31, Aug. 6–Sept. 1, 8-29, Oct. 9-23, Nov. 17, Dec. 4, 25, 1788).

136. Corn-cutter's journal. 1733(?)-34(?).
CtY (Nov. 13, 1733).

Country journal; or, The craftsman. *See* Craftsman.

137. Country magazine. 1763. m.
MH (v. 1).

138. Country spectator. *Ed.* T. F. Middleton. Gainsborough, nos. 1-33, Oct. 9, 1792–May 21, 1793. w.
CtY, MB.

139. County magazine. *Continued as* Western county magazine (from 1790). Salisbury, v. 1-6, 1786-92. m.
CtY (v. 1-2, Jan. 1786–Dec. 1788), DLC (v. 1-2, Jan. 1786–Oct. 1788), MH, NN (v. 1-2).

140. Courier and evening gazette. 1792+. d.
NN (Oct. 9, 11, 14-16, 19-21, 24, 25, 29, 30, Nov. 1, 4, 13, 25, 29, Dec. 6, 14, 19, 25, 26, 1799; Jan. 1, 2, 4, 17, 18, 21-23, 28, 30, 31, Feb. 1, 11, 13, 18, 20, 21, 25, 27–Mar. 7, 10, 12, 15, 21, 22, Apr. 9, 22, 23, 30, June 26, 27, 1800).

141. Courrier de l'Europe. London; Boulogne, 1776-92. (From U. L.)
DLC (v. 4-5, 7-10), MB (v. 1-23), N (v. 1-2).

142. Court and city register. *Continued as* Court and city

kalendar; or, Gentleman's register (from 1763?); *as* Court and city register; or, Gentleman's complete annual calendar (from 1779?); *as* London kalendar; or, City and court register (from 1783?). 1746(?)-97(?). a.
MH (1767), **PPAP** (1746, 1763, 1765, 1779, 1783), **PPL** (1748, 1753, 1775, 1780, 1786, 1791, 1794, 1797).

Court and city magazine. *See* Court magazine; or, Royal chronicle.

143. Court and city magazine; or, A fund of entertainment for the man of quality. . . . 1770-71. m. (From U. L.)
DLC.

Court, city and country magazine. *See* Court magazine; or, Royal chronicle.

144. Court, city and country magazine; or, Gentleman and lady's universal and polite instructor. 1788. m.
CtY (Jan.–Apr. 1788).

145. Court magazine; or, Royal chronicle. *Continued as* Court and city magazine (from Mar. 1763); *as* Court, city and country magazine (from Feb. 1764). *Ed.* Hugh Kelly. 1761-65. m.
CtY (v. 1-8, Sept. 1761–Nov. 1765), **NN** (Nov. 1761).

146. Court mercurie. John Cotgrave(?). 1644.
CtY (nos. 5, Aug. 3; 8, Aug. 31, 1644).

147. Court miscellany; or, Ladies new magazine. *Continued as* Court miscellany; or, Gentleman and lady's new magazine (from v. 2, 1766). Matilda Wentworth, etc. 1765-71. m.
CtY, DLC (v. 2), **MB** (v. 1-4, 1765-68), **WH** (v. 5-7).

148. Covent Garden journal. Henry Fielding. Nos. 1-72, Jan. 4–Nov. 25, 1752. s. w.; w. (from no. 53).
CtY (rotograph), **TxU.**

149. Covent Garden journal extraordinary. Bonnell Thornton(?). 1752. A parody on Fielding's Covent Garden journal.
CtY (no. 1, Jan. 20, 1752).

150. Covent Garden journal; or, The censor. *Continued as* Censor; or, Covent Garden journal (from no. 83, July 26, 1753). *Printed by* James Hoey. Dublin, nos. 1-234, 1752-56. w. Reprinted much material from Fielding's Covent Garden journal.
CSH (nos. 1-100, Jan. 23, 1752–Nov. 22, 1753), **CtY** (nos. 1-86, Jan. 23, 1752–Aug. 16, 1753).

Coventry mercury. *See* Jopson's Coventry mercury.

151. Crab-tree. 1757. w.
    TxU (nos. 12-14, July 12-26, 1757).

152. Craftsman. *Continued as* Country journal; or, The craftsman (from no. 45, May 13, 1727). Amhurst, Bolingbroke, Pulteney, etc. Nos. 1-1111(?), 1726-47(?). t. w.; w. The political parts were reprinted at various times as The craftsman, by Caleb d'Anvers, of Gray's Inn, esq. [*pseud.*]. The reprint of 1731-37 (in 14 v.) contains nos. 1-511, Dec. 5, 1726–Apr. 17, 1736, omitting nos. 301-02, 310, 323, 354, 388, 397, 401, 408-09, 427-29, 432, 434, 458, 460, 479, 481, 504.
    CtY (nos. 49-60, 63-72, 72-78, 80, 82-90, 93-94, 96-100, 102, 105-13, 115-20, 122-23, 126-29, June 9, 1727–Dec. 30, 1728; 1729-43, inc.; also nos. 1-44, Dec. 5, 1726–May 8, 1727, rep. 1727; also rep. 1731-37), **CU** (rep. 1731-37), **DLC** (rep. 1731-37), **ICJ** (rep. 1731-37), **ICU** (rep. 1731-37, v. 1-12, 14), **IU** (rep. 1731-37), **MB** (rep. 1731-37), **MH** (rep. 1731-37), **MdBP** (rep. 1731-37), **NIC** (rep. 1731-37), **NjP** (rep. 1731-37), **NN** (rep. 1731-37), **NNC** (rep. 1731-37, lacking v. 1, 11), **TxU** (nos. 139-368, 438-555, Mar. 1, 1728–Feb. 19, 1737, lacking nos. 200-01, 206, 249, 268, 277-88, 303-05, 311-50, 458-59, 473, 514-17, 532; also rep. 1731-37), **WH** (nos. 103, 108, 112, 114-18, 121, 123, 126, 130, 136, 138, 140, 143, 151, 162-64, 166, 168, 170, 174, 181-85, 193, 199, 202, 209, 211, 214-16, 218-20, 222-26, 231, 233-35, 237, 240, 242, 243, 245-48, 251, 253, 254, 256-73, 275, 276, 278-83, 285-88, 292, 302, 305, 307, 308, 312, 317-28, 330, 333, 336, 342, 345, 361, 362, 363, 381, June 22, 1728–Jan. 14, 1737).

153. Crisis. *Ed.* William Moore(?). Nos. 1-91, Jan. 21, 1775–Oct. 12, 1776. w. A supplement, The crisis extraordinary, was issued on Aug. 9, 1775.
    CSH (v. 1, rep. N. Y., 1776), **CtY** (also rep. 1775, 1776), **DLC** (nos. 1-73; also Crisis extraordinary), **ICN** (nos. 1-75, 78, 80-91), **MB** (nos. 1-80), **MH** (nos. 1-81), **MHi** (nos. 1-65), **MiUC**, **N** (nos. 1-76), **NIC** (nos. 1-28, rep. N. Y., 1776), **NN** (also Crisis extraordinary), **WH** (nos. 1-81).

154. Crisis. 1793. w.
    CtY (rep. 1794).

155. Critical observations on books, antient and modern. Thomas Howes. 1776-83(?). ir.
    CtY (nos. 1-8, 1776-83).

156. Critical review; or, Annals of literature. *Ed.* Smollett and others. 1756+. m.
    CtY, DLC, ICN, IU, MBB, MdBP, MH, N (lacking v. 22, 57, 84, 90, 93), **NjP, NN, NNC** (inc.), **PPL** (lacking 1789-90), **RPB** (v. 1-2, 4-10, 12-13, 17-18, 20+), **VaU, WU** (v. 1-2).

157. Critick: a review of authors and their productions. Thomas Brereton. Nos. 1-22, Jan.–June 1718; rep. as The criticks, being papers upon the times, 1719.
ICS, TxAG.

158. Cumberland magazine; or, Whitehaven monthly miscellany. Whitehaven, 1779-80(?). (From U. L.)
Ia (v. 2-4, 1779-80).

159. Currant. 1642.
ICN (July 12).

160. Currant intelligence, published by authority. Henry Muddiman. 1666. s. w.
CSH (nos. 1-24, June 4–Aug. 23, 1666), CtY (no. 12, July 12, 1666), MnU (nos. 1-24).

161. Currant intelligence; or, An impartial account of transactions both forraign and domestick. *Continued as* Smith's currant intelligence; or, An impartial account . . . (from no. 10, Mar. 16, 1680); *as* Currant intelligence (from Apr. 1681). J. Smith. Feb. 14, 1679/80– Dec. 24, 1681. s. w.
MnU (nos. 24, May 1, 1680; 38-70, Aug. 30–Dec. 24, 1681), NN (Feb. 17–Mar. 13, 16–Apr. 10, 17-27, 1680), WH (May 1-4, 1680).

162. Currant intelligence; or, An impartial account of transactions both forreign and domestick. *Continued as* Banks' currant intelligence . . . (from no. 2). A. Banks. 1680. w.
NN (Mar. 13, 20, Apr. 3), TxU (nos. 1-4, Mar. 13–Apr. 3, 1680).

Curtis' botanical magazine. *See* Botanical magazine. . . .

163. Daily advertiser. 1730+. d.
CtY (Apr. 29, 1734; Mar. 1, 1738; Feb. 21, Mar. 7, 19, 27, 1741; Aug. 16, Dec. 1, 1755), DLC (nos. 286-20929, Jan. 1, 1731–Dec. 31, 1795), NN (Feb. 25–Mar. 4, 1771).

164. Daily courant. 1702-35. d. There seems to have been also a country edition, issued tri-weekly. See below under IWS.
CtY (nos. 1, 97-1208, 1210-2555, Mar. 11, 1702–Dec. 31, 1709; Jan. 3, 1715–Dec. 30, 1717; 7118, Aug. 8, 1724; 5979, 5984, June 2, July 7, 1735), ICU (July 22, 24, 1710; nos. 3121-3371, Oct. 13, 1711–Aug. 1, 1712, badly cut up), IWS (nos. 33-84, May 27–July 25, 1702, chiefly country issues; also nos. 100, 106, Aug. 13, 20, 1702), TxAG (nos. 9255, 9256, 5070-71, 5206, 5498-99, 5505, 5507, 5547, July 7, 1731–Jan. 16, 1733), TxU (nos. 1159-1470, Jan. 1– Dec. 3, 1706; 1834-60, Jan. 1-31, 1708, lacking nos. 1844, 1847,

1856; 2799, Oct. 12, 1710; 3631, 3641, 3665, 3705, 3715, 3725, 3737, June 3–Oct. 5, 1713; 4005, 4033, Aug. 25, Sept. 27, 1714; 5149, 5152, Apr. 25, 26, 1718; 5813-5934, June 8–Oct. 27, 1720; 9286, 9287, Aug. 13-14, 1731; 5939, 5945, 5946, 5949, 5953, 5959, 5960, 5965, 5967, 5969, 5975, 5981, 5982, 5986, 5987, 5989, 5993, 5995, 5997, 5999, 6001, Apr. 16–June 27, 1735), **WH** (nos. 1395, Oct. 3, 1706; 1711, Aug. 8, 1707).

165. Daily gazetteer. 1735-48. d.
CtY (Jan. 2, Sept. 1, 1736), **IU** (nos. 1747-48, June 8-10, 1741), **TxU** (nos. 3-159, with some omissions, July 2–Dec. 31, 1735).

166. Daily journal. 1720-42. d.
CtY (Mar. 27–Nov. 6, 1733; Apr. 24, May 20, 22, 24, 25, Nov. 15, 29, 1736; Mar. 15, 17, 19, 1737), **TxU** (no. 3250, June 5, 1731).

167. Daily post. 1719-46(?). d.
CtY (June 3, 1723–Dec. 31, 1724; June 4, Nov. 17, 1733), **NN** (Sept. 29, 1738), **TxU** (no. 7820, Sept. 25, 1744), **WH** (no. 2783, Aug. 22, 1728).

Daily post boy. *See* Post boy, with foreign and domestick news.

168. Daily universal register. *Continued as* Times; or, Daily universal register (from Jan. 1, 1788); *as* Times (from May 18, 1788). 1785+. d.
CtY (1789, 1790, 1791, 1793, 1797-98, all inc.), **TxU** (nos. 2517, Jan. 26, 1793; 3936, July 3, 1797; 4298, Oct. 3,. 1798), **WH** (nos. 2517, 3936, 4298).

169. Delphick oracle. Sept. 1719–Mar. 1720. m.
CSH (lacking Mar. 1720).

170. Devil; containing a review and investigation of all public subjects whatever. 1786-87. w.
CSH (v. 1, nos. 1-13), **CtY** (nos. 1-13, 1786, 3rd ed.), **DLC** (v. 1), **MH**.

171. Devil's pocket-book. 1786-87. w.
CtY (nos. 1-10, 1786-87).

172. Devil upon crutches in England; or, Night scenes in London. 1755. (From U. L.)
DLC, ICN, NNC.

173. Diary, or an exact journall, faithfully communicating the most remarkable proceedings of both Houses of Parliament. . . . 1644-46.
MnU (no. 66, Aug. 21, 1645), **TxU** (no. 7, Aug. 16, 1644).

174. Diary; or, Woodfall's register. 1789-93(?). d.
CtY (May 26, 1789; Mar. 2-4, 16, 30, Apr. 1, 17, 27, 1790), **WH**

(nos. 67-111, 113-29, June 15–Aug. 26, 1789; 502, 504, 510, 522, 537, 547-49, 551, Nov. 4–Dec. 31, 1790; 752-53, 761-62, 769-70, 774, 790, 794, 798, 813, 819-20, 831-33, 836, 844, 850-51, 857, 863, Aug. 20–Dec. 28, 1791; 1090, Sept. 18, 1792).

Diatelesma. *See* Principall passages of Germany, Italy, France, etc.

175. Dilucidator; or, Reflection upon modern transactions. 1689.
CSH (nos. 1-3), **NIC** (no. 5).

175a. Diurnall occurances in Parliament. *Printed for* F. Coules and T. Banks. 1642. w.
ICN (no. 2, Jan. 24; no. 6, Feb. 21, 1642), **MnU** (Jan. 10).

Diurnall occurrences in Parliament. *See* Heads of severall proceedings in the present Parliament.

175b. Diurnall occurrences in Parliament. June 1642.
TxU (nos. 1-2, June 6-13, 1642).

Diurnall occurrences; or, The heads of severall proceedings in both Houses of Parliament. *See* Heads of severall proceedings in the present Parliament.

175c. Diurnall occurrences; or, The heads of the proceedings in both Houses of Parliament. *Printed for* I. G. 1642.
ICN (Jan. 10-17, Feb. 7-14, 1641/2).

Diurnall; or, The heads of all the proceedings in Parliament. *See* Heads of severall proceedings in the present Parliament.

176. Diverting muse; or, The universal medley. 1707.
NNC (pt. 1).

177. Diverting post. Henry Playford. 1704-06. w. (to June 30, 1705); m.
MH (nos. 3-5, Nov. 4-25, 1704; 27-29, Apr. 21–May 12, 1705; 32-35, May 26–June 23, 1705), **TxAG** (Feb. 1706), **TxU** (Jan. 1706).

178. Domestick intelligence; or, News both from city and country. *Continued as* Protestant (domestick) intelligence (from no. 56, Jan. 16, 1680). Benjamin Harris. Nos. 1-114, July 9, 1679–Apr. 15, 1681 (not published Apr. 16–Dec. 28, 1680). s. w. *See also* True Protestant (domestick) intelligence.
CSH (nos. 1-25, 1679; 83-84, 1680), **CtY** (photostat; also no. 21, Sept. 16, 1679, orig.), **ICN** (nos. 56-114, photostat), **IU** (photostat), **MB** (nos. 1-50), **MnU** (nos. 1-114, photographic facsimiles; also orginals of nos. 9, 10, 12-14, 20, 21, 39, 44, 57, 59, 61, 63-65,

69-71, 74, 78, 79, 81, 84, 87, 90-95, 97-114), **NIC** (photostat), **NN** (nos. 52-82), **NNC, WH** (photostat).

179. Domestick intelligence; or, News both from city and country. *Continued as* True domestick intelligence (from no. 19, Sept. 9, 1679); *as* Loyal Protestant, and true domestick intelligence (from no. 1, Mar. 9, 1681). Nathaniel Thompson. 1679-83. s. w.; t. w. (from Mar. 9, 1681).
    CtY (Mar. 12, 1680–Mar. 20, 1682; Mar. 23, June 20, July 1, 1682), **NN** (nos. 52-63, 65-85, Jan. 2–Apr. 27, 1680), **WH** (nos. 87-90, May 4-14, 1680; 28, 32, 37, 43, 46, 50, 52, 53, 56-61, 66-69, 71, 81-84, 86-89, 91, 93-95, 98, 100-04, 107-09, 111-16, 118-23, 125, 127-29, 134, 136-37, 140, 143-45, 147-48, 150-57, 159-65, 167-70, 172-91, June 11, 1681–Aug. 8, 1682).

180. Domestick intelligence; or, News both from city and country impartially related. T. Benskin. 1681-82.
    CtY (no. 112, June 19, 1682), **MnU** (nos. 5, June 9, 1681; 21, Aug. 4, 1681), **NN** (June 23, 1681), **TxU** (nos. 1-155, May 13, 1681–Nov. 16, 1682).

181. Dramatic censor, being remarks upon the conduct, characters and catastrophe of our most celebrated plays. No. 1, 1751.
    CtY (no. 1), **MH** (no. 1).

182. Dramatic censor; or, Critical companion. V. 1-2, 1770.
    CtY, DLC, ICN, ICU, IU, MB, NcU, NIC, NN, NNC.

183. Dramatic censor; or, Weekly theatrical report. T. Dutton. 1800+. w.
    CtY (nos. 1-26, Jan. 4–June 28, 1800), **DLC, IU** (v. 1-2), **MB, MH, MiU** (v. 1-2).

184. Dublin chronicle. Dublin, 1787-93(?). t. w.
    CtY (May 3, 1787–Dec. 31, 1791), **TxU** (nos. 8, 94, 126, 151, 257, 259, 260, 263, 271, 273-76, 481, 574, 773, 790, 858, 870, May 17, 1787–Nov. 21, 1792).

185. Dublin gazette. Dublin, 1750(?)-52(?). s. w.
    IU (no. 155, Feb. 11, 1752).

186. Dublin journal. George Faulkner. Dublin, 1725+.
    TxU (no. 666, Mar. 4, 1732).

187. Dublin magazine. Dublin, 1762-64(?).
    ICU (v. 1-3, 1762-64), **WH** (v. 2-3, 1763-64).

188. Dublin magazine and Irish monthly register. Dublin, 1788-1800. m.
    CtY (Dec. 1798), **DCU** (v. 4-5).

189. Dublin news-letter. Dublin, 1737-44. s. w.
NN (June 27, 1741), **WH** (no. 468, June 27, 1741, facsim.).

190. Eaton chronicle; or, The salt-box. Chester, nos. 1-20, Aug. 30–Sept. 26, 1788.
NN (rep. 1789).

191. Echo; or, Edinburgh weekly journal. Edinburgh, 1729-34. w.
TxAG (nos. 4-14, 18, 24, 27, 38, 39, Jan. 29–Oct. 1, 1729).

192. Edinburgh advertiser. A. Donaldson. Edinburgh, 1764+. s. w.
CtY (nos. 1-145, Jan. 3, 1764–May 21, 1765; 575-626, July 4–Dec. 29, 1769; 732-835, Jan. 4–Dec. 31, 1771; 2194-3339, Jan. 7, 1785–Dec. 29, 1795; 3550-3652, Jan. 5–Dec. 28, 1798), **ICU** (v. 59-60, Feb. 26–Dec. 31, 1793, lacking a few nos.), **MB** (v. 28, nos. 1417-74, 1747, July 22, 1777–Sept. 26, 1780, inc.), **N** (v. 27-30, Jan. 1, 1777–Dec. 29, 1778), **NN** (June 28, 1772–Dec. 31, 1773), **PPL** (v. 59-63, inc., Apr. 9, 1793–Apr. 14, 1795), **WH** (v. 3, no. 105–v. 4, no. 209, Jan.–Dec. 1765; v. 18-19, July 1772–June 1773; 21-22, Jan.–Dec. 1774; 31-32, Jan.–Dec. 1779; 40-45, July 1783–June 1786).

193. Edinburgh chronicle. Edinburgh, 1759-60(?). s. w.; t. w. (from Sept. 15, 1759); w. (from Apr. 1760).
CtY (nos. 1-35, Mar. 22–July 19, 1759), **WH** (v. 1, nos. 1-52, Mar. 22–Sept. 15, 1759; v. 3, nos. 131-73, Mar. 17–Oct. 8, 1760).

194. Edinburgh courant. *Continued as* Scots courant (from no. 707, Mar. 22, 1710). Edinburgh, 1705-20. t. w.
NN (Mar. 5-7, 1716; Mar. 17, 1717), **TxU** (nos. 202-400, Sept. 30, 1708–Mar. 24, 1709).

195. Edinburgh evening courant. Edinburgh, 1718+. t. w.
CtY (Sept. 25–Nov. 10, 1740), **MB** (no. 7686, Oct. 15, 1745), **NN** (Apr. 3, 1760; Nov. 14, 1764; Apr. 20–June 29, July 4-18, Aug. 10–Sept. 12, 16, 19, 1778; Jan. 1–Sept. 8, 15-22, Oct. 1–Dec. 26, 1781), **WH** (nos. 249-402, inc., Jan. 2–Dec. 28, 1727).

196. Edinburgh gazette. *Continued as* Scots postman; or, New Edinburgh gazette (from Sept. 7, 1708) *as* Edinburgh gazette; or, Scots postman (from Mar. 11, 1714). James Donaldson. Edinburgh, 1699-1715, with several interruptions and minor changes in title. On the complicated history of this periodical, see W. J. Couper, Edinburgh periodical press, I, 202-12, 223-25, 228-33, 238-42; II, 11-15.
TxAG (nos. 429, May 3, 1703; 27, July 14, 1707; 58, May 11, 1710; 252, Oct. 11, 1711).

197. Edinburgh gazette. Edinburgh, 1793+. s. w.
NN (July 2, 9–Oct. 29, Nov. 5–Dec. 31, 1793; 1794).

198. Edinburgh magazine and review. *Ed.* William Smellie and Gilbert Stuart. Edinburgh, v. 1-5, 1773-76. m.
CtY, DLC, ICN (v. 1-4), NN (v. 1, no. 4–v. 2, no. 12, Jan.–Sept. 1774; v. 2, no. 14–v. 3, no. 16, Nov. 1774–Feb. 1775).

Edinburgh magazine; or, Literary amusement. *See* Weekly magazine; or, Edinburgh amusement.

199. Edinburgh magazine; or, Literary miscellany. *Ed.* James Sibbald (to 1792); Robert Anderson. Edinburgh, 1785+. m.
DLC (v. 1, Jan.–June 1785; 3-4, 1786; 7, Jan.–June, 1788; 11, Jan.–June 1790), MB (1786), MH (v. 13, no. 78, June 1791; v. 15, no. 87, Mar. 1792), MiD-B (1778, 1790, 1796, 1799, inc.), NN (Feb. 1796), PPL (n. s., v. 1-11, Jan. 1793–June 1798).

200. Edinburgh quarterly magazine, intended to promote the knowledge, belief, and influence of divine revelation. Edinburgh, 1798-1800. q., with also an annual supplement.
CtY (v. 1, Mar. 31–Dec. 29, 1798; also suppl. 1798).

201. Edinburgh review. A. Wedderburn, Adam Smith, Hugh Blair, William Robertson. Edinburgh, nos. 1-2, 1755-56. s. a.
CtY (also rep. 1818), DLC, ICN, NcU (v. 1, rep. 1802), NN (rep 1818), PPL (rep. 1818).

202. Edinburgh review. Edinburgh, 1773-99.
TxU.

Edinburgh weekly magazine. *See* Weekly magazine; or, Edinburgh amusement.

203. Englands memorable accidents. 1642-43.
TxU (Jan. 2, 1642/3).

204. England's moderate messenger. 1649.
CSH.

204a. English chronicle. *Continued as* English chronicle, and universal evening-post (from Mar. 31, 1781?). 1779(?)-1800(?). t. w.
CtY (nos. 1355-1533, May 15, 1788–July 16, 1789, lacking 3 nos.), NN (Jan. 2, 1779), WH (nos. 2829, Aug. 8, 1797; 3164, 3184, 3189, 3216, Aug. 31–Dec. 31, 1799).

205. English currant. *Printed for* R. B. 1688-89.
CSH (nos. 1-9, Dec. 12, 1688–Jan. 9, 1689).

206. English currant; or, Advice domestick and forreign. *Printed for* Tho. Burrell. 1679-(?).
CSH (no. 1, Sept. 8, 1679).

207. English freeholder. Nos. 1-14, June 1–Aug. 27, 1791.
CtY, PPAP (nos. 1-7).

208. English gazette. *Continued as* Westminster gazette (from no. 8, Jan. 15, 1681). 1680-81.
CSH (nos. 1-3, Dec. 22-29, 1680), TxU (nos. 1, 3, 7, Dec. 22-29, 1680, Jan. 29, 1681).

209. English intelligencer. Nos. 1-8, 1679.
CSH, MH.

210. Englishman. Nos. 1-12(?), June 11–Aug. 20(?), 1768. (From U. L.)
DLC (nos. 1, 6, 8-12).

211. Englishman. Nos. 1-17, Mar. 13–June 2, 1779.
MiU.

212. Englishman: being the sequel of the Guardian. Richard Steele. Nos. 1-57, Oct. 6, 1713–Feb. 15, 1714; second series, nos. 1-38, July 11–Nov. 21, 1715. t. w.
CtY (first series, nos. 1-53, 55-56; also nos. 1-57, rep. 1714), DLC (first series), ICU (first series), IEN (first series, rep.), IWS (no. 57), MB (first series), NN (first series), NNC (first series), PU (first series), RPB (first series, rep. 1714), TxU (first series, nos. 1, 3, 6, 7, 8, 10-14, 18, 19, 23, 26, 30, 31, 35, 37, 39, 40, 41, 45, 46, 47, 48, 54, 57; also reps. 1713, 1714; second series, nos. 13, 14, 15, 34, 35, 36, 38, Aug. 22–Nov. 21, 1715; also rep. 1716).

213. English review; or, An abstract of English and foreign literature. *Continued as* English review of literature, science, discoveries, etc. (v. 27-28, 1796). Jan. 1783–Dec. 1796. m.
CtY, MeB (1787-92, inc.), MH (v. 2, Aug. 1783; v. 16, Oct. 1790), NjP (v. 17-21, 1791-93), NN, NNC (v. 1-21, 1783-93), PU (v. 4, 1784).

214. Entertainer. Nos. 1-12, Sept. 3–Nov. 19, 1754. w.
CtY, MiU (no. 1, Sept. 3, 1754), TxU (no. 1).

215. Entertainer, containing remarks on men, manners, religion, and policy. Nos. 1-43, Nov. 6, 1717–Aug. 27, 1718. w.
CtY, DLC, ICS (rep.), ICU (2nd ed.), MH, TxU (rep. by N. Mist).

216. Ephemeris; or, An astronomical state of the heavens. George Kingsley. Nos. 1-7, 1717-23. (From U. L.)
DLC (nos. 5-7), PPAP, WH (no. 1).

217. Epitome of the weekly news. 1682.
    TxU (nos. 1, 2, Aug. 28, Sept. 4, 1682).

Etherington's York chronicle. . . . *See* York chronicle. . . .

218. European magazine and London review. Jan. 1782+. m.
    CtY, CU (v. 1-7, Jan. 1782–June 1785; 9-30, Jan. 1786–Dec. 1796), DLC, ICN, IU, MB, MBB, MH (v. 3-7, 9-15, 17-26, 28), MHi, MiU, MnU (v. 1), N (v. 3-7, 9-18, 20-38), NcU (v. 16, 18, 21, 24), NIC, NjP (v. 1-5, 7-8, 10-21, 23, 25-33, 35-36), NN, NNC, PPL, PU (1784-90, inc.; 1791+), TxU (v. 1-35), WH.

219. Evangelical magazine. 1793+. m.
    CSH (Jan., Feb. 1799), CtY (v. 1, July–Dec. 1793; 3+, Jan. 1795+), DLC (v. 3-5, 1795-97), ICN, MB, MiU (v. 1-3, 5-13), NN (one no. in 1793; Jan. 1799).

220. Evening advertiser. 1754-58(?). t. w.
    CtY (nos. 2-4, 10-27, Mar. 5–May 2, 1754; 142, 160, 170, 223, 283, Jan. 25–Dec. 23, 1755), WH (no. 457, Feb. 3, 1757).

221. Evening mail. 1789+.
    CtY (July 20, 1789), NN (Feb. 14, June 23, 1794).

222. Evening post, with the historical account. 1706; 1709-30(?). t. w.
    CtY (nos. 516-29, Nov. 29–Dec. 30, 1712; 530-83, 585-93, 640-83, 685-86, Jan. 1–Dec. 31, 1713; 687-741, Jan. 2–May 8, 1714; 853, Jan. 25, 1716; 1939, 1941, 1942, Mar. 8-20, 1722), MB (nos. 1814, 1832, 1721), NN (Dec. 9, 1721), TxU (nos. 436, 510, 778, 979, 990, 991, 1025, 1040, 1101, 1145, 1233, 1235, 1411, 1415, 1418, 1419, 1426, 1432, 1433, 1434, 1436, 1438, 1441, 1450, 1699, 2981, May 27, 1712–Aug. 29, 1728).

223. Every man's magazine; or, Monthly repository of science, instruction, and amusement. 1771-72. m.
    CtY (v. 1, July 1771–June 1772).

Exact accompt. *See* Particular advice from the office of intelligence.

224. Exact and true collection of the weekly passages. 1646. m.
    ICN (one no., Jan. 1–Feb. 16, 1646).

225. Examiner. Dublin, 1710-13.
    TxU (v. 1-3, Aug. 14, 1710–Apr. 9, 1713).

226. Examiner; or, Remarks upon papers and occurrences. *Ed.* W. King; J. Swift; Mrs. Manley; W. Oldisworth. Aug. 3, 1710–July 26, 1714. w.
    CtY (v. 1, no. 1–v. 6, no. 19, Aug. 3, 1710–July 26, 1714), DLC (rep. 1712-14), ICU (v. 1, nos. 1-50, Aug. 3, 1710–July 26, 1711), IU (v. 1, nos. 1-52, Aug. 3, 1710–July 26, 1711), MB (Aug. 3,

1710–May 11, 1714), **NN** (v. 1, nos. 1-11; v. 4, no. 12, Aug. 3, 1710–June 26, 1713), **NNC** (Aug. 3, 1710–July 26, 1711, rep.), **TxU** (v. 1-6, Aug. 3, 1710–July 26, 1714; also nos. for Nov. 13-Dec. 11, 1714).

227. Exchange intelligencer. 1645.
    TxU (no. 7, July 10, 1645).

    Extract of letters. *See* Late proceedings of the Scottish army.

228. Extraordinary North Briton. William Moore. 1768-70. w.
    DLC (nos. 1-47), **N** (nos. 1-90, May 16, 1768–Jan. 20, 1770), **NN** (nos. 43-91, Mar. 4, 1769–Jan. 27, 1770).

229. Faithfull intelligencer from the Parliaments army in Scotland. Edinburgh, 1659.
    CtY (Dec. 3, 1659).

230. Faithfull mercury, imparting news domestick and foreign. 1679.
    CSH (no. 1, July 21, 1679).

231. Faithfull relation of the late occurences and proceedings of the Scottish army. *Printed for* R. Bostock and S. Gellibrand. 1644.
    CtY (Feb. 21, 1644).

231a. Faithful post. *Continued as* Great Britain's post (from no. 136, Nov. 9, 1653); *as* Politique post (from Jan. 11, 1654); *as* Grand politique post (from ?); *as* Weekly post (from Apr. 18, 1654). *Printed for* George Horton. No. 89, Apr. 1, 1653–June 19, 1655. w.
    CtY (no. 196, Sept. 19, 1654).

    Fame's palladium; or, Annual miscellany. *See* Gentleman and lady's palladium.

232. Family magazine. Mrs. Trimmer. 1788-89.
    ICU (Jan. 1788–June 1789).

233. Farmer's magazine. *Ed.* Robert Brown. Edinburgh, 1800+. q.
    CtY, N, NIC, NN, PPL (rep. 1802), **PU.**

234. Farmer's magazine and useful family companion. 1776-80.
    DA, NN (v. 1-2, Apr. 1776–Dec. 1777), **TxU** (v. 1).

235. Female spectator. Eliza Haywood. V. 1-4, 1744-46. m.
    CtY (also reps. 1748, 1766), **DLC, ICU** (3rd ed., 1750), **IEN** (rep. 1771), **IU, MB** (v. 1, 4, rep. 1755), **MH** (rep. 1748), **MnU, NNC** (v. 1-3, rep. 1748; v. 4, rep. 1766; also Dublin rep., 1747), **TxU** (rep. 1755).

236. Female tatler. Thomas Baker. 1709-10. t. w.
   MH (nos. 1-111, July 8, 1709–Mar. 29, 1710), **NN** (no. 56), **TxU** (nos. 1-12, 87-88, 91-92, 94).

237. Financial pamphlets. 1796+. (From U. L.)
   DLC.

238. Fine design discovered and Irish rebels landed. 1643.
   TxU (June 13, 1643).

239. Finn's Leinster journal. Kilkenny, 1766+.
   NN (Dec. 25, 28, 1799; Jan. 18, 25, Feb. 5, Apr. 12, 1800).

240. Flagellant. Robert Southey. 1792. w.
   CtY (nos. 1-5, Mar. 1-29, 1792).

241. Flapper. Dublin, nos. 1-75, Feb. 2, 1796–Feb. 4, 1797.
   CtY, DCU, MH, NN, TxU.

242. Flying post. *Continued as* Flying post; or, The post master (from no. 129, Mar. 10, 1696?). *Ed.* George Ridpath (to 1713); Stephen Whatley. 1695-1731(?).
   CtY (nos. 3321-3340, Jan. 10–Feb. 24, 1712/3; 3656, 3689, 3708, 3721, 3731, 3742, June 11–Dec. 29, 1715; 3758, 3806, 3818-3821, 3824, 3826, 3829, 3830, 3835-39, 3841, 3844-46, 3848, 3849, 3852, 3854, 3855, 3857, 3858, 3861-67, 3869-78, 3880-84, 3886-3900, Feb. 4–Dec. 29, 1716; 3904-12, 3926, Jan. 8–Mar. 5, 1717), **IU** (1696-99, inc.), **IWS** (no. 1134, Aug. 13, 1702), **MB** (nos. 4153, Aug. 21; 4171, Oct. 14, 1718), **MHi** (1695-1714, inc.), **TxU** (nos. 3280, 3282, 3292, Oct. 7–Nov. 4, 1712; also issues for June 1, 6, 1723).

Fog's weekly journal. *See* Weekly journal; or, Saturday's post. . . .

244. Fortnight's register; or, A chronicle of interesting and remarkable events, foreign and domestic. 1762. (From U. L.)
   NN (nos. 1-11, July–Dec. 1762).

245. Free Briton. F. Walsingham. 1729-35. w.
   CtY (Mar. 9, 1731), **RPB** (no. 50, 1730), **TxAG** (nos. 10, 13, 15, 16, 18, 25-27, 30-31, 55, 61, 64-66, 68-69, 73, 75-78, 82-85, 90, 94, 96, 100-01, 103, 111, 114-15, 120, 124-25, 131-32, 147, 157-59, 172, 200-01, 204-05, 207, 225, 228-29, 245, 247-48, 251, 259-60, 264, 266, 278, Feb. 5, 1730–Mar. 6, 1735).

246. Free Briton; or, The opinion of the people. 1727-(?).
   RPB (no. 2).

247. Free enquirer. *Ed.* P. Annet. 1761.
   CtY (v. 1, nos. 1-9, Oct. 17–Dec. 12, 1761).

248. Freeholder; or, Political essays. Joseph Addison. Nos. 1-55, Dec. 23, 1715–June 29, 1716. s. w.
  CtY (nos. 1-20; also rep. 1716), DLC, ICU (3rd ed., 1723), IU (rep. 1758), MH, MHi, TxAG (rep. 1732), TxU.

249. Freeholder extraordinary. 1717-18.
  TxU (May 2, 1718).

250. Freeholder's journal. 1722-23.
  CtY (nos. 1-36, Jan. 31, 1721/2–Aug. 29, 1722), NN (nos. 1-76, Jan. 31, 1721/2–May 18, 1723).

251. Freeholder's magazine; or, Monthly chronicle of liberty. By a patriotic society. 1769-70. m.
  MB (Jan.–Dec. 1770), NN (v. 1-2, Sept. 1769–Aug. 1770), RPB (Nov.–Dec. 1769; July–Aug. 1770).

252. Freemason's magazine; or, General and complete library. 1793-98. m. Single numbers for 1797 entitled Scientific magazine and freemasons repository.
  DLC (v. 1, 1793; Jan.–June, 1797).

253. Freethinker. 1711. s. w.
  TxU (no. 4, Nov. 27, 1711).

254. Freethinker. *Ed.* A. Philips. 1718-21. s. w.
  CtY (nos. 1-210, 216-339, Mar. 24, 1718–June 19, 1721, lacking no. 318; also rep. 1739), DLC (nos. 1-159, Mar. 24, 1718–Sept. 28, 1719, rep. 1722-23), ICU (nos. 1-159), IEK (rep. 1723), IU (nos. 1-350, Mar. 24, 1718–July 28, 1721), MB (nos. 1-159), MiU (nos. 1-159), MnU (rep. 1722-23), NN (nos. 1-159, rep, 1723), NNC (nos. 1-159, rep. 1723), PU (Mar. 24, 1718–Mar. 23, 1719), TxU (nos. 4, 57).

255. Freethinker extraordinary to Freethinker in ordinary. 1719.
  TxU (no. 7, Dec. 2, 1719).

256. Friendly intelligence. 1679.
  CSH (no. 2, Sept. 15, 1679).

257. Friendly writer and register of truth. 1732-33. m.
  ICU (nos. 1-6, Sept. 1732–Feb. 1732/3).

258. Fumbler. 1762.
  CtY (rep. in Political controversy, 1762).

260. Gallery of fashion. 1794+. m.
  MH, NN.

261. Gazetteer and London daily advertiser. *Continued as* Gazetteer and new daily advertiser (from April 27, 1764). 1741(?)-96(?). d.
  CtY (May 28, 1755; Jan. 2–Apr. 29, 1769; Dec. 3, 1770–July 17,

1771; Feb. 26, Mar. 6, July 21, 1789; Apr. 2–Dec. 31, 1790), ICU (nos. 13054-13202, Jan. 1–June 24, 1771).

Gazetteer and new daily advertiser. *See* Gazetteer and London daily advertiser.

General advertiser. *See* London daily post and general advertiser.

261a. General advertiser and morning intelligencer. *Continued as* Parker's general advertiser and morning intelligencer (from May 11, 1782?); *as* General advertiser (from Nov. 24, 1784). 1776-90(?).
NN (Dec. 24-29, 31, 1778; Jan. 1-7, 9, 15, Feb. 2, 10, 13, Oct. 1–Nov. 8, 10-22, 24, 25, 27–Dec. 11, 14, 16, 17, 22, 27-31, 1779; Jan. 1, 5-7, 12-15, 18–Feb. 5, 9-12, 16-25, 28–Mar. 8, 10-31, 1780).

262. General evening post. 1733+. t. w.
CtY (nos. 668-821, Jan. 3–Dec. 30, 1738; 1855-2218, Aug. 8, 1745–Dec. 26, 1747; 2221-22, Jan. 2-5, 1748; 2225-26, 2228, 2230-42, 2244-79, 2281-91, 2293-95, 2297-2305, Jan. 12–June 30, 1748; 3135-43, Jan. 15–Feb. 2, 1754; 3359, 3405, July 5, Oct. 23, 1755), WH (nos. 3588-90, 3592-3600, 3602-12, 3614-29, 3631-49, 3651-63, 3666-67, 3671-78, 3680-85, 3687-90, 3692-95, 3697-3705, 3708-09, 3712-67, 3769-72, 3775-80, 3782-87, 3789, 3792-3803, 3805-06, 3808-10, 3812-51, 3853-54, 3856, 3858-71, 3873-3908, 3910-43, 3945-54, 3956-79, 3981-4012, 4014-15, 4017-20, 4022-23, 4025, Jan. 4, 1757–Aug. 2, 1758; 6367, Nov. 29, 1774).

General history of Europe. *See* Present state of Europe; or, The historical and political monthly mercury.

263. General history of trade. Daniel Defoe. 1713. m.
CtY (nos. 1-2, June–Sept. 1713).

264. General London evening mercury. 1743-45(?). t. w.
WH (nos. 94-105, 106-37, 140-58, 161-76, 178-83, 185-86, 188, 190-94, 196-212, 214-24, 227-30, 232, 234, 236-45, 247, 251-58, 260, 264-65, 267-74, 277, 279-80, 282-84, 286-87, 289, 291-92, 295-98, 300, 303-05, 307-08, 310-12, 314-19, 323-26, 328-40, 343-48, 350-51, 353, 357-60, 363, 365, 368-69, 372-73, 375-77, Dec. 6, 1743–Sept. 26, 1745).

265. General magazine and impartial review. 1787-92.
CtY, MB (v. 4, July–Dec. 1790), MH (v. 1-4, 1787-90), MHi (1789-90), NN (v. 4), NNC (June 1787; Mar. 1788), PPL (v. 1-4).

266. General magazine of arts and sciences, philosophical, philological, mathematical, and mechanical. Benjamin Martin. 1755-65. This publication was issued under the following heads: pt. 1, The young gentlemen's and ladies philosophy (2 v.); pt. 2, The natural history of the

world (2 v.); pt. 3, A compleat system of all the philological sciences (2 v.); pt. 4, A body of mathematical institutes or principles of science (2 v.); pt. 5, Miscellaneous correspondence . . . [subtitles vary] (4 v.); Biographia philosophica (1 v.); and The general magazine, etc., on a new plan (1 v.).

CtY (pt. 5, v. 1-3, Jan. 1755–Dec. 1757), **DLC** (pt. 5, v. 1-2), **ICN** (pt. 5, v. 1-3, Jan. 1755–Dec. 1760), **MH** (pt. 5), **MHi** (pts. 1, 2, 5, v. 3-4), **NjP** (pt. 1), **NN** (pt. 1, v. 1-2, 1755-58; pt. 4, v. 2, inc., 1756; pt. 5, Jan. 1755–Dec. 1763), **NNC** (pt. 5), **WH** (pt. 5).

267. General magazine: or, Compleat repository of arts, sciences, politics, and literature. Jan.–Dec. 1776. m.
DLC, MB (inc.).

General proceedings of state affairs. *See* Severall proceedings in Parliament.

268. General review; or, Impartial register. 1752.
IaU, MH (nos. 1-5, 1752).

269. General treatise of husbandry and gardening. R. Bradley. 1725-26.
CtY (Aug. 1725).

270. Gentleman. 1755.
CtY.

271. Gentleman and lady's palladium. *Continued as* Gentleman and lady's military palladium (from 1759); *as* Gentleman and lady's palladium (from 1760); *as* Palladium extraordinary (from 1763); *as* Palladium enlarged (from 1764); *as* Palladium of fame; or, Annual miscellany (from 1765); *as* Fame's palladium; or, Annual miscellany (from 1766); *as* British palladium (from 1768). J. Tipper. 1752-79. a.
DLC (1752).

272. Gentleman and lady's weekly magazine. Edinburgh, 1774-75. w.
CtY (Feb. 4, 1774–Mar. 29, 1775).

Gentleman's and London magazine; or, Monthly chronologer. *See* London magazine and monthly chronicler.

274. Gentleman's diary; or, The mathematical repository. 1741+. a.
CtY, DLC, ICJ, MB (1764-67, 1769-82, 1784-86), **MH** (1744-45, 1759-63), **NNC** (rep. 1814), **PPAP** (nos. 1-12, 1741-52), **PU** (1785-90), **WH** (1741, 1748-49).

275. Gentleman's journal and tradesman's companion. 1721.
   DLC (nos. 1-18, Apr. 1–July 29, 1721).

276. Gentleman's journal; or, The monthly miscellany. *Ed.* Peter Motteux. Jan. 1692–Nov. 1694. m.
   CtY, CSH (Nov. 1692), DLC (1692-93), ICU (lacking June 1692 and a few pages of Oct. and Nov. 1692 and of Apr. 1693), IWS (Jan. 1692–Dec. 1693), MH, PPL, TxU (Apr., May, June, July, Sept. 1692; Jan.–Dec. 1693).

277. Gentleman's magazine; or, Monthly intelligencer. *Continued as* Gentleman's magazine and historical chronicle (from 1736). *Ed.* E. Cave, etc. 1731+. m.
   CSH, CSt, CtY, CU, DLC, ICN, ICU, IEN, IU, MB, MBB, MdBP, MH, MHi, MiU, MiUC, MnU, N, NcU, NIC, NjP, NN, NNC, PPL, TxU, WH.

278. Gentleman's mathematical companion. *Ed.* W. Davis, J. Hampshire. 1798+. a.
   IU, NIC, NNC, PU, RPB, TxU.

279. German museum; or, Monthly repository of the literature of Germany, the North and the Continent in general. 1800+. m.
   CtY, DLC, NN.

280. Ghost. Edinburgh, nos. 1-46, Apr. 25–Nov. 16, 1796. s. w.
   CtY (nos. 1-25, Apr. 25–July 20, 1796).

281. Glasgow courant. *Ed.* R. and A. Foulis(?). Glasgow, Oct. 21, 1745–Oct. 1760. w.
   DLC (Mar. 10, 1746–Sept. 7, 1747).

282. Glasgow courier. Glasgow, 1791+.
   CtY (Apr. 27–Dec. 28, 1799).

283. Glasgow magazine and review; or, Universal miscellany. Glasgow, 1783-84.
   NN (v. 1), PU (v. 1).

284. Gloucester journal. *Founded by* Robert Raikes and William Dicey. Gloucester, 1722+. w.
   WH (v. 54+, 1775+).

285. Gospel magazine and theological review. 1796+. (From U. L.)
   NjP (v. 1-5, 1796-1800).

286. Gospel magazine; or, Spiritual library, designed to promote religion, devotion and piety, from Evangelical principles. V. 1-8, Jan. 1766–Dec. 1773.
   NNU (v. 7), NjPT (v. 2), OO (v. 1), RPB (v. 1-2, 7).

287. Gospel magazine; or, Treasury of divine knowledge. *Ed.* A. M. Toplady. 1774-84. Merged into Spiritual magazine (1784).
NNU (v. 1-6), **NjPT, OO** (v. 8-10), **RPB** (no. 60, Dec. 1778).

Grand magazine of magazines; or, Universal register. *See* Magazine of magazines; or, Universal register.

288. Grand magazine of universal intelligence and monthly chronicle of our own times. V. 1-3, 1758-60. m.
CtY, DLC (v. 1-2), **IaU** (v. 1-2), **MB** (v. 1), **NN, WH** (v. 1).

Grand politique post. *See* Faithful post.

289. Gray's Inn journal. Arthur Murphy. Nos. 1-52, Sept. 29, 1753–Sept. 21, 1754; reprinted, with alterations and with 52 additional numbers (the whole extending from Oct. 21, 1752 to Oct. 12, 1754), in 1756, 2 v. w.
CtY (also rep. 1756), **DLC** (rep. 1756), **ICN** (rep. 1756), **ICU** (rep. 1756), **IU** (rep. 1756), **MB** (rep. 1756)), **MH** (also rep. 1756), **MnU** (rep. 1786), **NN** (rep. 1756), **NNC** (rep. 1756).

Great Britain's post. *See* Faithful post.

290. Grub-Street journal. *Ed.* Alexander Russel and John Martyn. Nos. 1-418, Jan. 8, 1730–Dec. 29, 1737. w. A reprint of numbers for the dates Jan. 8, 1730–Aug. 24, 1732 appeared in 1737 under the title of Memoirs of the Society of Grub-Street (2 v.). *See also* Literary courier of Grub-Street.
CtY (also Memoirs), **DLC** (nos. 314-400, Jan. 1, 1736–Aug. 25, 1737), **ICU** (Memoirs), **IU** (Memoirs), **MH** (Memoirs), **NN** (nos. 43, 95, 147; also Memoirs, v. 2), **NNC** (Memoirs), **TxU** (lacking nos. 14, 48, 67, 263, 272, 370, 373, 408; also Memoirs), **WH** (nos. 11-295, Mar. 19, 1730–Aug. 21, 1735, inc.).

292. Guardian. Steele, Addison, and others. Nos. 1-175, Mar. 12–Oct. 1, 1713. d.
CSt, CtY (nos. 1-20; also reps. 1714, 1723, 1793), **ICU, IEK** (rep. 1714), **IU, MH, NN** (rep. 1751-67), **NNC** (reps.), **TxU** (nos. 22-44, 81-175, lacking nos. 23, 33, 40, 97, 110, 121, 128, 148; also rep. 1797).

293. Haerlem courant truly rendered into English. Haarlem and London, 1680.
TxU (nos. 1, 7, 9, Jan. 16-17, 13-17, 18-21, 1680).

294. Hampshire chronicle. Southampton, 1772(?)-78(?). w.
WH (v. 3, no. 112, Oct. 1774; v. 6, nos. 298-300, May 4-18, 1778).

Harrison's Tatler. *See* Tatler.

295. Have at you all; or, The Drury Lane journal. Bonnell Thornton. 1752. w.

CtY (nos. 1-12, Jan. 16–Apr. 9, 1752), **IU, MB** (no. 1, Jan. 16, 1752), **MH** (nos. 1-11, 13, Jan. 16–Apr. 9, 1752, no. 12 omitted in numbering).

295a. Heads of severall proceedings in the present Parliament. *Continued as* Diurnall; or, The heads of all the proceedings in Parliament (Dec. 6-13, 1641) ; *as* Diurnall occurrences; or, The heads of severall proceedings in both Houses of Parliament (from Dec. 13-20, 1641) ; *as* Diurnall occurrences in Parliament (from Jan. 3-10, 1642) ; *as* Perfect diurnall of the passages in Parliament (from Jan. 24-31). Samuel Pecke for various booksellers. Nov. 29, 1641–April 4(?), 1642. w.
ICN (Dec. 6-13, 1641; Dec. 27–Jan. 3, 1641/2; Feb. 21-28, 1641/2), **TxU** (Jan. 24-31, 1641/2).

296. Henry's Winchester journal. Reading, 1743(?)-46(?). w.
CtY (nos. 128, 142, Mar. 31, June 24, 1746).

297. Heraclitus ridens; or, A discourse between Jest and Earnest. . . . Thomas Flatman. Nos. 1-82, Feb. 1, 1681–Aug. 22, 1682.
CtY, DLC, ICN (rep. 1713), **ICU** (rep. 1713), **MH, NN** (Apr. 26, May 10, 17, 31–June 14, 28, July 5, Nov. 15, 1681; Jan. 3, Mar. 14, Apr. 25, May 30–June 13, 21, 1682), **NNC** (nos. 51, 54, 66, 71, Jan. 17–May 2, 1682; also rep. 1713).

298. Herald; or, Patriot proclaimer. Sept. 17, 1757–Apr. 6, 1758. w.
CtY (rep. 1758), **ICU** (rep. 1758), **IU** (v. 1, rep. 1758).

299. Hermes straticus. No. 1, Aug. 17, 1648.
CSH.

300. Hermit; or, A view of the world. Nos. 1-30, Aug. 4, 1711–Feb. 23, 1712. w.
CtY, TxU (nos. 12-19, Aug. 18–Dec. 8, 1711).

301. Hibernian magazine; or, Compendium of entertaining knowledge. *Continued as* Walker's Hibernian magazine . . . (from 1786). Dublin, 1771+. m.
CtY (Apr.–May, 1795; July–Dec., 1796), **DLC** (1781), **ICN** (lacking Jan.–Mar., May–Nov. 1771; Jan.–Mar., May, July–Sept. 1772), **MH** (July–Dec. 1792; July–Dec. 1796), **NN, WH** (1773-78, 1779, 1782, 1783, 1797).

303. High-German doctor. Philip Horneck. 1714-15. s. w. Vol. 2 of 1719-20 rep. has appendix entitled The High-German doctor concluded. . . . [Aug. 1715], London, 1719.
CtY (rep., v. 1, 1720; v. 2, 1719), **DLC, ICU** (rep.), **IEK** (rep.

1720-19), **IU** (rep. 1720-19), **MB, NN** (nos. 1-11, Apr. 30–June 8, 1714), **NNC** (rep. 1715-19), **TxAG** (rep., v. 1, 1720; v. 2, 1719).

304. Hippocrates ridens; or, Joco-serious reflections on the impudence and mischief of quacks and illiterate pretenders to physick. 1686. w.
CSH (nos. 1-4, Apr. 26–May 17, 1686).

305. Historia litteraria; or, An exact and early account of the most valuable books. *Ed.* A. Bower. V. 1-4, 1730-33. m.
CtY, DLC, ICN (v. 1, impr. 1731), **ICS, ICU** (v. 1-4, impr. 1731-34), **IU** (v. 1-2, 1730-31), **MH, NN, RPB, WH.**

Historical account. . . . *See* Account of the publick transactions. . . .

306. Historical, biographical, literary, and scientific magazine. 1799-1800. m.
MH, TxU.

307. Historical chronicle. 1785(?)-86(?). m.
MB (v. 3, Jan.–June 1786).

308. Historical journal; or, An impartial account in English and in French, of the most considerable occurrences in Europe. 1697.
DLC (Feb. 3-17, 1697).

309. Historical magazine; or, Classical library of public events. 1789-92. m.
CtY, DLC (v. 1, 1789), **NN, TxU** (nos. 15-26, Jan.–Dec. 1790).

310. Historical register, containing an impartial relation of all transactions, foreign and domestick. 1716-38. q.
CtY (v. 1-21, 1716-36), **DLC, ICN** (v. 1-8, 1716-23), **ICU, IU, MdBP, MHi, MiU, MnU, NIC, NN, NNC** (v. 1-21, 1716-36), **PPL** (v. 2, no. 5–v. 12, no. 48, 1718-27), **TxU, WH.**

311. Historical register of publick occurrences, foreign and domestick. 1772-74(?).
CtY (Sept. 1, 1772–Apr. 8, 1774).

312. History of learning, giving a succinct account and narrative of the choicest new books, etc. 1694.
DLC (no. 1, May 1694), **ICU** (no. 1), **IU** (no. 1).

313. History of learning; or, An abstract of several books lately published. J. de la Crose. 1691.
ICU.

314. History of reformation, in a dialogue between Philanax and Erasmus. 1681.
CtY (no. 1, May 12, 1681).

315. History of the reign of Queen Anne, digested into annals. Abel Boyer. 1702-13. a.
ICU (v. 4, 11, 1705/6, 1712), TxU (1705).

316. History of the works of the learned. Jan. 1737–Dec. 1743. m. *See also* Literary magazine; or, The history of the works of the learned *and* Present state of the republic of letters.
CtY, DLC (1737-42), ICN, ICU (1737, v. 1; 1738-39; 1741-42), MH (1739-41), N (1737, pt. 2; 1738; 1739, pt. 2; 1741), PPL, WH (1738-39).

317. History of the works of the learned; or, An impartial account of books lately printed in all parts of Europe. V. 1-14, Jan. 1699–Mar. 1712. m.
CtY (v. 1-14), DLC (v. 1-13), ICJ (v. 1-12), ICN (v. 1-13, Jan. 1699–Dec. 1711), IU (v. 1-7, 10-13), IWS (v. 1-6, 1699-1704), MB (v. 1-12), MH (v. 1-12), N (v. 1, no. 5, May, 1699; v. 2, nos. 5, 10, May, Oct. 1700), NNC (v. 1-13), TxAG (v. 4-5), TxU (v. 1-4; v. 1, no. 1, 2nd ed., 1701).

318. History of our own times. 1741. s. m.
ICU (nos. 1-4, Jan. 1–Mar. 5, 1741).

319. Hog's wash; or, A salmagundy for swine. *Continued as* Hog's wash (from no. 2, Oct. 5, 1793); *as* Hog's wash; or, Politics for the people (from no. 6, Nov. 2, 1793); *as* Politics for the people; or, Hog's wash (from no. 7, Nov. 9, 1793); *as* Politics for the people (from no. 10, Dec. 14, 1793). D. I. Eaton. Nos. 1-15, Sept. 9, 1793–Jan. 18, 1794; pt. 2, nos. 1-14, Jan. 25–Apr. 1794; [pt. 3], nos. 1-30, 1794-95. w.
CtY, ICJ (v. 1, rep. 1794), MH.

Holland pacquet-boat; or, An historical account. *See* Account of the publick transactions. . . .

320. Honest gentleman. Nos. 1-25, Nov. 5, 1718–Apr. 22, 1719.
TxU (nos. 1-2, Nov. 5–Dec. 24, 1718; 11-25, Jan. 14–Apr. 22, 1719).

321. How do you do? *Ed.* Chas. Dibden and F. G. Waldron. 1796. s. m.
MH (nos. 1-8, July 30–Nov. 5, 1796).

Howgrave's Stamford mercury. *See* Stamford mercury.

322. Hue and cry. Dublin(?), 1755. w.
CtY (no. 3, June 18, 1755).

323. Humanist. Nos. 1-15, Mar. 26–July 2, 1757. w.
CtY, MiU (no. 1), TxU.

324. Hyp-doctor. John Henley. Nos. 1-534, Dec. 15, 1730–Jan. 20, 1741.
    CtY (no. 140, 1733).

326. Impartial intelligencer: communicating a perfect collection of the weekly passages in Parliament. . . . 1649. w.
    CSH (nos. 1-9, 11-18, 1649), DLC (July 25–Aug. 1, 1649).

Impartial London intelligence. *See* Protestant Oxford intelligence.

Impartial Protestant mercury. *See* True Protestant mercury . . . (Janeway).

Imperial magazine. *See* Biographical and imperial magazine.

328. Imperial magazine; or, Complete monthly intelligence. 1760-62. m.
    MH (v. 1, nos. 1-13, and suppl., 1760; v. 3, nos. 26-30, Jan.–May, 1762), NN (v. 3, Jan.–June, 1762), PPL (v. 1, 1760-61), O.

329. Independent Whig. *Ed.* J. Trenchard and Thomas Gordon. Nos. 1-53, Jan. 20, 1720–Jan. 4, 1721. w.
    CSH, CtY (also rep. 1743; also rep. Hartford, Conn., 1816), CU (rep. 1722), DLC (rep. 1721, 1752-53), ICN (rep. 1721), ICU (rep. 1721, 1735), IU (rep. 1726), MnU (rep. 1721), NIC (rep. 1722), NN (v. 1-2, Jan. 20, 1720–Jan. 18, 1721, 7th ed., with additions and amendments, 1743; v. 3, 2nd ed., 1741; v. 4, 1747), TxU (nos. 1-30), WH.

331. Inspector, containing a concise and impartial collection of news. Oxford, nos. 1-3, 1751.
    DLC.

Intelligence from the Scottish army. *See* Late proceedings of the Scottish army.

332. Intelligence from the south borders of Scotland. *Printed for* Robert Bostock and Samuel Gellibrand. 1664.
    CtY (no. 8, Apr. 24, 1664).

333. Intelligencer. J. Swift and T. Sheridan. Dublin, nos. 1-20, 1728-29. w.
    CtY (nos. 1-11, 13-16; also nos. 1-19, rep. London, 1729), DLC (nos. 1-19, rep. London, 1729), IU (2nd ed. London, 1730), MH (nos. 1-19, rep. London, 1729), MnU (nos. 1-19, rep. London, 1729).

334. Intelligencer, published for the satisfaction and information of the people. Sir Roger L'Estrange. Aug. 31, 1663–Jan. 29, 1666. s. w. Published on Mondays; on Thursday of each week (from Sept. 3, 1663) was published the Newes, published for satisfaction and information

of the people; this had separate numbering through no. 18; then was issued as a Thursday supplement of the Monday Intelligencer, with numbering and pagination continuous throughout both papers.
CSH (nos. 1-18, Aug. 31–Dec. 31, 1663; 1-102, Jan. 4–Dec. 29, 1664; 1-95, Jan. 2–Nov. 23, 1665; 1-9, Dec. 2-28, 1665; 1-9, Jan. 1-29, 1666), **CtY** (nos. 1-2, Sept. 3, 7, 1663; 27-28, 31-47, 51-69, 75-95, 99, 101, Apr. 4–Dec. 26, 1664; 38, 40, 44-48, May 18, 25, June 8-22, 1665), **DLC** (nos. 4, 6, 12, Jan. 14, 21, Feb. 11, 1663; 1-13, 15-16, Sept. 3–Dec. 17, 1663; 16, 18, 22, 24, 26, 28, 32, 34, 38, 42, 44, 46, 48, 50, 52, 56, 62, 64, 66, 70, 72, 76, 84, 86, 88, 90, 100, Feb. 25–Dec. 22, 1664; 2, 6, 8, 12, 14, 16, 18, 20, 20 [bis], 22, 28, 32, 34, 42, 44, 46, 50, 52, 54, 56, 60, 62, 64, 73, 75, 77, 79, 81, 83, 85, 87, 89, 91, Jan. 5–Nov. 16, 1665), **IU** (v. 1, no. 4–v. 2, no. 47, 51-101, 1663-64), **MdBJ** (Aug. 1–Dec. 31, 1663; Jan. 4–Mar. 24, 1664), **WH** (nos. 1, 15, 37, 41, 69, 70, 85, Jan. 4–Oct. 31, 1664; 3-4, Jan. 9-16, 1665; 49, June 26, 1665).

335. Intrepid magazine. *Ed.* W. Hamilton. 1784.
 MBB.

336. Ipswich journal. Ipswich, 1720+. w.
 CtY (June 22 [no. 332]–Sept. 1, Oct. 26–Nov. 2, Nov. 23–Dec. 28, 1745; Jan. 4–July 5, July 26–Nov. 1, Nov. 15, 29–Dec. 27, 1746; Jan. 3-17, 31, Feb. 14–Mar. 7, 21, Apr. 18-25, May 9–Oct. 10, Oct. 24–Dec. 26, 1747; Jan. 2-29, Feb. 20, Apr. 16-23, May 7–Oct. 29, Nov. 26–Dec. 31, 1748; Jan. 7-21, Feb. 4–Dec. 9, 30, 1749; Jan. 6–Feb. 24, Mar. 10–May 12, June 9-23, 1750; Sept. 7 [no. 1387], 1765), **ICU** (nos. 325-516, May 1745–Dec. 1748), **TxU** (no. 887, Jan. 31, 1756).

337. Ireland's true diurnall. *Continued as* True diurnall; or, A continued relation of Irish occurrances (from no. 2, Mar. 8). William Bladen. Feb. 3–Mar. 22(?), 1642. ir.
 CtY (no. 1, Feb. 3, 1642), **TxU** (Mar. 8, 22, 1642).

338. Irish agricultural magazine. Dublin, 1798+. ir.
 NN.

Italian mercury. *See* Mercurio italico.

Jackson's Oxford journal. *See* Oxford journal.

339. Jacobite's journal. Henry Fielding. 1747-48. w.
 CtY (nos. 1-40, 42-49, Dec. 5, 1747–Nov. 5, 1748, photographs).

340. Johnson's British gazette, and Sunday monitor. 1779+. w.
 CtY (Feb. 7, 28–June 27, 1790).

341. Jones's Coventry and Warwick ledger. Coventry, 1765(?)–(?). w.
 CtY (Aug. 24, Sept. 7–Oct. 19, 1765).

342. Jones's sentimental and masonic magazine. Dublin, 1792(?)-95(?). m.
   DLC (v. 3, 1793).
343. Jopson's Coventry mercury; or, The weekly country journal. Coventry, 1741+. w.
   CtY (Jan. 7–May 27, June 10–Sept. 2, Oct. 21–Dec. 30, 1765; Jan. 6, 1766–Dec. 25, 1769; Jan. 1–May 28, June 11–July 30, 1770).
344. Journal étranger de littérature, des spectacles, et de politique. June 1777–May 1778. (From U. L.)
   MH.
345. Journal of natural philosophy, chemistry, and the arts. *Ed.* William Nicholson. 1797+. m.
   CSt, CtY, CU, DLC, ICJ, IU, MB, MdBP, NcU, NIC, NN, PPAP, PU.
346. Joyfull and happy news from the west of Ireland. 1642.
   TxU (May 2, 1642).
347. Kapelion; or, Poetical ordinary. William Kenrick. 1750-51.
   CtY.
348. Kemmish's new weekly miscellany; or, Amusing companion. 1787. w.
   WH.

Kentish chronicle. *See* Kentish weekly post; or, Canterbury journal.

349. Kentish gazette. Canterbury, 1768+. s. w.
   ICU (Nov. 18, 1775; Apr. 24, Nov. 20, 1776), NN (Jan. 7-14, 28, Feb. 22–Mar. 7, 24–Apr. 28, May 5, 16-23, June 13, 16, 23, 27, July 4-14, 21, 28–Aug. 4, 29, Sept. 1, 8, 12, 19–Oct. 17, 24–Nov. 11, 18–Dec. 5, 23, 26, 1772; Jan. 2, 6, 23, 30, Feb. 3, 10-17, 24–Mar. 3, 10, 17, 24, Apr. 7-17, 24–May 5, 19, 22, June 2-12, 30–July 10, Aug. 7, 11, 21-28, Sept. 8, 25–Oct. 9, 16, 23, Nov. 3-20, 27–Dec. 4, 15, 18, 29, 1773; Jan. 1–Feb. 2, 16–Mar. 5, 12–Apr. 13, 20, 30, May 4, 14, 25–June 1, 11, 25, July 9, 23, Aug. 3, 6, 13, 17, 27, 31, Sept. 17–Oct. 29, Nov. 5–Dec. 10, 17-28, 1774; Jan. 4-25, Feb. 1-8, 15, 18, Mar. 4, 11, 15, 22, 29, Apr. 5, 12-19, 26, May 3-17, 24, 31, June 3, 14-24, July 4, 12, 19, 29, Aug. 5, 12, 16, 26, Sept. 6-13, 20-30, Oct. 11, 14, 21–Nov. 29, Dec. 6-27, 1775; Apr. 27, May 18, 22, Aug. 21, 28, Sept. 14-21, 28–Oct. 16, 30, Nov. 6-13, 20-27, Dec. 11, 18-28, 1776).

Kentish post and Canterbury journal. *See* Kentish weekly post; or, Canterbury journal.

350. Kentish register and monthly miscellany. Canterbury, 1793-95. m.
   DLC.

351. Kentish weekly post; or, Canterbury journal. *Continued as* Kentish post and Canterbury journal (from Nov. 21, 1769); *as* Canterbury journal (from Apr. 3, 1770); *as* Kentish chronicle and Canterbury journal (from May 27, 1778); *as* Kentish chronicle (from June 1791). Canterbury, 1768+. w.
    ICU (v. 1, nos. 1-61, Sept. 19, 1768–Nov. 13, 1769).

352. Kingdomes faithfull scout. D. Border. Feb. 2, 1648/9–Oct. 12, 1649. w.
    CSH (no. 4, 1648/9).

    Kingdomes intelligencer. *See* Parliamentary intelligencer.

353. Kingdomes weekly intelligencer, sent abroad to prevent misinformation. Richard Collings(?). Jan. 3, 1643–Oct. 9, 1649. w.
    CtY (nos. 1, 10, 12, 15, 16, 18, 21, Jan. 3–May 30, 1643; 59, June 18, 1644; also rep. of no. for Jan. 23, 1648/9), **MH** (nos. 4-52), **MnU** (no. 113, Aug. 19, 1645), **NN** (rep. of no. for Jan. 23, 1649), **TxU** (nos. 11, 13, 14, 15, 56, 60-62, 77, 78, Mar. 7, 1643–Oct. 29, 1644).

354. Kingdom's scout. 1645. w.
    TxU (nos. 1-2, Dec. 2–Dec. 9, 1645).

355. Ladies' diary. 1704+. a. (From U. L.)
    DLC (1706-07, 1711-12, 1715, 1718-95, 1797+), **MH** (1722, 1744, 1762, 1794-95, 1797), **NjP** (1728, 1740, 1745, 1749, 1757, 1767, 1776, 1785-92, 1797+), **PPAP** (1706-15, 1717, 1718-52).

356. Ladies' magazine; or, The universal entertainer. 1749-53.
    CtY (v. 1-2, Nov. 18, 1749–Nov. 16, 1751), **ICU** (v. 1).

357. Lady's gazette and evening advertiser. 1789.
    CtY (May 5, 1789).

358. Lady's magazine; or, Entertaining companion for the fair sex. 1770+. m.
    CtY, ICU (v. 1-9, 12, 15-16, 18-25, 28, 1770-97; v. 12, 15, inc.), **MB** (1774, 1781, 1783, 1786, 1794, inc.), **MH** (v. 1-28, 1770-97), **NN** (v. 6-9, 14, 21-27), **PPL, WH** (v. 1-7, 9-10, 12, 14, 15+).

359. Lady's monthly museum; or, Polite repository of amusement and instruction. 1798+. m.
    CtY, DLC (v. 1, July–Dec. 1798; v. 3+), **MB, MHi** (v. 1, 3, 5-6), **NN** (v. 2-3, 1799), **WH**.

360. Lady's poetical magazine; or, Beauties of British poetry. 1781-82.
    CtY, DLC, ICU, IU, MB, NNC.

361. Late proceedings of the Scottish army. *Continued as*

Intelligence from the Scottish army (no. 6); *as* Extract of letters (no. 7). Nos. 1-7, 1644.
CtY (no. 7, Apr. 20).

362. Lawyer's and magistrate's magazine. V. 1-6, 1790-94.
DLC (v. 1-3), MH-L, N (lacking v. 6; v. 1-3, Dublin rep.), NIC, NN (v. 1-3).

363. Lawyer's magazine. 1761-62. (From U. L.)
MH-L, NIC, NNC.

Lay monastery. *See* Lay monk.

364. Lay monk. Sir Richard Blackmore and John Hughes. Nos. 1-40, Nov. 16, 1713–Feb. 15, 1714; reprinted, 1714, as Lay monastery. t. w.
CtY (rep. 1714), IU (rep. 1714), MiU (rep. 1714), MnU (rep. 1714), NIC (rep. 1714), TxAG (rep. 1727), TxU (nos. 1, 5, 8, 19, 22, 24, Nov. 16, 1713–Jan. 8, 1714; also rep. 1754).

365. Leeds intelligencer. Leeds, 1754+. w.
CtY (Oct. 14, 1777; Jan. 14, 1793–Dec. 14, 1795; Jan. 1, 1798–June 30, 1800), WH (v. 4, no. 176, Nov. 15, 1757).

366. Leeds mercury. Leeds, 1767+. *Cf.* no. 1503.
TxU (v. 17, no. 896, Apr. 13, 1784).

367. Leicester and Nottingham journal. *Continued as* Leicester journal (from 1787). Leicester, 1753(?)+. w.
NN (May 21, July 16, 30, Aug. 6, Sept. 10, Oct. 8, 1790).

368. Letters and papers on agriculture, planting, etc. 1780+. (From U. L.)
DLC, NIC.

369. Library; or, Moral and critical magazine. . . . By a society of gentlemen. *Ed.* A. Kippis. V. 1-2, Apr. 1761–May 1762. m.
CtY, DLC, ICN, RPB (inc.).

Lincoln, Rutland and Stamford mercury. *See* Stamford mercury.

371. Literary and philosophical society of Newcastle-upon-Tyne. Reports. Newcastle-upon-Tyne. 1793+. (From U. L.)
DLC.

372. Literary amusements; or, Evening entertainer. Dublin, 1782.
ICN, ICU, MB, N.

373. Literary courier of Grub-Street. Nos. 1-30, Jan. 5–July 27, 1738. w. A continuation of the Grub-Street journal.
CtY, TxU (nos. 3-30, lacking nos. 15, 16, 19).

374. Literary fly. 1779. w.
CtY (nos. 1-17, Jan. 18–May 8, 1779), MiU (nos. 1-17).

375. Literary journal. Dublin, 1744-49. q. and a.
CtY, MH, NN.

376. Literary journal; or, A continuation of the Memoirs of literature. M. de la Roche. V. 1-3, 1730-31. m.
CtY (v. 1), RPB (v. 1-3).

377. Literary leisure; or, The recreations of Solomon Saunter, Esq., Sept. 26, 1799–Dec. 18, 1800. w.
DLC, NN (v. 2, nos. 32-60, May 1–Dec. 18, 1800).

378. Literary magazine and British review. 1788-94. m.
CtY, DLC (v. 1-11, July 1788–Dec. 1793), ICN, ICU (v. 3, 10), MB, MBB, MH (v. 4, 5), NIC (v. 7), NjP (v. 3-5), NN, NNC (v. 1-4, 6-9), PPH (v. 4), PPL, PU, WH.

379. Literary magazine; or, Select British library. J. Wilford. Jan.–June, 1735. m.
DLC, NNC (Mar. 1735).

380. Literary magazine; or The history of the works of the learned. *Ed.* E. Chambers. 1735-36. m. This periodical and the Present state of the republic of letters were superseded in 1737 by the History of the works of the learned.
CtY, ICU, NNC (Jan. 1736), PPL.

381. Literary magazine; or, Universal review. *Ed.*(?) Samuel Johnson. 1756-58. m.
CtY, MH (v. 1, Apr. 15, 1756–Jan. 15, 1757).

382. Literary miscellany; or, Selections and extracts, classical and scientific. Stourport, 1800+.
CtY, ICU.

383. Literary register; or, A weekly miscellany; being a review of publications in the year. . . . Newcastle-upon-Tyne, 1769-72. w.
CtY (v. 1-3, 1769-71).

Little review. *See* Weekly review of the affairs of France.

384. Living world; or, The history of the last fortnight. 1750. (From U. L.)
RPB (nos. 1-3, 1750).

385. Lloyd's evening post and British chronicle. 1757+. t. w.
CtY (nos. 1-853, July 22, 1757–Dec. 31, 1762; 931-1713, July 1, 1763–June 29, 1768; 1793-4451, Jan. 2, 1769–Dec. 30, 1785), ICU (v. 6, 1760, inc.), IU (v. 1-10, 41-46), NN (Mar. 8–June 7, 12–

July 14, 19, 24–Aug. 7, 11–Oct. 2, 6–Dec. 18, 22-29, 1758; 1777-79; Jan. 3–Oct. 4, 9–Dec. 29, 1780; 1781), **TxU** (nos. 2106, Jan. 1, 1771; 2302, Apr. 3, 1772; 2359, Aug. 14, 1773; 2761, Mar. 10, 1775; 3730, May 18, 1781; 3731, May 21, 1781; 3755, July 16, 1781; 3760, July 27, 1781; 3769, Aug. 17, 1781), **WH** (v. 2-3, 1758; 5-6, July 1759–June 1760; 8-11, 1761-62; 13-25, July 1763-1769; 35, Aug. 7–Oct. 26, 1774; 46, Jan. 17–Apr. 5, 1780).

386. Loiterer. *Ed.* James Austen. Oxford, 1789-90. w.
     CtY (v. 1-2, Jan. 31, 1789–Mar. 20, 1790), **DLC** (nos. 1-37, Jan. 31–Oct. 10, 1789), **MH** (v. 1-2).

387. London and country journal, with the history of the Old and New Testament. 1739-42.
     DLC (nos. 18-33, 35-122, 1739-41).

388. London and Dublin magazine. Dublin, 1734-35(?).
     IU (v. 1-2), **PPL** (v. 2, Jan.–Dec. 1735).

389. London chronicle; or, Universal evening post. *Continued as* London chronicle (from July 2, 1765). 1757+. t. w.
     CSH (v. 55-64, Jan. 5, 1784–Nov. 8, 1788), **CSt** (Jan.–June 1762), **CtY** (lacking nos. 1408, 1487-95, 1497-1501, 1512-16, 1521, 1597, 1600, 1607, 4620-97; also Boswell's file with his annotations, v. 21-38, Dec. 30, 1766–Dec. 29, 1775, lacking 17 nos.), **DLC**, **ICN** (v. 1-68, 1757-90), **ICU** (1758, 1760-65, 1771-72, 1773-82, 1785-96, 1800, many nos. missing before 1773 and a few later), **IU** (v. 1-7, 9, 11-47, 59, 1757-85), **MB** (1757-79, 1781-84, Dec. 1788–Mar. 1789, 1793), **MdBP** (v. 35), **MH** (v. 1-88, 1757-1800, lacking v. 77, Mar. 31–June 4, 1795, and v. 78), **MiU** (v. 1-11, 39, 71-72, 82-88), **N** (inc.), **NIC** (v. 1-54, 1757-84), **NN** (lacking v. 27-28, 39, 57, 59-60, 73, 76-80, 84-88), **NNC** (v. 3-4), **PPL** (1773-78), **RPB** (v. 1-83, 1757-98), **TxU** (nos. 628-702, 706, 1761; 2192, 1771), **WH** (v. 1-23, 26-34, 45-50, 53-60, 69-78).

     London corresponding society. *See* Moral and political magazine. . . .

390. London courant. 1688-89. s. w.
     CSH (nos. 1-9, Dec. 12, 1688–Jan. 8, 1689).

391. London courant. *Continued as* London courant; or, New advertiser (from Dec. 1746?). 1745-47(?). d.
     CSH (no. 306, June 23, 1746).

392. London courant and Westminster chronicle. *Continued as* London courant, Westminster chronicle and daily advertiser (from Oct. 10, 1781); *as* London courant, noon gazette, and daily advertiser (from Jan. 21, 1782); *as* London courant, morning gazette, and daily advertiser (from Mar. 11, 1782); *as* London courant and daily

advertiser (from Apr. 9, 1782); *as* London courant, Westminster chronicle, and daily advertiser (from Apr. 15, 1782); *as* London courant and daily advertiser (Sept. 6, 1782). Nov. 25, 1779(?)–Sept. 6, 1782(?). d.
MB (Nov. 25, 1779–Apr. 18, 1780), NN (Nov. 26–Dec. 31, 1779; Jan. 1–Mar. 21, 27–June 30, 1780).

London courant; or, New advertiser. *See* London courant, 1745-47(?).

393. London daily post and general advertiser. *Continued as* General advertiser (from Mar. 12, 1744); *as* Public advertiser (from Dec. 1, 1752); *as* Oracle and public advertiser (from Mar. 1, 1794). 1734-98. d. Incorporated with Daily advertiser in 1798.
CtY (Mar. 15, 17, May 20, 22, 25, 26, Sept. 4, 14, Nov. 27, 30, 1736; Apr. 26, 1737; Feb. 24, Apr. 9, 1741; June 24, 1766; Feb. 7, 1767–July 17, 1771; Jan. 2, 1775–Dec. 30, 1780), NN (July 16, 1772; Dec. 21, 1779; Mar. 9, 1780), TxU (Dec. 24, 1746; Jan. 21, 1754; Jan. 24, 1775–Dec. 6, 1776; Sept. 23, Oct. 22, 25, 31, Nov. 1, 2, 12, 18, 19, 20, Dec. 4, 5, 6, 22, 1794), WH (Mar. 5, 1772; Mar. 16, 1778).

394. London evening post. 1727+. t. w.
CSH (no. 2926, Aug. 7, 1746), CtY (nos. 1001-1580, Apr. 20, 1734–Dec. 31, 1737; 3146-3302, Jan. 2–Dec. 31, 1748; 4122, Apr. 13, 1754; 4216-34, Nov. 19–Dec. 31, 1754; 4235-4546, Jan. 2, 1755–Dec. 28, 1756; 4548-4677, Jan. 1–Oct. 29, 1757; 4717-4856, Jan. 31–Dec. 21, 1758), IU (Mar. 25, 1742–Mar. 29, 1748), NN (June 21, July 3, 1735; Oct. 10, 1738; Oct. 11, 1739; Nov. 6, 23, 1742; Jan. 20, 1770, Dec. 24-29, 1778; Jan.–Dec. 1779; Jan.–Mar. 1780), TxU (nos. 113-1387, Aug. 29, 1728–Oct. 7, 1736, inc.), WH (no. 929, Nov. 3, 1733).

London gazette. *See* Oxford gazette.

395. London intelligence. 1689. s. w.
CSH (nos. 1-10, Jan. 15–Feb. 16, 1689), CtY (no. 10).

396. London journal. John Trenchard, etc. 1719-44. w.
CtY (Sept. 3, 10, Oct. 1-15, Nov. 12–Dec. 31, 1720; Jan. 7–Dec. 30, 1721; Jan. 6–Dec. 22, 1722; Jan. 5–Dec. 21, 1723; Jan. 3–Dec. 26, 1724; Feb. 13, 1725; July 2, Oct. 8–Dec. 31, 1726; Jan. 14–Dec. 30, 1727; Jan. 17–Apr. 18, May 30, June 6, July 11, Aug. 6, Nov. 21, 28, Dec. 12, 1730; Feb. 13–Nov. 20, 1731; Feb. 3, 17–Mar. 17, 31–Apr. 14, Apr. 28–May 5, 26–June 9, 23–July 14, Aug. 11-25, Sept. 22–Oct. 6, 20–Nov. 17, Dec. 15, 1733; Jan. 5–Dec. 31, 1735), IU (no. 113, Sept. 23, 1721), NN (nos. 77-78, Jan. 14-21, 1721; 86, Mar. 18, 1721; 107, Aug. 12, 1721; 185-87, Feb. 9-23, 1723),

56   A Census of British Newspapers and Periodicals, 1620-1800

TxAG (nos. 731, June 30; 743, Sept. 22; 746, Oct. 13, 1733), **TxU** (nos. 79-177, Jan. 28, 1721–Dec. 15, 1722, lacking nos. 155, 156, 160, 161, 169, 170, 172; 261, July 25, 1724; 522, 528, 577, 597, 598, 613, 626, 630, Aug. 2, 1729–Aug. 21, 1731), **WH** (nos. 74-164, 169, 180, 196, 201, 207, 221, 240, 242, 259, 265, 280, 282, 294, 296, 299, 315, 321, 322, 382, 383, 394, 397, 399, 400, 402, 404-06, 420, 421, 499, Dec. 1, 1720–Feb. 22, 1729).

London kalendar; or, City and court register. *See* Court and city register.

397. London magazine and monthly chronicler. *Continued as* Gentleman's and London magazine; or, Monthly chronologer (from 1753). Dublin, 1742-83(?). m.
CtY (v. 47, 1777), **MB** (v. 39, 1769), **MH** (v. 29-30, 35, 40, 41, 50, 1760-80), **NN** (Jan. 1770, 1783), **PPL** (1779).

398. London magazine; or, Gentleman's monthly intelligencer. *Continued as* London magazine and monthly chronologer (from 1736); *as* London magazine enlarged and improved (from 1783). J. Wilford, etc. 1732-85. m.
CSH (1770-75; Apr. 1778; 1779-80; 1783-85), **CSt** (v. 1-41, 1732-72), **CtY** (lacking Jan.–June, 1784), **DLC**, **ICU** (v. 1-50, 1732-81), **IU** (v. 11, 13-46, 48-52), **MB** (v. 1-52), **MBB**, **MdBP** (v. 25, 27, 28, 31, 33, 35, 43-45, 47, 48, 50), **MH** (v. 1-52), **MHi**, **MiUC** (v. 31-32), **N** (v. 9, 25-26, 28-30, 33-34, 36-41, 44), **NIC** (v. 1, 19, 23, 25, 31), **NN** (v. 1-51), **NNC**, **PPL**, **TxU** (1732-48, 1750-57, 1775, 1782), **VaU** (v. 47-52), **WH**.

399. London medical journal. *Continued as* Medical facts and observations (from 1791). *Ed.* S. F. Simmons. 1781-1800. q.
DSG, ICJ, PU (1797-1800).

400. London medical review and magazine. *Ed.* W. Blair. 1799+. m.
DSG, ICJ.

401. London mercury. 1669.
CSH (nos. 1-2, Jan. 6, 27, 1669).

402. London mercury. 1682. s. w.
CSH (nos. 1-56, Apr. 6–Oct. 17, 1682), **MB** (nos. 1-50, 1682), **IWS** (nos. 1-50, Apr. 6–Sept. 26, 1682), **TxU** (nos. 1-56, Apr. 6–Oct. 17, 1682).

403. London mercury, containing the history, politics, and literature of England. 1781 (for the year 1780)-(?).
DLC (1780), **WH**.

404. London mercury; or, Moderate intelligence. *Continued as*

London mercury; or, The Orange intelligence (from Jan. 1689). 1688-89. s. w.
   CSH (nos. 1-9, Dec. 18, 1688–Jan. 10, 1689), CtY (nos. 1-2, 4, 5, Dec. 18-27, 1688), MH (nos. 1-2, 4), NN (Dec. 15, 22, 27, 1688; Jan. 7, 1689).

405. London monthly review. 1787(?)+. (From U. L.)
   DGU (v. 5-6, 9-10, 11-12, 1791+).

London morning penny post. *See* Universal London morning advertiser.

406. London museum of politics, miscellanies and literature. V. 1-4, Jan. 1770–Dec. 1771. m.
   ICN (v. 1, nos. 1-3, Jan.–Mar. 1770), MB (Feb., Mar., Oct. 1770; Jan. 1771), NN.

407. London news letter, with foreign and domestick occurrences. 1696.
   NN (no. 14, May 29, 1696).

408. London packet; or, New evening post. *Continued as* London packet; or, New Lloyd's evening post (from Apr. 17, 1772). 1770+. t. w.
   CtY (Dec. 30, 1799+), IU (1796+), IWS (nos. 966-1123, Jan. 1–Dec. 30, 1776), N (May 28, 1770–June 24, 1771; June 22, 1772–July 30, 1773), NN (1772-80, inc.), TxU (no. 2310, Aug. 17, 1785).

409. London post, faithfully communicating his intelligence of the proceedings of Parliament. John Rushworth and Gilbert Mabbott. 1644-45. w.
   MH (nos. 5, 23), TxU (nos. 2, Aug. 20, 1644; 21, Jan. 28, 1645).

409a. London register; or, Historical notes of the present times. Jan.–June 1762. m.
   CtY.

410. London review of English and foreign literature. *Ed.* W. Kenrick and others. V. 1-12, 1775-80. m.
   CtY, DLC (v. 1-2), NN (v. 1-11, Jan. 1775–June 1780).

411. London spy. Edward Ward. 1698-1700. m.
   CtY (v. 1-2, Nov. 1698–Apr. 1700), MHi (v. 1-2, no. 6), NNC, TxU (Nov. 1698, rep. 1700; Jan., Mar.–May, July, Oct., Dec. 1699, Apr. and Dec. rep. 1701; Jan., Mar. 1700).

London spy and Read's weekly journal. *See* Weekly journal; or, British gazetteer.

412. Looker-on. William Roberts, James Beresford, Alexander Chalmers, etc. Nos. 1-86, Mar. 10, 1792–Jan. 11, 1794; extended to 92 nos. in collected ed. s. w.; w. (from Dec. 1, 1792).

CSt (rep.), CtY (nos. 1-86; also rep. 1794, 1796), ICU (Mar. 10, 1792–Dec. 21, 1793), MB (rep. 1795, 1796), MH (nos. 1-86, Mar. 10, 1792–Dec. 21, 1793), NN (rep.), PU (rep.).

413. Lottery magazine; or, Compleat fund of literary, political and commercial knowledge. 1776-77(?). m.
CtY (June–Nov. 1777), MB (July–Nov. 1777), NN (July–Oct. 1776).

414. Lounger. *Ed.* Henry Mackenzie. Edinburgh, nos. 1-101, Feb. 5, 1785–Jan. 6, 1787. w.
CSt, CtY, DLC, ICN, ICU (2nd ed.), MB (rep.), MH (lacking nos. 96-97), MnU, NIC (nos. 1-100), NN, NNC, (rep. N. Y. 1789), PU, TxU.

415. Lounger's miscellany; or, The lucubrations of Abel Slug, Esq. 1788-89. s. m.
CtY (nos. 1-20, May 31, 1788–Mar. 7, 1789), MB (nos. 1-20).

416. Lover. Steele. Nos. 1-40, Feb. 25–May 27, 1714. t. w.
CSH (rep. 1715), CtY (rep. 1715, 1723), ICU (rep. 1789), IEN (rep. 1723), IU (rep. 1789), MH, NIC (rep. 1789), NN (rep. 1789), TxU (nos. 19-26; also rep. 1715).

417. Loyal impartial mercury; or, News both forreign and domestick. 1682. s. w.
TxU (nos. 1-46, June 9–Nov. 17, 1682).

418. Loyal intelligence; or, News both from city and country. 1680.
NN (nos. 1-3, Mar. 6-31, 1680), TxU (nos. 1-3).

419. Loyal London mercury; or, The moderate intelligencer. *Continued as* Loyal London mercury; or, The currant intelligence (from no. 8). 1682.
MB (nos. 1-20), TxU (nos. 1-25, June 14–Nov. 15, 1682).

Loyal Protestant, and true domestick intelligence. *See* Domestick intelligence. . . . (N. Thompson).

419a. Loyal weekly journal: the phoenix; or, Sir Roger reviv'd. Francis Clifton. 1717.
TxU (no. 4, Jan. 26, 1716/7).

420. Lying intelligencer. 1763. w.
CtY (rep. in Political controversy, 1763).

421. Macaroni and theatrical magazine. *Continued as* Macaroni, savoir vivre, and theatrical magazine (from Apr. 1773). Oct. 1772–Dec. 1773.
ICU (Oct. 1772–Nov. 1773), MB, MH (Jan., Aug., Nov., Dec. 1773).

422. Magazine of magazines. Limerick, 1751-61. m.
CtY (v. 1-2, Jan.–Dec. 1751; 4-12, July 1752–Dec. 1756), NN (v. 4, 8, 9, 11-14, 18, July 1752–July 1759).

423. Magazine of magazines; or, Universal register. *Continued as* Grand magazine of magazines; or, Universal register (from v. 2). V. 1-3, 1758-59.
CtY (v. 1, nos. 1-16, July–Dec. 1758; v. 3, no. 16, Oct. 1759), MB, MH, MHi (Nov. 1759), NjP, NN (v. 2-3, no. 13, Jan.–July, 1759).

424. Man: a paper for ennobling the species. Peter Shaw. 1755. w.
CtY (nos. 1-53, Jan. 1–Dec. 31, 1755).

425. Manchester literary and philosophical society. Memoirs. Manchester, 1785+. ir.
CSt (v. 1-2, 1785; v. 3, 1790; v. 4, pt. 1, 1793; v. 4, pt. 2, 1796; v. 5, pt. 1, 1798; v. 5, pt. 2, impr. 1802), CtY, CU, DLC, ICU, IU (inc.), MH (v. 1-5, 1785-98), MiU, MnU, NIC, NN, NNC, PPAP.

426. Man in the moon, discovering a world of knavery under the sunne. John Crouch. 1649-50. w.
CSH, CtY (Nov. 21, 1649, rep.), MdBJ (Nov. 21, 1649), MH (Aug. 23, 1649), NN (Nov. 21, 1649, rep.).

427. Many remarkable passages from both Houses of Parliament. 1642.
CtY (May 17, 1642), TxU (May 20, 1642).

428. Marine intelligencer; or, An account of sea affairs. (?)-1711(?).
NN (Apr. 28, 1711).

Martin's magazine. *See* General magazine of arts and sciences.

429. Mathematical and philosophical repository. 1795+. (From U. L.)
MdBP, NN, NNC.

430. Mathematician. 1745-50. (From U. L.)
MB, RPB.

431. Matrimonial magazine; or, Monthly anecdotes of love and marriage for the court, the city and the country. 1775. Merged into Westminster magazine, *q. v.*
DLC (v. 1, Jan.–June 1775).

432. Matter of great note. 1641.
TxU (Mar. 2, 1641/2).

Maty's new review. *See* New review. . . .

433. Meddler. Dublin, 1744. w.
CtY (v. 1, nos. 1-26, Jan. 4–June 28, 1744).

434. Medical and chirurgical review; or, Compendium of medical literature, foreign and domestic. *Ed.* Henry Clutterbuck. July, 1794+. m.
ICJ, MdBJ.

435. Medical and philosophical commentaries. *Continued as* Medical commentaries (from 1780); *as* Annals of medicine (from 1796). Edinburgh, 1773+. q.; a. (from 1783).
CtY, ICJ, MB, PU.

436. Medical and physical journal. *Ed.* T. Bradley, etc. 1799+. m.
CSt, CtY (v. 2+, Aug. 1799+), DLC, ICJ, MB, N, PU.

Medical commentaries. *See* Medical and philosophical commentaries.

437. Medical essays and observations. Philosophical society of Edinburgh. Edinburgh, 1733-44. (From U. L.)
CtY (rep.), DLC (v. 2), ICJ, NNC, PU.

Medical facts and observations. *See* London medical journal.

438. Medical museum; or, A repository of cases, experiments, researches, and discoveries, collected at home and abroad. V. 1-3, 1763-64. m. Reprinted as Medical museum; or, Select cases, experiments, enquiries, and discoveries in medicine, pharmacy, anatomy . . . , v. 1-4, 1781.
MBM (v. 1-2, rep. 1781), MdBJ, MdBM (v. 1-3, rep. 1781), PU (v. 1-3; v. 1, rep. 1781), WU.

439. Medical observations and inquiries. 1757-84.
CtY, MB, MdBJ, PU.

440. Medical society of London. Memoirs. 1792+. (From U. L.)
CtY (v. 3), ICJ, MB, MdBJ (v. 1-3), PU, WU.

441. Medical spectator. 1791-94(?). w.
PU (nos. 1-43, 45, Oct. 1, 1791–Feb. 23, 1793).

442. Medley. *Ed.* Arthur Maynwaring, with occasional assistance from Steele, Anthony Henley, and John Oldmixon. 1st series, nos. 1-45, Oct. 5, 1710–Aug. 6, 1711; 2nd series, nos. 1-45, Mar. 3–Aug. 7, 1712; 1st series rep. in 1712 as Medleys for the year 1711. w. (1st series); s. w. (2nd series).
CtY (1st ser.; 2nd ser., nos. 1-44; also rep. 1712), DLC (rep. 1712), IU (1st ser.; also rep. 1712), IWS (rep. 1712), MH (rep. 1712), NIC, NN (rep. 1712), NNC (rep. 1712), PPL (rep. 1712), TxAG (rep. 1712), TxU (1st ser.; 2nd ser., nos. 1-40, inc.).

443. Memoirs for the curious. *Published by* James Baldwin. 1701. m.
     NNC (v. 1, nos. 1, 2, n. d.).

444. Memoirs for the ingenious, containing curious observations in philosophy, mathematicks, physick, philology, and other arts and sciences. J. de la Crose. 1693. m.
     CtY (nos. 1-6, Jan.–June 1693; 8, Aug. 1693), **ICU** (Jan.–Dec. 1693), **NN** (nos. 1-3).

445. Memoirs for the ingenious; or, The universal mercury. No. 1, Jan. 1694. m.
     CtY, IU (no. 1, Jan. 1694), **NN** (no. 1).

446. Memoirs of literature, containing an account of the state of learning both at home and abroad. Michel de la Roche. March 1710–Sept. 1714; Jan.–Apr.(?) 1717; 2nd ed., rev. and cor., 1722.
     CtY (v. 1, Mar. 13, 1710–Dec. 31, 1711; also rep. 1722), **DLC** (1722), **ICN** (1722), **ICU** (1722), **IU** (1722), **MB** (1722), **MBB** (1722), **MH** (1722), **NIC** (1722), **NN** (v. 4, nos. 1-9, Jan. 4–Sept. 1714; also 1722), **NNC** (1722).

447. Memoirs of science and the arts. 1793-94. (From U. L.)
     CtY (v. 1), **DLC** (rep. 1798), **NjP**.

Memoirs of the present state of Europe. *See* Present state of Europe; or, The monthly account of all occurrences. . . .

Memoirs of the Society of Grub-Street. *See* Grub-Street journal.

449. Mercator; or, Commerce retrieved. D. Defoe. 1713-14. t. w.
     CtY (nos. 1-181, May 26, 1713–July 20, 1714), **NN** (nos. 1-181), **TxU** (nos. 14, 21, 25, 26-31, 34, 38-45, 103, 114, 119, 123, June 25, 1713–Mar. 6, 1714).

450. Merchants and manufacturers magazine of trade and commerce. 1785-86.
     DLC.

451. Merchants news-letter. 1703-(?). w. (From U. L.)
     DLC (nos. 2-5, 15-18, 1703).

452. Mercure britannique; ou, Notices historiques et critiques sur les affaires du temps. J. Mallet du Pan. 1798-1800. m.
     CtY, NIC, NN (v. 1, no. 8, 1798; no. 17, 1799).

453. Mercure de France. Dublin, 1775.
     CtY (v. 1-2, no. 1, Apr.–July 1775).

454. Mercure turc. Nos. 1-7, 1781.
    DLC (nos. 1-7, 1781).

455. Mercurio britannico. J. Mallet du Pan. Nos. 1-32, Aug. 1798–Jan. 10, 1800. s. m.
    DLC.

456. Mercurio italico; o sia, Ragguaglio generale intorno alla letteraturo . . . di tutta l'Italia. The Italian mercury; or, A general account concerning the literature, fine arts, useful discoveries, &c. of all Italy. *Ed.* Francesco Sastres. 1789-90(?). m. In Italian and English.
    DLC (v. 1-3, pt. 1, 1789-90), MBB (v. 1-2, 1789), NN (v. 1-2), NNC (v. 1-2), RPB (v. 1-2).

456a. Mercurius academicus, communicating the affairs of Oxford to the rest of the passive party thorowout the kingdom. No. 1, Apr. 15, 1648.
    IWS (no. 1).

457. Mercurius Anglicus. 1648.
    CSH (no. 1, Aug. 3, 1648).

458. Mercurius Anglicus. 1681. (From U. L.)
    MH (nos. 1-3, Oct. 10-17, 1681).

459. Mercurius Anglicus; or, The weekly occurrences faithfully transmitted. *Continued as* True news; or, Mercurius Anglicus (from no. 11, Dec. 27, 1679). 1679-80. s. w.
    CSH (nos. 1-10, Nov. 13-Dec. 24, 1679), CtY (no. 8, Dec. 17, 1679), NN (nos. 13-17, 19-28, 30-45, Jan. 3-Apr. 24, 1680), WH (nos. 47-51, May 1-15, 1680).

460. Mercurius anti-Britannicus. 1645.
    CSH.

461. Mercurius anti-melancholicus. No. 1, Sept. 24, 1647.
    CSH, MH.

462. Mercurius anti-mercurius. John Harris. 1648. w.
    CSH, IWS (one no., n. d.).

463. Mercurius anti-pragmaticus. Oct. 19, 1647–Feb. 3, 1648. w.
    CSH (nos. 2-5, 16-19, 1647-48), CtY (nos. 4, Nov. 11, 1647; 18, Jan. 27, 1648), ICU (Oct. 19, 1647; 1648), MH (nos. 4, 8).

464. Mercurius aquaticus. 1648.
    CSH.

465. Mercurius aulicus, againe communicating intelligence from all parts touching all affaires, designes, humours, and conditions throughout the kingdome. Samuel Sheppard. 1648. w.

DLC (no. 2, Feb. 10, 1648), MB (no. 3, Feb. 17, 1648), MnU (nos. 2-3, Feb. 3-17).

466. Mercurius aulicus, communicating the intelligence and affaires of the Court to the rest of the kingdome. Peter Heylin and Sir John Berkenhead. Oxford, 1643-45. w.
CSH (1642/3), CtY (Jan. 7, 28, Feb. 11, 25, 1643; Apr. 20, Nov. 23, 1644; Feb. 9, Mar. 2, 1645), IU (52 nos., 1642/3), IWS (Jan. 8, 1643–Nov. 23, 1644), MH (Nov. 11, 1643), MnU (Mar. 5–May 20, July 16–Dec. 16, 1643; Jan. 14-27, Feb. 11–Oct. 12, Oct. 27–Nov. 23, 1644; Jan. 5-18, 26, Feb. 1, 9-15, Mar. 2-8, 16-22, Apr. 13-19, 1645), WH (May 14, July 23, 30, Aug. 6, 13, 20, 27, Sept. 3, 10, 17, 25, Nov. 19, 25, 1643; Jan. 6, 13, Feb. 3, 10, 17, Mar. 2, 9, 16, 23, Apr. 6, 20, June 8, 15, 29, July 6, 20, Aug. 10, 17, Sept. 14, 21, 28, Oct. 5, 1644; Jan. 12, 19, Feb. 2, 16, Mar. 2, 9, 23, 30, Apr. 20, 27, May 4, June 8, July 20, Aug. 17, 1645).

467. Mercurius bellicus; or, An alarum to all rebels. Sir John Berkenhead. 1647-48.
CSH (nos. 1-7, 9-11, 16-19, 21-24, 26-27, Nov. 23, 1647–July 26, 1648), DLC (no. 2, Nov. 29, 1647), ICU (July 26, 1648).

468. Mercurius bellicus: the fourth intelligence from Reading. 1643. (From U. L.)
MH (May 1, 1643).

469. Mercurius bifrons; or, The English Janus. 1681.
CtY (no. 1), MH (no. 1), TxU (nos. 1, 2, 3, Feb. 10–Mar. 3, 1681).

470. Mercurius Britannicus. *Printed by* B. W. 1647. w.
CSH (nos. 1-3), MH (nos. 1-2, June 17–July 24, 1647).

471. Mercurius Britannicus. 1718.
NN (Jan.-Mar. 1718), RPB.

472. Mercurius Britannicus, communicating the affaires of Great Britaine for the better information of the people. Thomas Audley and Marchamont Nedham. 1643-46. w.
CSH (nos. 1-5, 7-81, 83-130, 1643-46), CtY (nos. 1-20, Aug. 29, 1643–Jan. 11, 1644; no. 3, mss. copy), DLC (nos. 1-130, lacking no. 106), IWS (nos. 1-130, lacking no. 35, Aug. 23, 1643–May 18, 1646), MH (nos. 11-109), MnU (nos. 1-100, Aug. 23, 1643–Oct. 6, 1645; also counterfeit, no. 27, Mar. 18, 1644), TxU (nos. 5, 6, 21, 24, 30, 37, 39, 40-43, 47, 48, 54, 55, 58, 64, 65, Sept. 26, 1643–Jan. 13, 1645).

Mercurius Britannicus; or, The weekly observator. *See* Mercurius reformatus.

474. Mercurius Britanicus [subtitles vary]. Nos. 1-13, May 16–Aug. 16, 1648. w.
    CSH (nos. 1-13).
475. Mercurius Brittannicus. Gilbert Mabbott. Nos. 1-7, May 4–June 5, 1649. w.
    CSH (nos. 1, 3-5, 7).
476. Mercurius Caledonius. Thomas Sydserf. Edinburgh, nos. 1-12, 1661.
    CtY (no. 1, Jan. 8, 1661), DLC (Jan. 8, 1661, rep.; 2 extracts in Clarendon hist. soc.), IU (2 extracts in Clarendon hist. soc., 1882), MH (no. 1).
477. Mercurius Catholicus. Father Thomas Budd(?). 1648.
    CSH.
478. Mercurius censorius; or, Newes from the Isle of Wight and other parts of the kingdom to the royalists. John Hall. 1648.
    CSH (no. 1, June 1, 1648), ICN (no. 1).
479. Mercurius civicus. Richard Collings(?). May 11, 1643–Dec. 10, 1646. w.
    CSH (nos. 148, 149, Apr. 2, 9, 1646), MH (nos. 11, 16), TxU (nos. 65, 114, 139, Aug. 22, 1644–Jan. 22, 1646).
480. Mercurius civicus; or, A true account of affairs both foreign and domestick. 1680.
    CSH, MnU (no. 10, Apr. 17, 1680), NN (nos. 1-2, 4-12, Mar. 22–Apr. 27, 1680), RPB (no. 4, Apr. 1, 1680), TxU (nos. 1-14, Mar. 22–May 6, 1680).
481. Mercurius clericus; or, News from Syon. 1647. w.
    CtY (no. 1, Sept. 24, 1647), MH (no. 1).
482. Mercurius clericus; or, News from the Assembly. 1647.
    CSH (no. 1).
483. Mercurius critticus. 1648.
    CSH (no. 1, Apr. 13, 1648).
484. Mercurius Democritus; or, A perfect nocturnal, communicating many strange wonders out of the world in the moon. . . . John Crouch. May 10–Aug. 10, 1659.
    ICU (no. 1, May 10, 1659), TxU (nos. 5, June 7; 11, Aug. 3, 1659).
485. Mercurius dogmaticus. Samuel Sheppard. 1648.
    CSH (no. 1, Jan. 13, 1648).
486. Mercurius domesticus. 1648.
    CSH (no. 1, June 5, 1648).

487. Mercurius domesticus; or, Newes both from city and country. *Printed for* B. Harris. 1679.
   WH (no. 1, Dec. 19, 1679).

488. Mercurius elencticus, communicating the unparallel'd proceedings at Westminster, the head-quarters, and other places. . . . Sir George Wharton and S. Sheppard. 1647-49. *Cf.* J. B. Williams, History of English journalism . . . , pp. 200-10.
   CSH (inc.), CtY (no. 34, July 18, 1648), DLC (nos. 11, Feb. 9; 21, Apr. 19, 1648), ICN (no. 43, Sept. 20, 1648), ICU (May 31, 1648), MB (no. 12, Feb. 1648), MH (no. 34), MnU (nos. 13, 15; 2nd ser., no. 8).

489. Mercurius, &c. Jan. 17–Apr. 10, 1644. w.
   CSH.

490. Mercurius fidelicus. Nos. 1-2, Aug. 24-31, 1648. w.
   CSH.

491. Mercurius fumigosus; or, The smoking nocturnall, communicating dark and hidden newes out of all obscure places in the Antipodes, either in fire, aire, earth or water. John Crouch. Nos. 1-70, 1654-55.
   CtY (no. 58, July 4, 1655).

491a. Mercurius fumigosus; or, The smoaking nocturnal, communicating many strange wonders out of the world in the moon, the Antipodes, Magy-land . . . and other adjacent parts [slight variations in title]. John Crouch. 1660.
   CtY (no. 2, Feb. 1, 1660; 1, Mar. 28, 1660), ICU (Jan. 18, 1660), TxU (Jan. 18, Feb. 1, 1660).

492. Mercurius Gallicus. 1648.
   CSH.

493. Mercurius Helonicus, or the result of a safe conscience. . . . *Printed by* Robert Ibbitson. No. 1, 1651.
   IWS (no. 1).

494. Mercurius honestus; or, Newes from Westminster. 1648.
   CSH.

495. Mercurius impartialis. Sir George Wharton. 1648. w.
   CSH.

496. Mercurius infernus; or, News from the other world, discovering the cheats and abuses of this. Nos. 1-6, 1680.
   TxU (nos. 1-4, n. d.), NN (nos. 1-5).

497. Mercurius insanus insanissimus. 1648.
   CSH (nos. 2-3), ICU.

498. Mercurius librarius; or, A catalogue of books. *Ed.* John Starkey and Robert Clavell. 1668-70. q. Nos. 1-8 reprinted in Edward Arber's Term catalogues, v. 1.
   CSH (nos. 1-8, 1668-70).

499. Mercurius medicus; or, A soveraigne salve for these sick times [slight variation in sub-title in no. 2]. Henry Walker. *Printed for* W. Ley. 1647.
   CSH, CtY (no. 1, [Oct. 11], 1647), IWS (no. 2, Oct. 15-22, 1647), MH.

500. Mercurius Mediterraneus; or, The Streights weekly mercury. 1694. w. (From U. L.)
   DLC (no. 1, Nov. 28, 1694).

501. Mercurius melancholicus; or, News from Westminster and other parts. John Hackluyt and others. 1647-49. w. Numerous counterfeits.
   CSH (no. 3, Sept. 17, 1647; 1649), CtY (nos. 2-4, Sept. 11-24, 1647; 24, Feb. 12; 30, Mar. 27; 33, Apr. 17; 38, May 15; 41, June 5; 42, June 12, 1648), DLC (nos. 2, Sept. 11; 4, Sept. 25, 1647; 21, Jan. 22; 23-24, Jan. 29-Feb. 12; 32-33, Apr. 3-17; 36, May 8, 1648), ICU (Oct. 30, 1647), IU (no. 2, Sept. 11, 1647), MB (nos. 6-8, Oct. 9-23, 1647; 21, Jan. 22; 22, Jan. 29; 25, Feb. 19, 1648), NIC (no. 4).

502. Mercurius melancholicus. John Crouch. 1648. w. A counterfeit of the preceding(?).
   CSH (no. 1, July 28, 1648).

503. Mercurius mercuriorum stultissimus. 1647.
   CSH.

503a. Mercurius militaris, communicating intelligence from the Saints militant dissembled at Westminster, the headquarters. . . . No. 1, Apr. 21-28, 1648.
   IWS (no. 1).

504. Mercurius militaris; or, The people's scout. . . . No. 1, Apr. 17-24, 1649.
   CSH.

505. Mercurius morbicus; or, Newes from Westminster and other parts. Henry Walker. 1647.
   CSH.

506. Mercurius musicus. *Ed.* Henry Playford. 1699-1702.
   MH (nos. 1-7, 10, 11, 1700-02).

507. Mercurius phanaticus; or, Mercury temporizing. 1660
   CtY (no. 1, Mar. 14, 1660), TxU (no. 1).

508. Mercurius poeticus, discovering the treasons of a thing called Parliament. 1648.
    CSH, IWS (one no., May 5-13, 1648).

509. Mercurius poeticus. Marchamont Nedham. 1654. w.
    CSH (no. 1, Feb. 27, 1653/4).

510. Mercurius poeticus. 1660.
    CtY (no. 1, July 16, 1660).

511. Mercurius politicus. Oliver Williams, etc. 1660.
    CtY (no. 8, May 17, 1660).

512. Mercurius politicus: being monthly observations on the affairs of Great Britain. Daniel Defoe. 1716-20. m.
    CtY (May 1716–Jan. 1717; May–Oct. 1718), MH (May 1716–Feb. 1718; Jan., Mar.–Oct. 1719; Jan.–Dec. 1720), TxU (May, Dec. 1716; Jan.–Mar., May, June, Sept., Nov., Dec. 1717; Feb., Mar., May, Sept., 1718; June, Aug., Sept., Dec. 1719).

513. Mercurius politicus, comprising the summ of all intelligence . . . in defence of the Commonwealth and for information of the people [variations in subtitle]. Marchamont Nedham, John Milton, John Hall, John Canne, etc. Nos. 1-615, 1650-60. w.
    CSH (nos. 157, 221, 552-64, 601-14, 1653-60), CtY (nos. 28, Dec. 19, 1650; 144-53, 155-60, 162-63, 165-66, 168, 171-72, 174-85, 186-237, 238-80, 282-339, 341-403, 405, 408-23, 425-44, 545-65, 567-602, 604-06, 609-11, 615, Mar. 17, 1653–Apr. 12, 1660), DLC (nos. 601-15, Jan. 5–Apr. 12, 1660), ICN (nos. 36-64, 66-87, Feb. 13, 1651–Feb. 5, 1652; 111, July 22, 1652), ICU (nos. 222, Sept. 14, 1654; 599, Dec. 22, 1659), IU, MBB (nos. 221, 552, 608, 1654, 1659, 1660), MdBJ (no. 103, May 27, 1652), MHi (nos. 605, 607, 614, 1660), MnU (nos. 284, Nov. 22, 1655; 292, Jan. 17, 1656; 560-61, 567, 570, Mar. 24–June 9, 1659), NIC (nos. 1-138, 200-615), PPH (1654-61), WH (nos. 93, Mar. 18, 1652; 319, 332, July 24, Oct. 23, 1656; 352, Mar. 12, 1657).

514. Mercurius politicus; or, An antidote to popular misrepresentation. . . . James Drake. Nos. 1-51, June 12–Dec. 4, 1705. s. w.
    CtY, MH.

515. Mercurius pragmaticus (for King Charls II). 1649. ir.
    CSH (nos. 1-11, Apr. 24–July 3, 1649).

516. Mercurius pragmaticus. 1658.
    CtY no. 1, Aug. 30, 1658).

517. Mercurius pragmaticus. 1659.
    ICU (Dec. 30), TxU (no. 1, n. d.; no. 2, Dec. 30, 1659).

518. Mercurius pragmaticus, communicating intelligence from all parts. . . . John Cleiveland, Samuel Sheppard, Marchamont Nedham, etc. 1647-50. w.
CtY (nos. 1, 4, 8, 10, 11, 13, 14, 16-18, 21-23, Sept. 21, 1647–Feb. 22, 1648; 2, 6, 9, 12, 19, Apr. 11–Aug. 8, 1648), DLC (Sept. 21, 1647–Mar. 28, Apr. 4, June 20, 1648), ICU (no. 25, Sept. 19, 1648), MB (nos. 5, 7, 8, Oct.–Nov. 1647), MH (1st ser., nos. 1-23; 2nd ser., nos. 1-41; 3rd ser., nos. 2-6, 8-10; Sept. 14, 1647–June 26, 1649), MnU (nos. 1-28, Sept. 14, 1647–Mar. 28, 1648; 1-5, 7-11, 13-17, Mar. 28–June 5, 1648), NIC (nos. 2, 10, 13, 16, 17, 20, 23, 25, 27, Sept. 21, 1647–Mar. 21, 1648; 4, 5, 7, 9, 10, 11, 14, 16-19, 20, 21-28, 30-33, 36-37, Apr. 18–Dec. 12, 1648).

518a. Mercurius pragmaticus, communicating intelligence from all parts. Nos. 1-50, Apr. 4, 1648–Apr. 17, 1649. w.
IWS (nos. 1-10, Apr. 4–June 6, 1648).

519. Mercurius psitacus; or, The parroting mercury. 1648. w.
CSH.

520. Mercurius publicus. 1648.
CSH (nos. 1-4).

521. Mercurius publicus; being a brief summary or rehearsal of the whole weeks intelligence. 1680.
NN (nos. 1-2, Feb. 28–Mar. 18, 1679/80).

522. Mercurius publicus, comprising the sum of forraign intelligence with the affairs now in agitation in England, Scotland, and Ireland [variations in subtitle]. Giles Drury and Henry Muddiman. 1660-63. w. This was the Thursday edition of the official newsbook, the Monday edition being entitled Parliamentary intelligencer, *q. v.*
CSH (nos. 15-54, 1660-61; 1-53, 1661-62; 1-52, 1662-63; 1-33, 1663), CtY (nos. 16-19, 21-25, 27, 31-33, 48, Apr. 22–Nov. 29, 1660; 11, 18, 20, Mar. 21–May 22, 1661), DLC (nos. 1-54, Apr. 9, 1660–Jan. 9, 1662), ICU (no. 16, Apr. 22, 1660; Oct. 3, 1661; May 15, 1662), MH (nos. 31, 36, Aug. 2, Sept. 6, 1660), MnU (nos. 16-54, 1660; 1-53, 1661; 1-12, 1662).

523. Mercurius reformatus; or, The new observator. *Continued as* Weekly observator (from Jan. 9, 1692); *as* Mercurius Britannicus; or, The weekly observator (from Apr. 15, 1692); *as* Mercurius Britannicus (from ?). 1689-94.
CSH (app. to 1692), CtY (v. 1-4, May 15, 1689–Oct. 24, 1691, v. 4 lacking no. 21), DLC (v. 1-3, May 15, 1689–Mar. 14, 1691), IWS (v. 1-4, May 15, 1689–Oct. 24, 1691), MH (v. 1-4), NN (Dutch trans., 1690), PPL (Aug. 14, 28, 1689; v. 5, nos. 2, 9, 10, 11, 12, Feb.–Apr. 1692), TxU (Sept. 4, 1691).

524. Mercurius republicus. 1649. w.
    CSH.
525. Mercurius Romanus. 1706-07.
    CtY (nos. 1-27, 29-34, 36, 1706-07).
526. Mercurius rusticus. 1647.
    CSH.
527. Mercurius rusticus. 1685.
    NN.
528. Mercurius rusticus; or, The country's complaint. . . . Bruno Ryves. Nos. 1-21, 1643-44. w. (with gaps).
    CtY (1st week, May 20, 1643), ICN (rep. 1685), ICU (19th week, Feb. 16, 1643/4; also rep. 1646).
529. Mercurius Scoticus. Sir George Wharton. 1648.
    CSH.
530. Mercurius theologicus; or, The monthly instructor. Nos. 1-12, 1700-01. m.
    CtY, NN (v. 1, nos. 1, 4, 8, 10, 11).
531. Mercurius urbanicus. 1648.
    CSH.
532. Mercurius urbanus. 1643.
    CSH.
533. Mercurius vapulans. No. 1, Nov. 27, 1647.
    DLC.
534. Mercurius veridicus. 1644.
    TxU (no. 5, Feb. 27, 1644).
535. Mercurius veridicus, communicating intelligence from all parts of Great Britaine. . . . 1648. w.
    CSH, IWS (nos. 1-3, Apr. 21–May 8, 1648).

Mercury, publishing advertisements of all sorts. . . . *See* True character of Mercurius urbanicus & rusticus.

537. Merlin: the weekly monitor predicting England's grandeur. 1692. w.
    NN (June 15, 1692).
538. Meteors. Nos. 1-12, Nov. 1799–May 1800. f.
    DLC, ICU.

Methodist magazine. *See* Arminian magazine.

539. Methodist magazine; or, Evangelical repository. Leeds, 1798+. (From U. L.)
    NNG.

540. Microcosm. G. Canning and others. Windsor, nos. 1-40, Nov. 6, 1786–July 30, 1787. w.
CSt, CtY (also 2nd ed., 1788), DLC, ICN, ICU, IEN, IU, MB (rep. 1788), MH (also 2nd ed., 1788; 3rd ed., 1790; 4th ed., 1809), MiU, NN (also 2nd ed.; 4th ed.), NNC (2nd ed.; 3rd ed.), PPL, TxU (2nd ed.).

Middlesex journal and evening advertiser. *See* Middlesex journal; or, Chronicle of liberty.

541. Middlesex journal; or, Chronicle of liberty. *Continued as* Middlesex journal; or, Universal evening post (from no. 508, July 2, 1772); *as* Middlesex journal and evening advertiser (from no. 729, Nov. 30, 1773). 1769-78(?). t. w.
CtY (nos. 1-272, Apr. 4, 1769–Dec. 29, 1770), WH (nos. 184-507, 744-64, 766-69, 771-72, 774-819, 821-32, 834-43, 845-84, 886-99, 1043, 1056-82, 1085-99, 1101-24, 1126, 1128-33, 1135-54, 1157-98, 1200-01, 1203-12, June 5, 1770–Dec. 31, 1776).

Middlesex journal; or, Universal evening post. *See* Middlesex journal; or, Chronicle of liberty.

542. Midwife; or, Old woman's magazine. *Ed.* Christopher Smart. 1750-53. ir.
CtY, DLC, MB (1751), NN (v. 2, nos. 1-6, 1751), NNC (v. 2, no. 1).

543. Mirror. 1757. s. w.
MiU (no. 1, Mar. 22, 1757).

544. Mirror. Henry Mackenzie and others. Edinburgh, nos. 1-110, Jan. 23, 1779–May 27, 1780. s. w.
CSt, CtY (also 7th ed., 1787; 8th ed., 1790; 1st Amer. ed., 1792), DLC, ICN (rep.), ICU (also 5th ed., 1783), IU (rep. 1794), MB, MnU (11th ed., 1811), N (Amer. ed., 1793), NN, NNC (nos. 37-74, June 1, 1779–Jan. 22, 1780, 5th ed., 1783), TxU, WH.

545. Mirror of the times. 1796(?)+. w.
CtY (Jan. 19, 1799+).

546. Miscellanea curiosa. 1723-27. (From U. L.)
NIC.

547. Miscellanea curiosa mathematica. *Ed.* F. Holliday. 1745-49.
MiU, NNC (nos. 1-7, 1745).

548. Miscellanea scientifica curiosa. 1766. (From U. L.)
CtY.

549. Miscellaneous antiquities; or, A collection of curious papers .... Horace Walpole. Nos. 1-2, 1772.
ICN.

Miscellaneous correspondence. . . . *See* General magazine of arts and sciences. . . .

550. Miscellaneous letters, giving an account of the works of the learned, both at home and abroad. 1694-96. w. (to Jan. 1695); m.
    CtY (v. 1, Oct. 17, 1694–Dec. 1695), NN (v. 2, nos. 22-24, Jan.–Mar. 1696), PPL (v. 1, no. 1–v. 2, no. 3, Oct. 17, 1694–Mar. 1696).

551. Miscellaneous observations upon authors, ancient and modern. John Jortin. 1731-32.
    CtY, DLC, ICN, MB, NIC (extracts in John Jortin's Tracts, philological, etc., v. 2, 1790), NN (no. 2, 1731), RPB.

552. Miscellanies over claret. 1697.
    CtY (nos. 1-2, 1697), MdBJ, MH.

553. Miscellany: giving an account of the religion, morality, and learning of the present times. *Continued as* Weekly miscellany; giving an account of the religion, morality, and learning of the present times (from no. 3); *as* Weekly miscellany (from no. 13). W. Webster. Nos. 1-444, 1732-41. w.
    CtY (nos. 4-53, 61-124, 126-27, 129-31, 133-296, 298-313, 315-49, 354-61, 363-77, 379-93, 395-98, 400-10, 412-18, Jan. 6, 1733–Dec. 27, 1740; also nos. 1-101, 2nd ed., 1738), NN (rep. 1736-38), NNC (nos. 1-51, rep. 1736), TxAG (rep. 1738).

554. Missionary magazine. Edinburgh, 1796+. m.
    CtY (v. 2, no. 7, Jan. 1797), N, NIC, NN (v. 6, no. 38, July 15, 1799), NNG.

Mist's weekly journal. *See* Weekly journal; or, Saturday's post. . . .

555. Mitre and crown; or, Great Britain's true interest. 1748-51. s. m.; m. (from Jan. 1749).
    DLC (v. 1-3, nos. 1-4, Oct. 1748–Feb. 1751), MnU (v. 3, nos. 1-4).

556. Moderate: impartially communicating martial affaires to the kingdome of England. Gilbert Mabbott. 1648-49.
    MH (nos. 31-32, 34-35, 38), MnU (nos. 24-25, 27, Dec. 19, 1648–Jan. 16, 1649).

557. Moderate intelligencer, impartially communicating martiall affaires to the kingdome of England. John Dillingham. 1645-54. w.
    CSH (1649), CtY (nos. 137-53, 155-57, 159-70, 179-88, 190-93, 204, 209, 217, Nov. 4, 1647–May 10, 1649; n. s., nos. 1, May 29, 1649; 169, Dec. 29, 1652; 175, Apr. 26, 1653), ICU (nos. 89, 90, Nov. 19, 26; 93, Dec. 17, 1646; 135, Oct. 21, 1647), MnU (nos.

16, 44-45, 48, 50, 52-54, 57-58, 62, 80, 82, 86-87, 90-91, 93-97, 100-02, 106-08, 110-13, 116, 125, 134-44, 146-50, 153-55, 157, 160-65, 168, 170-72, 179, 185, 188, 190-94, 197, 200-01, 203-11, 213, 217-18, 221-23, 225, 227, 230-31, 233-34, 236, June 12, 1645–Sept. 27, 1649).

Moderate publisher of every dayes intelligence. *See* Perfect passages of every daies intelligence.

558. Moderator. Nos. 1-50, May 22-Nov. 10, 1710. s. w.
CtY, MiU, TxU.

559. Moderator. Steele. 1719.
CtY, ICN, MH (2nd ed., 1719), NN, NNC, TxU.

560. Modern history; or, A monthly account of all considerable occurrences, civil, ecclesiastical, and military, with all natural and philosophical productions and transactions. 1687-89. m.
CSH (v. 2, nos. 1, 2, 11, Oct., Nov. 1688, Aug. 1689), DLC, NN (v. 2, no. 5, Feb. 1689).

561. Modest narrative of intelligence. 1649. w.
CSH (nos. 1-14).

562. Momus ridens; or, Comical remarks on the weekly reports. 1690-91. w.
CtY (nos. 17-18, Feb. 18-25, 1691), MH (nos. 17-18).

563. Monethly account. 1688-89(?). m.
NN (Feb. 1689).

564. Monitor. *Published by* J. Morphew. 1714.
TxU (nos. 1-4, Apr. 22-29, 1714), MH (nos. 1-36, Apr. 22–July 12, 1714).

565. Monitor. *Printed for* J. Roberts. 1724-26(?). w.
IU (June 5, 1726).

566. Monitor; or, British freeholder. 1755-65. w.
CtY (nos. 1-504, Aug. 9, 1755–Mar. 20, 1765), DLC (Aug. 9, 1755–July 31, 1756), ICU (nos. 1-52, Aug. 9, 1755–July 31, 1756), IU (nos. 357, 360, rep.), MB (v. 1-2, Aug. 9, 1755–July 16, 1757), NNC (v. 1-4, nos. 1-208, Aug. 9, 1755–July 14, 1759; rep. 1760), WH (nos. 1-104, Aug. 9, 1755–July 16, 1757; 197-387, Apr. 28, 1759–Jan. 1, 1763).

567. Monthly account of the Land Bank. 1695. m.
CtY (no. 3, Oct. 1, 1695).

568. Monthly amusement. 1709. m.
CtY (nos. 1-6, Apr.–Sept. 1709).

568a. Monthly catalogue. B. Lintot. 1714-15. m.
ICN.

569. Monthly catalogue: being a general register of books, sermons, plays, poetry, and pamphlets [variations in subtitle]. J. Wilford. 1723-30.
    DLC (1723-29), ICN (1723-29).

570. Monthly chronicle. 1728-32. m. Includes monthly "Register of books."
    CtY (v. 1-3, Jan. 1728–Dec. 1730), DLC (v. 1-4), ICU (v. 1-4, 1728-31; v. 5, nos. 1-3, Jan.–Mar. 1732), N, TxU (v. 1-5, no. 3, Jan. 1728–Mar. 1732).

571. Monthly epitome and catalogue of new publications. 1797+. m.
    CtY (v. 2-4, Jan. 1798–Dec. 1800), DLC (v. 2-3, 1798-99), ICN, MB, PPL.

572. Monthly extracts; or, Beauties of modern authors. 1791-92. m.
    ICN (v. 1).

573. Monthly journal of the affairs of Europe. July 1704-(?). m. (From U. L.)
    CtY (no. 1).

574. Monthly ledger; or, Literary repository. V. 1-3, 1773-75. m.
    CtY (v. 1-3, 1773-75), DLC, IU, PPL.

575. Monthly magazine, and British register. *Published by* R. Phillips. 1796+. m.
    CSH (v. 2, July–Dec. 1796; v. 4, July–Dec. 1797), CtY (v. 1, no. 2, Feb. 1796+), DLC, ICU, MB, MBB, MdBP, MH, MiU, N (v. 7, Jan.–July, 1799), NjP (v. 2, July–Dec. 1796), NN (v. 1-7, Feb. 1796–July 1799), NNC, PPL, TxU (v. 2-3), WH.

576. Monthly masks of vocal musick, containing all the choicest songs by the best masters made for the play-houses, public consorts, and other occasions. 1703-07. m. (From U. L.)
    MH.

577. Monthly mirror, reflecting men and manners, with strictures on their epitome, the stage. 1795+. m.
    CtY, DLC, ICN, ICU, MB, MBB (v. 7, Jan.–June 1799), MH, MHi (Jan.–June 1799), MiU, NIC, NjP, NN, PPL, WH.

578. Monthly miscellany; or, Gentleman and lady's compleat magazine. 1774-75. m.
    CtY, NN (v. 1-2, 1774).

579. Monthly register; or, Memoirs of the affairs of Europe. Samuel Buckley. 1703-07(?). m.
    DLC (1707).

580. Monthly review. *Ed.* R. Griffiths. 1749+. m.
   CtY, DLC, ICN, ICU, IU, MB, MBB, MdBP, MH, MHi (1762-99, inc.), MiU, MnU (1749-89; n. s., v. 2+), N (v. 1-46, 1749-72), NIC, NjP, NN, NNC, PPH, PPL, PU, RPB (v. 1-81), TxU, WH.

581. Monthly visitor and entertaining pocket companion. 1797+. m.
   CtY, MBB, NN.

582. Moral and political magazine of the London corresponding society. 1796. m.
   CtY (v. 1, June–Dec. 1796), NNC (v. 1, June–Dec. 1796).

583. Morning advertiser. 1794+. d.
   TxU (nos. 66, 80, 400, 657, 665, 768, 774, 797, 801, 993, Apr. 25, 1794–Apr. 1, 1797).

584. Morning chronicle, and London advertiser. *Continued as* Morning chronicle (from 1789 or 1790). 1769+. d.
   CSH (Sept. 4, 1794), CtY (Apr. 21, 23, May 7-9, 13-16, 18, 21-28, 31–June 6, 8-17, 20, 22-23, 25, July 1-5, 7-15, 18, 20, 1785; Jan. 16, Dec. 13, 1788; June 10, 1789; Dec. 4-6, 13-14, 17, 1792; Jan. 1, 7, 15, 23, 25-26, Feb. 4, 1793; Jan. 1-9, 11-22, 24–Apr. 27, 30–Sept. 20, 23–Nov. 12, 14–Dec. 31, 1799; Apr. 1, 1800+), MB (1794+), NN (July 3, 5, 15, 17, 1779; Mar. 1, 1780), WH (nos. 3485, 3549, 3561-63, 3567, 3570, 3572-73, 3575-87, 3589-3603, 3607-08, 3610-14, 3618, 3621, July 19–Dec. 27, 1780; 6150-51, 6153-6205, Jan. 23–Mar. 28, 1789).

585. Morning herald and daily advertiser. 1780+. d.
   CtY (May 15, July 15, 20, 21, Nov. 19, Dec. 11-13, 17, 19-23, 25-29, 31, 1788; Jan. 2-5, 7, May 20-26, 28, 30, June 5-11, July 20-21, Nov. 19, 1789; Feb. 4, 10-26, Mar. 1-5, 8-25, 27-30, Apr. 1-5, 7-24, 27-30, May 3-8, 12, 13, 17–June 11, 29, Aug. 9–Dec. 4, 1790; Jan. 10, May 13, Nov. 22, 24, 25, Dec. 5-7, 10-20, 26-31, 1791; Jan. 2-7, 11-13, 16–Feb. 6, 9-10, 14-27, Mar. 1-9, 13-20, 23–Apr. 6, 10-13, 16, 18–May 5, 8-9, 11–June 21, 23-30, July 3-7, 9-10, 13-25, 27–Aug. 22, 31, Sept. 4-11, 14-27, Oct. 27–Nov. 20, 23-24, 26-27, 29, Dec. 1-4, 6-21, 25-31, 1792; Jan. 1-15, 17-21, 23, 28–Mar. 14, 16–Apr. 2, 4, 8-11, 13-20, 23–May 9, 11-14, 17-22, 24-30, June 3-5, 7–July 2, 4, 10-19, 22–Aug. 3, 1793), TxU (nos. 454, Apr. 13, 1782; 1604, Dec. 16, 1785; 4069, 4083, 4111, 4121, Mar. 16, Apr. 2, May 4, 16, 1792).

586. Morning post and daily advertiser. 1772+. d.
   CtY (Dec. 29-31, 1777; Jan. 1, 3–Mar. 14, 17–May 19, 21-29, June 1–July 8, 1778; Jan. 19–May 19, 1789), NN (Jan. 2-28, 30–Dec. 31, 1777; Dec. 28, 30, 1778), TxU (1797, inc.).

Morning star. *See* Star and evening advertiser.

587. Muses' gazette. 1720.
    MB (no. 8, Apr. 20, 1720, rep. in The theatre, by Sir Richard Steele, ed. John Nichols, 1791).

588. Muses mercury; or, The monthly miscellany. 1707-08. m.
    DLC (v. 1, 1707), TxU (v. 1, nos. 1, 2, 6, Jan., Mar., June 1707; v. 2, no. 1, Jan. 1708).

589. Museum; or, The literary and historical register. *Ed.* R. Dodsley. Nos. 1-39, Mar. 29, 1746-Sept. 12, 1747. s. m.
    CtY, DLC, ICU, IU, NIC, NN, NNC, PPL.

590. Museum rusticum et commerciale. 1763-66.
    CtY, ICJ, IU, N, NNC (3rd ed., 1766), WH.

591. National journal; or, The country gazette. 1746. t. w.
    CtY (rep. 1748).

592. Naturalists' miscellany. G. Shaw and E. Nodder. 1789+. m.
    CU, DLC, MB, NIC.

593. Naval biography. 1800+.
    CtY.

594. Naval chronicle. J. S. Clarke, S. Jones, J. Jones, etc. Jan. 1799+. m.
    CSt, CtY, DLC, ICN, ICU, IU, MB, MH, MHi, NIC, NN, NNC, PPL.

595. New annual register. A. Kippis and others. 1781 (for the year 1780)+. a.
    CtY, DLC, ICU, MB, MH, MnU (1780-89, 1791-97, 1799+), N (v. 5, 1784), NN, NNC (1783, 1786), PU (1782, 1795+), WH.

New anti-Roman pacquet. *See* Pacquet of advice from Rome.

597. Newcastle chronicle. Newcastle-upon-Tyne, 1764+. w.
    CtY (Aug. 28, 1790; Apr. 27, Aug. 10, 1793).

598. Newcastle courant, with news foreign and domestick. Newcastle-upon-Tyne, 1711+. t. w.; w. (from 1725?).
    CtY (nos. 5856-6116, Jan. 3, 1789–Dec. 28, 1793).

599. Newcastle general magazine. Newcastle-upon-Tyne, 1747-60. m.
    CtY (v. 1-12, 1747-59), DLC (v. 12), NN (Mar., Sept., Dec., and app., 1748; Jan., Mar., Sept., Nov. 1749).

600. Newcastle journal. Newcastle-upon-Tyne, 1739-76(?). w.
    DLC (Dec. 21, 1745), NN (Mar. 29, 1746).

Newcastle-upon-Tyne. Literary and philosophical society.

See Literary and philosophical society of Newcastle-upon-Tyne.

602. New Christian's magazine, being a universal repository of divine knowledge. V. 1-5, 1782-86. (From U. L.)
OO (v. 1-5).

603. New Cork evening post. Cork, 1791+. s. w.
NN (Jan. 3, Mar. 4, 7, 14, 18, Apr. 1, 8, 11, 18–May 9, 20, June 3–July 8, 15, 18, 25–Aug. 1, 8, 15, 19, 26–Sept. 5, 12-19, 26–Oct. 7, 17–Nov. 4, 11–Dec. 2, 9, 12, 19, 23, 1799).

604. New dialogue between Somebody and Nobody; or, The Observator observed. 1681.
TxU (nos. 3-5, Dec. 5-19, 1681).

605. New Heraclitus ridens; or, An old dialogue between Jest and Earnest revived. 1689.
CtY (no. 1, May 24).

606. New lady's magazine; or, Polite and entertaining companion for the fair sex. C. Stanhope. 1786-95. m.
CtY (v. 1, Feb.–Dec. 1786, and suppl.; v. 9-10, Jan. 1794–Dec. 1795), IU (v. 3), MB (v. 4, 1789), MBB (v. 1-6, Feb. 1786–Dec. 1791), NN (v. 1-6).

607. New London magazine, being an universal and complete monthly repository of knowledge, instruction and entertainment. 1785-92. m.
CtY (July 1787), DLC (v. 1-3, 1785-87), IU (v. 2-8, 1786-92), MH (v. 1, 1785; 5, 1789), NN (v. 1, July–Dec. 1785), WH (v. 2, 1786).

608. New London medical journal. 1792-93. m.
CtY (v. 1-2, 1792-93; v. 2, inc.).

609. New London price courant. 1786.
CtY (Apr. 14, 1786).

610. New London review; or, Monthly report of authors and books. 1799-1800. m.
CtY, NN.

611. New magazine; or, Moral and entertaining miscellany. Dublin, 1799-1800.
DCU, PPL (Jan.–Oct. 1799).

612. New memoirs of literature. M. de la Roche. V. 1-6, Jan. 1725–Dec. 1727. m.
CtY, DLC, ICN, ICU (v. 6, 1727), IU, MB, MH, NN, NNC (lacking v. 6), PPL, RPB (v. 1, Jan.–June 1725).

613. New miscellany for the year. . . . J. Swift, etc. 1734-39. a.

CtY (1734, 1737-38), ICU (1737, pts. 1-9), MB (1737), MH (1737-38), NN (1738).

614. New musical and universal magazine. 1774-75(?).
DLC (v. 1-3, 1774-75).

615. New novelist's magazine. 1786-87. m.
MB, NN (v. 2, 1787).

616. New plain dealer; or, Freeman's budgets. 1792-96. ir.
MH (nos. 1, 2nd ed., n. d.; 2-3, May 1792), NNC (no. 1, 1792).

617. New review, with literary curiosities and literary intelligence. Ed. H. Maty. 1782-86. m.
CtY (v. 1-10, no. 2, Feb. 1782–Aug. 1786), DLC, MB (v. 1-9), MBB, MH, NN (v. 1-9), NNC (v. 1-9), WH (v. 1, 5, 7-9).

618. New royal and universal magazine; or, The gentleman and lady's companion. 1752(?)-59(?). m.
CtY (v. 16, nos. 4-5, Oct.–Nov. 1759).

619. New spectator, with the sage opinions of John Bull. 1784-86. w.
CtY (nos. 1-22, Feb. 3–June 29, 1784), MiU (nos. 1-9, Feb. 3–Mar. 30, 1784).

620. New theological repository. Liverpool, July 1800+. m.
MBB.

621. New town and country magazine; or, General monthly repository of knowledge and pleasure. 1787-88. m.
CtY (v. 2, Jan.–Dec. 1788).

622. New universal magazine; or, Gentleman's and lady's polite instructor. 1751-59. m.
ICU (v. 1, nos. 1-9, Sept. 1751–May 1752), MH (v. 5, Jan.–June 1754).

623. New weekly chronicle; or, Universal journal. *Continued as* Owen's weekly chronicle; or, Universal journal (from no. 2, Apr. 15, 1758). 1758-67(?). w.
CtY (Apr. 8, 1758–Dec. 29, 1759), NN (v. 1, nos. 1-39, Apr. 8–Dec. 30, 1758), WH (v. 2, no. 74, Sept. 1, 1759).

624. Newes of this present weeke from Germany, Italy, and Spaine. N. Butter. 1640.
ICN (century 3, no. 27, June 6, 1640).

Newes, published for satisfaction and information of the people. *See* Intelligencer, published for the satisfaction and information of the people.

625. News from Parnassus. *Continued as* Advice from Parnassus (from no. 2). 1681.
TxU (no. 1, Feb. 2, 1681).

626. News from the dead; or, The monthly packet of true intelligence from the other world. Pts. 1-8, 1714-15. (From U. L.)
    DLC.

627. News from the land of chivalry. 1681.
    TxU (nos. 2-3, n. d. [1681]).

Nicholson's journal. *See* Journal of natural philosophy, chemistry, and the arts.

628. Night walker; or, Evening rambles in search after lewd women. John Dunton. 1696-97. m.
    DLC (Sept. 1696–Mar. 1697).

629. Northampton mercury; or, The Monday's post. Northampton, May 2, 1720+. w.
    DLC (v. 3-4, 1722-23), TxU (v. 27, no. 7, May 19, 1746), WH (v. 11, nos. 22-24, 48, 50-52, Sept. 21, 1730–Apr. 19, 1731; v. 12, nos. 1-5, 7, 9-17, 22-36, 38, 51, Apr. 26, 1731–Apr. 10, 1732; v. 13, nos. 5-7, 17-26, 29, 34, 36, 37-39, 45-47, 49, 52, May 22, 1732–Apr. 16, 1733; v. 14, nos. 3-4, 6-7, 9, 11-12, 15-18, 20, 23-24, 29, 32-36, 49, 51-52, May 7, 1733–Apr. 15, 1734; v. 15, nos. 1, 7, 13-22, 25-26, 38-39, 40, 42, 44, 47, 49-51, Apr. 23, 1734–Apr. 14, 1735; v. 16, nos. 2, 5-8, 11, 18-19, Apr. 28–Aug. 25, 1735).

630. North British intelligencer; or, Constitutional miscellany. Edinburgh, 1776-77. w.
    NN (v. 1, 3, 5, 1776-77), PPL (1776-77).

631. North British magazine; or, Caledonian miscellany. Edinburgh, Oct. 16, 1782–Oct. 24, 1783.
    CtY (no. 9, Feb. 20, 1783).

632. North Briton. John Wilkes. *Printed for* G. Kearsley (nos. 1-45) and E. Sumpter (no. 46). Nos. 1-46, June 5, 1762–May 28, 1763. w. (with some interruptions). After the close of Wilkes' editorship (with no. 46), the North Briton was continued as follows: (1) nos. 47-235(?), June 4, 1763–Dec. 6, 1766 (with pagination continuous from Wilkes' no. 46; printed for E. Sumpter [through no. 181, Dec. 21, 1765] and T. Peat [from no. 182, Dec. 28, 1765]); (2) nos. 47-218, May 10, 1768–May 11, 1771 (with double numbering from no. 65, Sept. 10, 1768, which is also called no. 19 " of the Continuation"; printed for W. Bingley); (3) after no. 218 in Bingley's journal; or, Universal gazette. Besides the no. 46 dated May 28, 1763, there were at least two other issues bearing this number but presenting quite different texts: (1) a fragment dated Apr. 30, 1763, " printed at

Strawberry Hill" and (2) an issue dated Nov. 12, 1763. There were also a good many "extras" bearing the title North Briton extraordinary.

CSH (nos. 1-46, 1762-63), **CSt** (nos. 1-93, June 5, 1762–Apr. 14, 1764; 95-170, Apr. 28, 1764–Oct. 5, 1765; 74, 2nd ed., **68, 3rd ed.**, 130, 4th ed.), **CtY** (nos. 47-199, May 10, 1768–Dec. 29, 1770 [Bingley's continuation]; also nos. 1-46, rep. 1769; nos. 1-44, Dublin rep., 1764-65; nos. 1-45, rep. 1766; Appendix to nos. 1-46, 1769), **DLC** (nos. 1-218, rep. 1769-71 [original series and Bingley's continuation]; also Appendix to nos. 1-46, 1769), **ICU** (nos. 1-46; also no. 46 of Apr. 30, 1763; also nos. 1-46 [Apr. 30 and Nov. 12, 1763], rep. Bingley, 1769; also nos. 47-100, May 10, 1768–Apr. 10, 1769, rep. Bingley, 1769), **IU** (nos. 5-46 of the original issue and 47-64, 66-73, 96, 101-206, 208-18 of Bingley's continuation; also nos. 1-45, rep. 1763), **MB** (nos. 1-218 [original issue and Bingley's continuation], rep. 1769-71), **MnU** (nos. 2-143, June 12, 1762–Mar. 30, 1765), **N** (nos. 1-45, June 5, 1762–Apr. 23, 1763; 50-189 [Bingley's continuation], May 28, 1768–Nov. 10, 1770), **NIC** (nos. 1-45), **NN** (nos. 1-46, June 5, 1762–May 28, 1763; 47-51, June 4–July 2, 1763; 131-235, Jan. 5, 1765–Dec. 6, 1766), **NNC** (nos. 1-52, 81, 100-03, 123, 149, 193-94, 1762-70; also nos. 1-46, rep. 1763), **TxU** (nos. 47-218 [Bingley's continuation]; also nos. 1-46, rep. 1772), **WH** (nos. 1-46, June 5, 1762–Apr. 30, 1763, and 47-153, May 10, 1768–Mar. 3, 1770, rep. Bingley).

633. Novelist's magazine. V. 1-23, 1780-88.
DLC (v. 2-8, 10-11, 13-18, 20-22), **ICU** (v. 1-20, 1780-86), **IU, MB, MHi, MnU, NjP, NN, NNC** (v. 7, 16, 23), **WU**.

634. Observator. John Tutchin (to Sept. 1707). 1702-12. w.; s. w. (from May 23, 1702).
CtY (v. 1-11, Apr. 1, 1702–July 30, 1712), **DLC** (nos. 11-23, Nov. 1–Dec. 12, 1707), **ICU** (v. 1-3, Apr. 1, 1702–Mar. 3, 1705), **MH** (v. 7, nos. 2-43, Feb. 21–July 14, 1708; v. 8, nos. 1-99, Feb. 2, 1709–Jan. 11, [1710]; v. 9, nos. 13-16, 25, 56, Mar. 1-11, Apr. 12, July 29, 1710), **NN** (v. 1, no. 5, Apr. 29, 1702; v. 3, no. 53, Sept. 23, 1704), **TxU** (v. 1-3, Apr. 1, 1702–Mar. 3, 1705).

635. Observator. *Continued as* Rehearsal (from no. 2, Aug. 12, 1704); *as* Rehearsal of Observator, &c. (from no. 5, Sept. 2, 1704, though with frequent recurrences of Rehearsal); *as* Rehearsal (from no. 51, July 21, 1705). Charles Leslie. August 5, 1704–Mar. 26, 1709. w. (to no. 93, Apr. 6, 1706); s. w.
CtY (also rep. 1750), **DLC, ICU** (also rep. 1750), **IEK, IU** (v. 1-3, 1704-08), **IWS, MH, MnU, NNC** (also rep. 1750), **TxAG, TxU, WH**.

636. Observator, in question and answer. Sir Roger L'Estrange. Apr. 13, 1681–Mar. 9, 1687. Sometimes called Observator in dialogue.
CSH (v. 1, nos. 1-470, Apr. 13, 1681–Jan. 9, 1684; v. 2, nos. 1-215, Jan. 10, 1684–Feb. 7, 1685; v. 3, nos. 1-246, Feb. 11, 1685–Mar. 4, 1687), **CtY** (v. 1-3, Apr. 13, 1681–Mar. 9, 1687), **DLC** (Apr. 23, 1681), **ICN** (v. 1, Apr. 13, 1681–Jan. 9, 1684), **ICU** (v. 1-3), **IU** (Apr. 13, 1681–Mar. 9, 1687), **IWS, MB** (Apr. 13, 1681–Mar. 9, 1686/7), **MH** (v. 1; v. 2, nos. 1, 39-45, 47-69, 71-76, 78-83, 86-88, 92, 94-103, 106-08, 111, 113, 114, 116-19, 121-23, 125-30, 132-43, 145-214, Jan. 10, 1684–Feb. 6, 1685; v. 3, nos. 201-02, Aug. 18-21, 1686), **MnU** (v. 1-3, Apr. 13, 1681–Mar. 9, 1687), **N** (v. 1, 3), **NN** (v. 1-3), **PPL** (Jan. 14, 1684–Mar. 9, 1686/7), **WH** (Apr. 13, 1681–Mar. 9, 1681/2).

637. Observator observ'd; or, Protestant observations upon anti-Protestant pamphlets. 1681.
NN (no. 2), **TxU** (nos. 1, May 6, [1681]; 2, 3, n. d.).

638. Observator reviv'd. 1707. (From U. L.)
DLC.

639. Observator, Tory, Trimmer, Whig, Nobs, Mob. 1688(?).
CSH (no. [1], Dec. [1688]).

640. Observator, with a summary of intelligence. Marchamont Nedham. Nos. 1-2, Oct. 24–Nov. 7, 1654. (From U. L.)
NN (no. 1).

641. Occasional paper, containing reflexions on books. . . . 1697-98.
IEK (nos. 1-3), **IU** (v. 1, no. 9, 1698), **NIC** (no. 2), **NNC** (nos. 1, 4, 8).

642. Occasional paper. S. Browne, B. Avery, and others. 1716-19. m. Titlepages of collected volumes read: A collection of the occasional papers for the year . . . ; sometimes referred to as "Bagweel" papers.
CSH (v. 3, no. 9, Sept. 1719), **CtY** (nos. 1-10, 12, 1716-18), **ICU** (v. 1, nos. 1-5, 7-12; v. 2, nos. 2-12; v. 3, no. 9, 1716-19), **IU** (v. 3, no. 9), **MB** (nos. 1-12, 1716; v. 3, no. 4, 1718; v. 3, nos. 9, 10, 1719), **MHi** (1717-18, inc.), **NIC** (v. 3, no. 12, Dec. 1719), **NNC** (v. 1-2, 1716-18), **TxU** (v. 3, no. 9).

643. Occasional writer. Bolingbroke. 1727.
CtY, ICU (nos. 1-3, 1727), **NIC** (nos. 1-3), **NNC** (no. 1, 1727), **TxU** (no. 2, 1727).

644. Occasional writer. 1738.
CtY, NNC (no. 4).

645. Occurrences from foreign parts, with an exact accompt of the publick affairs of . . . England, Scotland and Ireland. Oliver Williams, John Canne, etc. Nos. 1-88(?), June 28, 1659–May 18, 1660. (From U. L.)
    MH (nos. 50, 88, 1660).

646. Oeconomist; or, Edlin's weekly journal. 1733-(?). w.
    CtY (no. 1, Sept. 1, 1733).

647. Oeconomist; or, Englishman's magazine. Thomas Bigge and others. Newcastle-upon-Tyne, 1798-99. m.
    CtY, ICJ (v. 1), IEK, IU, NNC (v. 1, 1798).

    Œdipus; or, The postman remounted. *See* Account of the publick transactions.

    Old common sense; or, The Englishman's journal. *See* Common sense; or The Englishman's journal.

648. Old England; or, The constitutional journal. *Continued as* Old England; or, The broadbottom journal (from Oct. 4, 1746); *as* Old England; or, The national gazette (from Apr. 6, 1751); *as* Old England's journal (from Feb. 24, 1753). 1743-53. w.
    CtY (nos. 8, [1743]; 146, Feb. 28, 1747), NN (Aug. 20, Sept. 1, 7, Oct. 1, 1743).

649. Old maid. Frances Brooke. Nos. 1-37, Nov. 15, 1755–July 24, 1756. w.
    CtY (rep. 1764), DLC (no. 10, Jan. 17, 1756), IU, IWS, TxU (nos. 1-9, Nov. 15, 1755–Jan. 10, 1756).

650. Old Whig. Joseph Addison. Nos. 1-2, Mar. 19–Apr. 2, 1719.
    CtY (nos. 1-2; also rep. in Town talk, 1789), IU (rep. in Town talk, 1790), MB (rep. 1790), MBB (rep. 1790), NN.

651. Old Whig; or, The consistent Protestant. 1735-38(?). w.
    CtY (Mar. 13, 1735–Mar. 30, 1738), MB (nos. 1-103, 1735-38), MH (nos. 1-160, 1735-38), NIC (rep. 1739), NNC (rep. 1739), PPL (Mar. 13, 1735–Mar. 13, 1738, rep. 1739), TxU (nos. 47-160, Jan. 29, 1736–Mar. 30, 1738, lacking nos. 50-53, 55, 58, 62, 80-81, 85-86, 97-98, 101-02, 104, 105-110, 111, 112-17, 118, 126, 130, 134-35, 140-41, 150, 152-55).

652. Olla podrida. T. Monro and others. Oxford and London, nos. 1-44, Mar. 17, 1787–Jan. 12, 1788. w.
    CtY (2nd ed., 1788), DLC (2nd ed.), ICU, IU, MB (2nd ed.), MH, MHi (2nd ed.), NIC (2nd ed.), NNC (2nd ed.), PPL (v. 1, nos. 1-37, Mar. 17, 1787–Nov. 24, 1787), WH.

    One pennyworth of pig-meat; or, Lessons for the swinish multitude. *See* Pigs' meat.

654. Opposition. 1755. ir.
   CtY, NN, NNC, RPB (no. 1?).

655. Oracle. V. 1, 1754. (From U. L.)
   TxU (v. 1).

   Oracle and public advertiser. *See* London daily post and general advertiser.

656. Oracle, Bell's new world. 1789-94. d. Incorporated with the Public advertiser in 1794. *See* London daily post and general advertiser.
   CtY (nos. 32-295, July 7, 1789–May 10, 1790; 478-804, Jan. 1–Dec. 24, 1791, inc.).

657. Orange gazette. 1688-89. s. w.
   CSH (nos. 1-8, 11-17), CtY (nos. 2, 10, Jan. 3, Feb. 8, 1689).

658. Oratory magazine. *Ed.* J. Henley. 1748.
   CtY (no. 3).

659. Ordinary weekly curranto. Nathaniel Butter and Nicholas Bourne. 1638-39.
   MnU (nos. 6-11, 21-23, 29-31, 35-40, 47-48, 50, 64-74, Jan. 1–May 27, 1639).

660. Oriental collections. Sir Wm. Ouseley. 1797-99. q.
   MB, NN (v. 1-2, 1797-98), NNC (v. 1-2), PU.

661. Oriental repertory. 1791-97. (From U. L.)
   DLC.

662. Original weekly journal, with fresh advices, foreign and domestick. *Continued as* Applebee's original weekly journal . . . (from July 16, 1720). 1715(?)-36(?). w.
   CtY (July 30, 1715, May 9, 1719–May 6, 1721, Jan. 19, 1722, May 4, 1723, Mar. 23, 1730), TxU (Aug. 4, 25, Sept. 1, 15, Dec. 29, 1716; Jan. 5, 12, 19, Feb. 2, May 18, 1717).

663. Orphan reviv'd; or, Powell's weekly journal. 1719-20. w.
   MH (nos. 23, 51, Apr. 18, Nov. 7, 1719).

   Owen's weekly chronicle; or, Universal journal. *See* New weekly chronicle. . . .

664. Oxford diurnall, communicating the intelligence and affaires of the court to the rest of the kingdome. Oxford, 1643. w.
   CtY (1st week, Jan. 7, 1642/3).

665. Oxford gazette. *Continued as* London gazette (from no. 24, Feb. 5, 1666). Oxford, 1665-66; London, 1666+. s. w. Numerous issues called Supplement to the London gazette; others, London gazette extraordinary.

CSH (no. 15, Jan. 1, 1666-1747; June 15, 1780), CtY (1665-1738, 1740-44, 1746-68, 1775, 1790), DLC, ICU (nos. 1-2369, 2371-3272, 1665-97; 1736, inc.; 1766-67, inc.), IU (nos. 1-3693, 4060, 1665-1704), IWS (nos. 255-2141, Apr. 27, 1668–May 27, 1686), MB (1665-94; 1701–Oct. 1708; June 10, 1775; Mar. 9, June 4, Aug. 3, Sept. 21, Oct. 10, Nov. 23, 1776; 1780-81; 1788-89; 1792-97; 1799+), MiU (nos. 1-6590, 1665-1727), MnU (1665-1722), NcU (nos. 2204-43, 1686-89; 3251-4013, 1696-1704), NIC (1799+), NN (Nov. 16, 1665–Feb. 1, 1666; Feb. 23, Sept. 21, Oct. 5, 9, Dec. 18-25, 1779; Feb. 12, 28, Mar. 4, 6, May 25, June 15, July 5, Oct. 9, Dec. 21, 30, 1780; Jan. 9, 16, Mar. 13, Apr. 23, May 11, June 5, 9, 12, 16, 23, 27, July 14, Aug. 4, 9, 11, 21, Oct. 15, Nov. 6, Dec. 18, 1781; Mar. 12, 26, 30, May 18-25, June 18, 1782; Feb. 8, 1785–Jan. 1, 1788; 1789-90; 1792-98), NNC (nos. 2020-2438, Mar. 30, 1685–Mar. 25, 1689, inc.), TxU (nos. 202-4210, Oct. 24, 1667–Mar. 18, 1705; 4785, Dec. 13, 1710; 5010-5246, May 27, 1712–July 31, 1741; 5517, Mar. 5, 1717; 5625, Mar. 18, 1718; 8499-8601, Jan. 7, 1745–Dec. 30, 1746; 11663, May 7, 1776; [?], Nov. 8, 1782; 13570, Sept. 14, 1793; 13572, Sept. 16, 1793; 13987, Mar. 3, 1797), WH (nos. [?], Sept. 10, 1666, rep.; 1508-1559, May 3–Oct. 28, 1680; 2929, Dec. 7, 1693; 2986-98, 3001-03, 3005-12, 3014, 3018-20, June 25–Oct. 22, 1694; 3073, Apr. 25, 1695; 3550, Nov. 20, 1699; 3568, 3600, 3602, 3622, Jan. 6, May 13, 20, July 29, 1700; 3784, 3808, 3762, 3770, Feb. 16, May 11, Dec. 1, 29, 1701; 3797, Apr. 2, 1702; 3983, 3991, Jan. 13, Feb. 10, 1703; 4086, 4102, 4044, 4054, 4057, 4058, 4065, Jan. 8–Oct. 26, 1704; 4102, 4168, 4099, Jan. 14, Oct. 22, Dec. 3, 1705; 5018-24, 5026, 5028-42, 5044-62, 5068, June 17–Nov. 15, 1712; July–Dec. 1767; 1768-99).

666. Oxford journal. *Continued as* Jackson's Oxford journal (from ?). W. Jackson. Oxford, 1753+.
TxU (no. 76, Oct. 12, 1754).

667. Oxford magazine; or, University museum. Oxford, 1768-76. m.
CtY (v. 1-13, July 1768–Dec. 1776), DLC (v. 1-3, 1768-69), MB (v. 1-7, 9-11, 1768-75), MdBP (v. 12, 1775), MH (v. 1-2, July 1768–June 1769; v. 7, July–Dec. 1771), NIC (v. 1-7, 1768-71), NN (v. 1-11, 1768-74, v. 11 inc.), PPH (v. 10, 1773), PPL (v. 1-2, 1768-69; v. 6, 1771).

668. Packets of letters from Scotland. *Printed by* Robert Ibbitson. 1648. w.
CtY (nos. 2, 13, 22, 23, 29, Mar. 29–Oct. 3, 1648).

669. Pacquet from Parnassus; or, A collection of papers. 1702.
CtY (v. 1, nos. 1-2, 1702), MH (nos. 1-2).

670. Pacquet of advice from Rome; or, The history of popery. *Continued as* Weekly pacquet of advice from Rome (from v. 1, no. 2) ; *as* New anti-Roman pacquet (from v. 3, no. 1 [*i. e.* 5], July 9, 1680) ; *as* Anti-Roman pacquet (from v. 3, no. 5 [*i. e.* 9]) ; *as* Weekly pacquet of advice from Rome restored; or, The history of popery continued (from v. 3, no. 22 [*i. e.* 26]) ; *as* Weekly pacquet of advice from Rome (from v. 4, no. 1). V. 1-5, Dec. 3, 1678–July 13, 1683; v. 6, Jan. 5–Feb. 8(?), 1689. w. There were two issues of v. 5: one edited by Henry Care (nos. 1-47, Aug. 25, 1682–July 13, 1683), the other by William Salmon (nos. 1-38, Aug. 25, 1682–May 17, 1683).
CSH (v. 1-3, 1678-81), **CtY** (v. 1-3, Dec. 3, 1678–Dec. 16, 1681; v. 5, Aug. 25, 1682–July 13, 1683), **ICU** (v. 1-5, 1678-83), **IWS** (v. 1-3), **MH** (v. 1-5), **MiU** (v. 1, nos. 1-31, Dec. 3, 1678–July 4, 1679; v. 2, nos. 1-47, July 11, 1679–May 28, 1680; v. 3, nos. 1-80, June 4, 1680–Dec. 16, 1681; v. 4, nos. 1-35, Dec. 23, 1681–Aug. 18, 1682; v. 5, both issues; v. 6, nos. 1-3, Jan. 5–Feb. 8, 1689), **NN** (v. 1-2), **NNC** (v. 1-5), **TxAG** (v. 3, nos. 29-80; v. 4, nos. 1-35; v. 5, nos. 1-47), **TxU** (rep.).

Palladium . . . *See* Gentleman and lady's palladium.

671. Papers concerning the Scots commissioners. *Printed by* A. Coe. 1647.
CtY (no. 5, Feb. 28, 1647).

672. Papers sent from the Scotts quarters. Samuel Pecke. 1646.
CtY (Sept. 24, 1646).

673. Papers of the resolution of the Parliament of Scotland. *Printed by* I. C. 1647.
CtY (no. 1, Jan. 21).

674. Paris gazette. 1673.
CSH (no. 1).

675. Paris pendant l'année. *Ed.* M. Peltier. 1795+. w.
CtY, NN (v. 27, no. 205, June 16, 1800), **NNC** (v. 1-4, lacking nos. 28-29; v. 7, lacking no. 59; v. 8, lacking no. 71; v. 9, lacking no. 73; 1795-96).

Parker's general advertiser and morning intelligencer. *See* General advertiser and morning intelligencer.

677. Parker's London news; or, The impartial intelligencer. *Continued as* Parker's penny post (from Apr. 28, 1725). 1718(?)-33(?). t. w.
MH (Oct. 26–Nov. 2, Nov. 9-13, 25, 30, Dec. 2, 9, 14, 16, 21, 28, 30, 1724; Jan. 1, 8-18, 22, 27, Feb. 3-8, 12, 19, Mar. 3-15, 24, 26,

Apr. 1, 1725), **TxU** (nos. 1186, 1194, 1213-16, 1221-23, 1225, 1227-29, 1231, 1234-35, 1244, 1247, 1249-77, 1280-84, 1292-98, 1300-02, Nov. 27, 1732–Aug. 24, 1733).

678. Parliamentary intelligencer. *Continued as* Kingdomes intelligencer (from Jan. 1, 1661). Henry Muddiman and Giles Drury. 1659-63. w. *See also* Mercurius publicus, 1660-63.
 CSH (nos. 15-53, Apr. 2–Dec. 31, 1660; 1661-63), **CtY** (nos. 17, 41, 43, Apr. 23–Oct. 22, 1660; [captions missing], Apr.–May, 1662; nos. 14, 17-19, 27-28, Apr. 6–July 13, 1663), **ICU** (Nov. 12, 1660; Dec. 29, 1662), **MH** (1660-63, inc.), **WH** (nos. 5, Feb. 4, 1661; 17, 36, 38, [?], 48, 51, Apr. 28–Dec. 22, 1662; 14, 18, 22-23, Apr. 6–June 8, 1663).

679. Parliamentary spy. 1769-70. w.
 CtY (nos. 1-23, Nov. 21, 1769–May 25, 1770), **IU** (nos. 1-23).

680. Parliament kite; or, The tell tale bird. 1648.
 CSH (nos. 1-15).

681. Parliament porter; or, The door keeper of the House of Commons. 1648.
 CSH (nos. 1-4).

682. Parliament scout, communicating his intelligence to the kingdome. John Dillingham. 1643. w.
 CtY (no. 5, July 27, 1643).

683. Parliament's post. 1645. w.
 TxU (nos. 4, June 3; 8, July 1, 1645).

684. Parliament's scrich-owle. 1648. w. In verse.
 CSH (nos. 1-3), **ICU** (no. 2).

685. Parliament's vulture. 1648.
 CSH (no. 1, June 22), **ICU**.

686. Parrot, with a compendium of the times. Eliza Haywood. Nos. 1-9, Aug. 2–Oct. 4, 1746. w.
 CtY (rep. 1746).

687. Particular advice from the office of intelligence. *Continued as* Exact accompt (from Jan. 6, 1660). Oliver Williams and others. 1659-60.
 CtY (no. 31, Oct. 21, 1659).

688. Pasquin. Duckett, Amherst, Steele. Nos. 1-120, Nov. 28, 1722–Mar. 26, 1724. w.; s. w.
 CtY (nos. 1-120), **DLC** (nos. 1-119, lacking nos. 57-69).

689. Patrician. 1719.
 CtY (no. 1), **DLC** (no. 1), **TxU** (also rep. 1719).

690. Patriot. *Ed.* John Harris. 1714-15. t. w.
TxU (nos. 11-12, Apr. 26-30, 1714).

691. Patriot. Nos. 1-5, June 17–July 17, 1762.
CtY (rep. in Political controversy, 1762).

692. Patriot. Edinburgh, nos. 1-23, June 3–Nov. 14, 1740. w.
CtY.

693. Patriot; or, Political, moral, and philosophical repository. 1792-93. s. m.
CtY (v. 1-2, 1792-93), **MH** (v. 1-3, 1792-93), **NNC** (v. 1), **PU** (v. 1, Apr. 3–Sept. 18, 1792).

694. Patriot; or, The Irish packet open'd. Nos. 1-7, Oct. 25–Dec. 6, 1753. w.
CtY (rep.), **MH, NNC.**

695. Peeper. 1796.
CtY (nos. 1-34), **IU.**

696. Pegasus, with news, an observator, and a Jacobite courant. *Printed for* John Dunton. 1696. t. w.
IU.

Penny London morning advertiser. *See* Universal London morning advertiser.

Penny London post; or, The morning advertiser. *See* Universal London morning advertiser.

698. Perfect diurnal of every day's proceedings in Parliament. *Continued as* Perfect diurnal; or, The daily proceedings in Parliament (from no. 8, Mar. 1, 1660). Nos. 1-21, Feb. 21–Mar. 16, 1660. d.
CtY (no. 1, Feb. 21).

699. Perfect diurnall of some passages and proceedings of . . . the armies in England and Ireland. John Rushworth and Samuel Pecke. Nos. 1-302, 1649-55. w.
CtY (nos. 1-14, 16-72, 77-79, 81-84, 86, 88, 90-92, 94-95, 97-101, 103-[120], Dec. 17, 1649–Mar. 19, 1652), **ICU** (no. 11, Feb. 25, 1649/50), **MB** (nos. 11-13, 15, 17, 18-20, 23, 24, 27, 30, 34-36, 38, Feb. 18–Sept. 9, 1650), **WH** (nos. 1-7, 10, 14-15, Dec. 10, 1649–Mar. 25, 1650).

700. Perfect diurnall of some passages in Parliament. Samuel Pecke. *Printed for* Francis Coles and Laurence Blaikelocke. 1643-49. w.
CtY (nos. 1, 3, 5, 6, 9, 10, 22, 179, 192, 193, 209, 241, 281, 293, July 3, 1643–Mar. 12, 1648), **ICU** (Apr. 2, July 23, Aug. 6, 1649), **MnU** (nos. 1-140, 191-200, 211-20, 231-40, June 26, 1643–Mar. 4, 1647/8), **IWS** (nos. 1-100, July 3, 1643–June 30, 1645; 121-60, Nov. 24,

1645–Apr. 24, 1646), **TxU** (nos. 2, 7, 13, 15-18, 20, 21, 23, 28-31, 33, 34, 38, 40, 43, 45-48, 56, 64, 69, 70, 74, 75, 77-80, 82, 84, 85, 87-90, 93, 95-98, 100-09, 111-17, 122-26, 129-31, 133-39, 141-47, 149-59, 161-82, July 10, 1643–Jan. 25, 1646), **WH** (nos. 231-39, 241-43, 246-47, 250-52, 254, 256, 258-61, 263-64, 269, 271, 287-91, 293, 295, 297-98, 300-01, 305, 307-14, 316-20, 323, Jan. 3, 1648–Oct. 8, 1649).

700a. Perfect diurnall of some passages of Parliament. Samuel Pecke(?). *Printed by* W. Hunt. (?)-1650.
CtY (nos. 324-25, July 22-29, 1650).

Perfect diurnall of the passages in Parliament. *See* Heads of severall proceedings in the present Parliament.

700b. Perfect diurnall of the passages in Parliament. *Printed for* W. Cook. Jan.–Mar. 1642. w.
TxU (Jan. 24-31).

701. Perfect diurnall of the passages in Parliament. Nos. 1-2(?), June 20-28, 1642. *Cf.* R. H. Griffith in Times literary supplement, Dec. 11, 1924, p. 849.
TxU (nos. 1-2).

702. Perfect diurnall of the passages in Parliament. *Printed by* J. Okes and F. Leach. 1642-43.
CtY (nos. 18, 25, 28, 33-35, 38-39, 41-46, 48, 30 [*i. e.* 50], 52-53, Oct. 17, 1642–June 19, 1643), **TxU** (nos. 38-40, 40 [*sic*], 43-44, 46-49, 30 [*i. e.* 50], 52-53, Mar. 6–June 19, 1643).

703. Perfect diurnall of the passages in Parliament. Samuel Pecke. Various publishers, including Thomas Cook, William Cook, Walter Cook, Robert Wood, etc. Nos. 1-52(?), June 20, 1642–June 5, 1643.
CtY (nos. 5, July 18, 1642; 26, 30-32, 36, 37, 41, 45, 46, 48, 50-52, Dec. 12, 1642–June 5, 1643), **TxU** (nos. [4], July 11, 1642; 36, 39, 40, 41-43, 46, 47, 52, Feb. 20–June 5, 1643).

704. Perfect occurrences of Parliament and chief collections of letters from the armies. 1644-45.
CtY (no. 37, Aug. 29, 1645), **DLC** (no. [15], Apr. 4, 1645), **TxU** (nos. 14, Mar. 28; 43, Oct. 10, 1645).

704a. Perfect occurrences of . . . Parliament and martiall affairs. No. 11, Mar. 13, 1646-1647. *See* J. B. Williams, A history of English journalism . . . , p. 231. Possibly a continuation of No. 704.
CtY (Dec. 25, 1646), **TxU** (Aug. 28, 1646).

705. Perfect passages of each dayes proceedings in Parliament. Henry Walker(?). 1644-46(?). w.

CtY (nos. 1-60, 63-71, Oct. 23, 1644–Mar. 4, 1646), TxU (nos. 53, 61).

706. Perfect passages of every daies intelligence from the Parliaments army under the command of his Excellency the Lord General Cromwell. *Continued as* Moderate publisher of every dayes intelligence (from no. 81, Jan. 21, 1653); *as* Certain passages of every dayes intelligence (from Jan. 27, 1654). Henry Walker. 1650-55. w.
CtY (no. 17, Nov. 15, 1650).

Perfect proceedings of state affairs. *See* Severall proceedings in Parliament.

Perfect weekly account, 1647. *See* Weekly account.

706a. Perfect weekly account. Mar. 29, 1647-1650. w.
CSH (1649), ICU (Oct. 2, 1650).

707. Periodical essays. 1780-81. w.
CtY (rep. 1810), MiU (nos. 1-5, 8-14, Dec. 2, 1780–Mar. 3, 1781).

708. Pharos. Nos. 1-50, Nov. 7, 1786–Apr. 28, 1787. s. w.
CtY (rep. 1787), MB.

709. Philadelphian magazine. 1788-89. m.
CtY (v. 2, nos. 12-22, Jan.–Nov. 1789), DLC (v. 1, Feb.–July 1788), MB (v. 2).

711. Philanthropist; or, Philosophical essays on politics, government, morals, and manners. Nos. 1-43, Mar. 16, 1795–Jan. 25, 1796. w.
CtY, DLC, NN.

712. Philological miscellany. 1761.
MH (v. 1, 1761).

713. Philosophical collections. R. Hooke. Nos. 1-7, 1679, 1681-82.
CSH, CSt, MB, MH, NNC, WU.

714. Philosophical magazine. 1798+. m.
CSt, CtY, CU, DLC, ICJ, IU, MB, MdBP (lacking v. 1, 1798), MHi, N, NIC, NN, NNC, PU, TxU, VaU.

715. Philosophical society of Edinburgh. Essays and observations. Edinburgh, v. 1-3, 1754-71.
MH, PPAP.

Philosophical transactions of the Royal society. *See* Royal society of London.

716. Philosophy of medicine. 1799.
ICU (v. 1, 4th ed., 1799), VaU.

717. Phoenix; or, Revival of scarce and valuable pieces. 1707-08.
    ICU (v. 1-2, 1707-08), NNC (v. 1-2, 1707-08).

Phoenix; or, Weekly miscellany improv'd. *See* Weekly miscellany of instruction and entertainment.

718. Picture of the times. 1795. w.
    CtY (nos. 1-31).

718a. Pig's meat; or, Lessons for the swinish multitude, published in weekly penny numbers. . . . Thomas Spence. 1793-95. w.
    CtY (v. 1-3, 1793-95), DLC, ICJ (v. 1-2), MH, NIC (v. 3, 1795).

719. Plain dealer. 1712. w.
    CtY (nos. 1-17, Apr. 12–Aug. 2, 1712), IEK (nos. 1-16), TxU (nos. 5, 11, 14, 16, May 10–July 26, 1712).

720. Plain dealer. Aaron Hill, William Bond, and others. Nos. 1-117, Mar. 23, 1724–May 7, 1725. s. w.
    CtY (nos. 47, 48, 53, 56, 59-68, 75-85, 87, 88, 1724-25; also rep. 1730-34), MB.

721. Plain dealer. Nos. 1-3, 1763. w.
    CtY (rep. in Political controversy, 1763).

722. Plain dealer. 1775-76.
    CSH (nos. 1-8, Dec. 25, 1775–Feb. 12, 1776).

723. Plebeian. Steele. Nos. 1-4, Mar. 14–Apr. 6, 1719. w.
    CtY, DLC, ICU, IU (rep. 1790), MB (rep. 1790), MBB (rep. 1790), NN, TxU (also rep. 1719).

724. Pocket magazine; or, Elegant repository of useful and polite literature. 1794-95. m.
    DLC, MB (1794), WH (v. 1, 2, nos. 7, 9, Aug. 1794–Apr. 1795).

725. Poetical courant. Samuel Philips. 1706. w.
    CtY (v. 1, no. 5, Feb. 23, 1706).

726. Political cabinet; or, An impartial review of the most remarkable occurrences of the world. 1744-45.
    CtY (no. 1, July 1744).

727. Political controversy; or, Weekly magazine of ministerial and anti-ministerial essays, consisting of the Monitor, Briton, North Briton, Auditor, and Patriot entire, with select pieces from the newspapers. *Ed.* John Wilkes. V. 1-5, 1762-63. w.
    CtY (v. 1, no. 1–v. 5, no. 8, July 19, 1762–Sept. 6, 1763), DLC v. 2-5, inc.), MdBP, MH (nos. 1-11, 27, 1762-63), NN, NNC (v. 1-4, 1762-63), PPAP, WH (v. 2, nos. 11-13; v. 3, no. 27; v. 5, nos. 4, 6-8; Dec. 7, 1762–Sept. 6, 1763).

728. Political herald and review. *Ed.* Gilbert Stuart. 1785-86. m.
    ICU (v. 1-2, 1785-86), **NNC, PU**.

729. Political magazine and parliamentary, naval, military, and literary journal. V. 1-21, 1780-91. m.
    CtY (v. 1-21, Jan. 1780–Dec. 1791, v. 2, 3, 6, 9, 14, 16, 20, inc.), **DLC** (v. 1-19), **IU** (v. 3, 1782), **MB** (v. 1-6, 8, 10, 1780-85), **N, NjP, NN** (1780-85; Feb.–Nov. 1789; July–Dec. 1791), **NNC, PU** (v. 1, 4, 6-10), **WH**.

730. Political register and impartial review of new books. *Ed.* J. Almon. V. 1-11, 1767-72. m.
    CtY, DLC (v. 1-8, 10, May 1767–June 1772), **ICN** (nos. 1-21, May 1767–Dec. 1768), **MB, MBB, MdBP** (v. 1), **MH, MiUC** (v. 1-9), **NIC, NN, NNC** (v. 1, nos. 1-8), **PPL** (v. 1-7, 9-11, 1767-72), **WH** (v. 1-8).

731. Political review of Edinburgh periodical publications. Edinburgh, nos. 1-7, June 20–Aug. 1, 1792. w.
    MB.

732. Political state of Europe. 1792-95. m.
    CtY, DLC (v. 3-10, 1793-95), **MH, NNC** (v. 1-8, 1792-94), **WH**.

733. Political state of Great Britain. *Ed.* Abel Boyer (to Oct. 1729). 1711-40. m. The second edition (1718-20) of v. 1-8, for the years 1711-15, is entitled Quadriennium annae postremum; or, The political state of Great Britain.
    CtY (v. 1-52, Jan. 1711–June 1739; also Quadriennium), **DLC** (v. 2-54, 56-60, July 1711–Dec. 1740), **IU** (v. 1-36, 38-39, 41-42, 44, 46-55, 1711-38), **MB** (Sept. 1711–Nov. 1739), **MH** (v. 1-60, 1711-40; v. 1-2, 7, 2nd ed.), **MdBP, NIC** (Mar. 1711), **NN** (v. 1-58), **NNC** (v. 1-6, 7 inc., 8-54, 56-60), **TxU** (1714; Sept. 1717; Jan. 1718–Dec. 1720; July–Dec. 1735; also Quadriennium), **WH** (v. 4-5, 7-28, 31-34, July 1712–Dec. 1727).

734. Politician. 1762.
    CtY (rep. in Political controversy, 1762-63).

735. Politicks of Europe; or, A rational journal concerning the affairs of the time. 1690-91(?).
    CSH (nos. 1, 2, 4, 6, 7, 9, 10, 11), **DLC** (nos. 1-17, July 2, 1690–Oct. 3, 1691).

Politics for the people. *See* Hog's wash; or, A salmagundy for swine.

Politics for the people; or, Hog's wash. *See* Hog's wash; or, A salmagundy for swine.

Politique post. *See* Faithful post.

736. Poor Gillian; or, Mother Redcap's weekly advice to city and country. 1677.
CSH (Nov. 23–Dec. 14).

737. Poor Robin's intelligence. *Continued as* Poor Robin's memoirs (from Dec. 1677). Henry Care. 1676-78.
CSH (nos. " A-Qqqq " [84 nos.], Mar. 23, 1676–Mar. 13, 1677; nos. 1-17, Dec. 10, 1677–Apr. 8, 1678), DLC (Jan. 2–Mar. 13, 1677).

738. Poor Robin's intelligence newly revived. *Continued as* Poor Robin's intelligence revived (from no. 4). Henry Care. 1679-80.
CSH (nos. 1-10, 12-38, Sept. 4, 1679–May 12, 1680), NN (nos. 20-35, Jan. 7–Apr. 21, 1680), TxU (nos. 24-38, Feb. 4–May 12, 1680).

Poor Robin's memoirs. *See* Poor Robin's intelligence.

739. Poor Robin's publick and private occurrances and remarks. 1688.
CSH (nos. 1-3).

740. Post angel. 1701-02. m.
CtY (v. 1-3, Jan. 1701–June 1702), ICU, MH (v. 1-2).

741. Post boy, with foreign and domestick news. *Continued as* Post boy, and historical account, &c., with foreign and domestick news (from no. 16, June 19, 1695); *as* Post boy (from Oct. 1695?); *as* Daily post boy (from Nov. 19, 1728?). Abel Roper, Abel Boyer, etc. 1695-1735. t. w. *See also* Account of the publick transactions. . . .
CSH (nos. 452-744, lacking nos. 480, 489-91, 499, 502, 504-05, 553, 588, 591, 638, 683, 705, 711, 760, 1698-1700), CtY (nos. 452-53, 455-589, 592-99, 601-738, 742-57, 759-61, 763-855, 857-978, 981, 1009, 1013-14, 1019, 1021-22, 1024, Mar. 29, 1698–Dec. 9, 1701; 2693, Aug. 14, 1712; 3066-4434, Jan. 1, 1715–Dec. 28, 1717; 4628-5097, Mar. 28, 1719–Mar. 24, 1722; 5411-5506, Mar. 26, 1724–Mar. 23, 1725; Jan. 28, Mar. 6, 27, 1732; June 3, 6, Sept. 9, 1735), IU (1695-1728, inc.), IWS (nos. 1049-98, Feb. 5–May 27, 1702), MB (1718), NN (Mar. 7, 1721), TxU (nos. 2807-09, 2810-13, 2819-2923, 2959, 2978, 3012, 4076, 4483, 4489, 4754, 4758, 4882, 4883, May 7, 1713–Nov. 10, 1720), WH (nos. 240, Nov. 19, 1696; 696, Sept. 23, 1699; 1048, Feb. 3, 1701).

Post man, and the historical account. *See* Account of the publick transactions. . . .

742. Prater. Nos. 1-35, Mar. 13–Nov. 6, 1756. w.
CtY (rep. 1757).

743. Present case of Europe in general. 1689.
CSH (no. 1).

744. Present state of Europe. Dublin, 1690(?)-93(?). m.
WH (v. 4, Jan.–Dec. 1693).

745. Present state of Europe; or, The historical and political monthly mercury. I. Phillips. 1690-1736(?). m. A translation of Mercure historique et politique, published at the Hague, 1686-1777. The title-page of v. 1 reads: The general history of Europe.
CSH (July–Dec. 1690), CtY (1690–Jan. 1736, inc.), DLC (1690-1728), ICU (v. 4, 14, 18-19, 1693, 1703, 1707-08; also Edinburgh rep. 1691-95), IWS (v. 1-24, 1690-1713, lacking v. 12, 1701), MB (1691), MHi (1692-1709), MnU (1692-98, 1700-01, 1716), NIC (Jan.–Dec. 1702), NjP (1704), NN (July 1690–Dec. 1693, 1699-1703, 1706-07, 1709, 1711-12, 1714, 1716-20), NNC (1690-1704, 1718, inc.), PPL (1698), WH (1692-98, 1700-04).

746. Present state of Europe; or, The monthly account of all occurrences, ecclesiastical, civil and military. *Continued as* Memoirs of the present state of Europe (from v. 1, no. 2). 1692-96. m. A translation of Lettres historique, published at the Hague.
CtY (v. 2, Jan.–Dec. 1693), WH (v. 1-2, 1692-93).

747. Present state of the republic of letters. *Ed.* Andrew Reid. V. 1-17 [*i. e.* 18], Jan. 1728–Dec. 1736. m. This periodical and The literary magazine; or, The history of the works of the learned were superseded in 1737 by The history of the works of the learned.
CtY, DLC, ICN (lacking v. 15), ICU (v. 1-13, 15-18), MB, MBB, MdBJ (v. 12), MH (v. 1-6, Jan. 1728–Dec. 1730), NN, NNC, PPL, TxAG (v. 12-13, 1733-34).

748. Press. Dublin, 1797-98. t. w.
CtY (Sept. 28, 1797–Mar. 3, 1798).

749. Principall passages of Germany, Italy, France, etc. *Continued as* Continuation of the actions, passages, and occurrences (no. 2, 1637); *as* Diatelesma (nos. 3, 4). N. Butter and N. Bourne. Nos. 1-4, 1636-38.
CSH (no. 1, 1636), MnU (nos. 2, 3, 4, 1637-38).

750. Prisoner. 1782.
MiU (no. 1, Nov. 30, 1782).

751. Proceedings of the society for preserving liberty and property against levellers. 1793(?)-(?).
CtY (2 v.).

752. Prompter. Aaron Hill, William Popple, etc. Nos. 1-173, Nov. 12, 1734–July 2, 1736. s. w.
CtY (lacking nos. 24, 84, 93, 116, 138, 152).

753. Prompter. Nos. 1-19, Oct. 24–Dec. 10, 1789.
    CtY (inc.).
754. Protestant courant. 1682.
    TxU (nos. 4-6, May 6-13, 1682).
755. Protestant dissenter's magazine. 1794-99. m.
    ICU (v. 1-5, 1794-98), MBB (v. 1-6, 1794-99).

    Protestant (domestick) intelligence. *See* Domestick intelligence (Harris).
756. Protestant mercury. 1696(?)-98.
    IU (Aug. 31, 1696).
757. Protestant observator; or, Democritus flens. 1681.
    TxU (nos. 1-10, Nov. 19–Dec. 24, 1681).
758. Protestant Oxford intelligence; or, Occurences foraign and domestick. *Continued as* Impartial London intelligence . . . (from Apr. 4, 1681). *Printed for* T. Benskin. 1681.
    CtY (Mar. 24, 1681), TxU (nos. 5-7, Mar. 24-31, n. d.; 2-4, Apr. 7-14, n. d.).
759. Protestant postboy. 1711-12. t. w.
    CtY (nos. 1, 31-32, 35-38, 42, 67-75, 78-100, 102-23, Sept. 4, 1711–July 12, 1712), TxU (nos. 36, [?], 41, 67, 79, 119, Nov. 24, 1711–June 14, 1712).
760. Protester, on behalf of the people. 1753. w.
    CtY (nos. 1-24, June 2–Nov. 10, 1753), IU (nos. 1-20).

    Public advertiser. *See* London daily post and general advertiser.

    Public characters. *See* British public characters.
761. Public gazetteer. Dublin, 1758-72. s. w.
    WH (1758-59).
762. Public intelligence. Sir Roger L'Estrange. No. 1, Nov. 28, 1665.
    CSH.
763. Publick intelligencer. Marchamont Nedham and John Canne (in 1659). Oct. 8, 1655–Apr. 9, 1660. w.
    CSH (nos. 161-73, 209-17, 1659-60), CtY (nos. 118, Jan. 25, 1658; 210, Jan. 9, 1660), ICU (no. 212, Jan. 1660), MnU (Feb. 2-9, 1657; Dec. 28, 1657–Mar. 7, 1659; May 23-30, 1659), WH (nos. 53, 68, 79, 83, 99, 113, 173, 194, Oct. 13, 1656–Sept. 19, 1659).
764. Public ledger; or, Daily register of commerce and intelligence. *Continued as* Public ledger (from Nov. 3, 1761). J. Newbery. 1760+. d.

CtY (nos. 272, 274-76, 285-87, 290-97, Nov. 24–Dec. 23, 1760), **NN** (v. 1, nos. 1-79, 81-130, 132-43, Jan. 12–June 26, 1760; v. 2, no. 531, Sept. 22, 1761, facsimile).

765. Public occurrences truely stated. Henry Care (to no. 25); Elkanah Settle. 1688. w.
CSH, CtY (nos. 3, 14, 19-20, 22, 30-31, 34, Mar. 6–Oct. 2, 1688), **NN** (Apr. 3, 10, June 19, July 17, 24, 1688).

767. Public register; or, Freeman's journal. Dublin, 1763+. s. w.
CtY (v. 1, no. 34, Jan. 3, 1764; v. 4, no. 33, Dec. 27, 1766), **PPL** (Sept. 13, 1763–Sept. 3, 1765; Sept. 5, 1767–Aug. 26, 1769; Aug. 31, 1771–Aug. 27, 1772).

768. Publick register; or, Weekly magazine. 1741. w.
CtY (nos. 1-24, Jan. 3–June 13, 1741).

769. Publisher, containing miscellanies in prose and verse. 1745.
CtY (nos. 1-3, 1745), **ICS** (nos. 1-4).

Quadriennium annae postremum. *See* Political state of Great Britain.

770. Quiz. Charles Dibden, Sir Robert Porter, Jane Porter, etc. 1797. f.
MH.

771. Rambler. Samuel Johnson and others. Nos. 1-208, Mar. 20, 1750–Mar. 14, 1752. s. w.
CSt, CtY (also reps.), **DLC** (rep. 1783), **ICN, IU** (1751), **MB** (nos. 160-208, Sept. 28, 1751–Mar. 14, 1752), **MdBJ** (rep. 1767), **MH, NN** (also rep. 1785), **NNC** (reps.).

772. Ramble round the world; or, The travels of Kainophilos. 1689. w.
CSH (2 pages).

773. Ranger. Martin Hawke and Sir R. Vincent. Brentford, 1794-95. w.
DLC (nos. 1-28, Jan. 1–July 5, 1794).

774. Reader. Steele. Nos. 1-9, Apr. 22–May 10, 1714. t. w.
CSH, CtY (rep. 1723), **ICU** (rep. 1789), **IEN** (rep. 1723), **IU** (rep. 1789), **NIC** (rep. 1789), **NNC** (rep. 1789), **TxU** (no. 4, Apr. 28, 1712; also reps. 1715, 1789).

775. Reading mercury; or, Weekly entertainer. Reading, 1723-24(?). w.
ICN (v. 1, no. 31, Feb. 1, 1724, facsim.), **MH** (v. 1, no. 1, July 8, 1723, facsim.).

Read's weekly journal. *See* Weekly journal; or, British gazetteer.

776. Reasoner. 1784.
    MiU (no. 1, Jan. 1, 1784).
777. Recreations in agriculture, natural history, the arts, and miscellaneous literature. J. Anderson. 1799+. m.
    CSt, MH, NNC, WU.
778. Reformer. 1780.
    CtY (nos. 1-4).
779. Register of the times; or, Political museum. 1794-96.
    CtY (v. 1-8, June 11, 1794–June 1796), DLC (v. 1-8), NIC (v. 1-8), PPL (v. 1-8), WH (v. 2-4, Oct. 20, 1794–Apr. 30, 1795).

Rehearsal. *See* Observator, 1704-09.

Rehearsal of Observator. *See* Observator, 1704-09.

780. Remembrancer; or Impartial repository of public events for the year. . . . *Ed.* J. Almon. 1775-84.
    CSH, CtY (v. 1-17, 1775-84; also suppl. 1777), DLC, IU (v. 1-7, 9-10, v. 1, 4th ed.), MB, MH, N (4th ed.), NIC, NN, NNC, PPAP, PPL (1775-82), PU (v. 1, rep. 1778), WH.
781. Repertory of arts and manufactures. 1794+. m.
    CtY, DLC, ICJ, ICU, IU, MB, NcU (v. 1-4, 1794-96), NN, NNC, PPL, WH (v. 1-10, 1794-99).
782. Repository. 1788-89. f.
    CtY (nos. 3, 5, Feb. 1, Mar. 1, 1788), MB (v. 2, pt. 2, Jan. 1, 1789), MHi (v. 2, pt. 2, 1789), NIC.
783. Repository: a select collection of fugitive pieces of wit. I. Reed. 1777-83.
    CtY (4 v.).
784. Repository, containing a . . . view of the most considerable transactions, occurrences, etc. 1752.
    CtY, NN.
785. Repository; or, Treasury of politics and literature. 1770.
    MH (v. 1-2, 1770, pub. 1771), NN (v. 1-2, 1770).
786. Republican queries answered.
    TxU (no. 2, n. d.).
787. Reveur. Edinburgh, 1737-38. w.
    CtY (nos. 1-28, Nov. 18, 1737–May 26, 1738).

Review of the affairs of France. *See* Weekly review of the affairs of France.

Review of the state of the British nation. *See* Weekly review of the affairs of France.

96 *A Census of British Newspapers and Periodicals, 1620-1800*

Review of the state of the English nation. *See* Weekly review of the affairs of France.

788. Review and Sunday advertiser. No. 1, June 22, 1789-1796.
IU (no. 191, Feb. 10, 1793).

789. Robin's last shift; or, Weekly remarks. *Continued as* Shift shifted (from May 5, 1716). G. Flint. 1716. w.
DLC (Feb. 18–Apr. 28, 1716), **TxU** (Feb. 25–Apr. 14, lacking nos. for Mar. 10, 17; May 5–Aug. 25, lacking nos. for June 30, July 14, 28, 30; Sept. 29, 1716).

789a. Robinson Crusoe's London daily evening post. [Publisher not named.] 1742. d.
MH (4 unnumbered issues, Sept. 21, Nov. 12, 13, 18, 1742).

790. Roman post-boy; or, Weekly account from Rome. 1689.
CSH (Mar. 23).

791. Rotterdam courant. 1680.
CSH (June 7, 1680).

792. Royal college of physicians. Medical transactions. 1785+.
CSt (v. 1-3, 1785-86; v. 1, 3, 3rd ed., v. 2, 2nd ed.), **ICJ**.

793. Royal female magazine. 1759(?)-60(?).
MH (v. 2, 1760).

794. Royal gazette and universal chronicle. *Continued as* Royal chronicle (from no. 13). 1761. t. w.
WH (v. 1, nos. 1-13, May 22–June 19, 1761).

795. Royal magazine; or, Gentleman's monthly companion. 1759-71. m.
CSH (Feb. 1761), **CtY** (v. 1-13, July 1759–Dec. 1765), **DLC**, **MB** (v. 1, 1759; 6-8, 1762-63), **MBB**, **N** (v. 1-3, 1759-60; 5-18, 1761-69), **NNC** (v. 2-3, 1760), **PPL** (1759-65), **WH** (v. 1-7, 10-15, 1759-66).

796. Royal magazine; or, Quarterly bee. 1750-51. q.
CtY (v. 1-3, Oct. 1750–June 1751).

797. Royal register. 1778-83.
MB (v. 2, 2nd ed.), **WH**.

798. Royal society of London. Philosophical transactions. *Ed.* Henry Oldenburg (to 1677). Mar. 6, 1665+.
CSH (v. 1-16, 1665-86), **CSt**, **CtY** (v. 1-10, 1665-75; 13-18, 1683-94; 20-24, 1698-1705; 31-32, 1721-23; 34-35, 1727-28; 40, 1738; 43-90, 1745-1800), **CU** (v. 47+, 1751+; also abridg., v. 1-10, 1749-56), **DLC**, **ICU**, **IU** (v. 1-3, 1665-67; 58+, 1768+), **MB**, **MBB**, **MdBJ**, **MdBP**, **MiU** (abridg.), **N** (v. 1-3, no. 33, 1665-68; 8-11, 1673-76; 12, nos. 137-42, 1677-78), **NIC** (v. 1-29, 1665-1716), **NN**,

NNC (v. 1-6, 1665-71; 35 inc., 1728; 46+, 1749+), **PPL** (1733+), **PU, RPB** (v. 47-89, 1751-99), **TxU** (v. 47+, 1751+; also abridg. v. 1-10), **WU**.

799. Ruddiman's weekly mercury. Edinburgh, 1777-83(?). w.
    CtY (Aug. 7, Dec. 31, 1777; Jan. 7–Dec. 30, 1778; Jan. 6-20, 1779).

800. St. James's chronicle; or, British evening-post. 1761+. t. w.
    CtY (nos. 285-1149, Jan. 1–July 7, 1763; 1224-1537, Jan. 3–Dec. 29, 1769; 1694-1853, Jan. 2–Dec. 31, 1772; 2009-2166, Jan. 1–Dec. 31, 1774; 2243-48, 2251, 2255-59, 2261-70, 2272-76, 2278-2306, 2309, 2311, 2313-18, 2320-21, July 1–Dec. 31, 1775; 2621-2933, Jan. 1, 1778–Dec. 30, 1779; 3095-3404, Jan. 2, 1781–Dec. 31, 1782; 3561-3716, Jan. 3, 1784–Jan. 1, 1785; 4398-4400, June 30–July 4, 1789), **NN** (June 6, 25, 1767; July 26, Aug. 23, 1768; Jan. 2–Feb. 29, Mar. 5–July 2, 11–Oct. 15, 20-24, 29–Dec. 31, 1772; Jan. 2-7, 14–Mar. 4, 9–May 22, 29–June 17, 22–July 1, 6–Aug. 7, 12, 17–Dec. 30, 1773; Jan. 1–Apr. 16, 21–Oct. 11, 15–Dec. 31, 1774; Jan. 3–Feb. 28, Mar. 4–Aug. 1, 5–Sept. 5, 9-21, 26–Oct. 26, 31–Dec. 16, 21-30, 1775; Jan. 2–Feb. 13, 17–Apr. 23, 27–Aug. 22, 27–Dec. 31, 1776; Jan. 2–May 31, June 5–Aug. 5, 9–Oct. 25, 30–Dec. 30, 1777; Jan. 1–July 23, 28–Oct. 1, 10, 15, Dec. 31, 1778; Jan. 2, Feb. 2, 25, 1779; Sept. 2, 1783), **TxU** (Dec. 24, 1771), **WH** (nos. 2127, 2129-30, 2133, 2135, 2137-38, 2140-42, 2146-49, Oct. 1–Nov. 22, 1774; 2164, 2166-67, Aug. 19-26, 1775; 2381, 2383, June 13, 18, 1776).

801. St. James's evening post. 1715-55(?).
    CtY (1715-17, 1720, 1734-37, 1743, 1745, 1746-47, 1755), **IU** (no. 5130, Dec. 4, 1742), **MB** (nos. 1665-1815, lacking nos. 1729, 1778, 1800, Jan. 8–Dec. 27, 1726), **NN** (Jan. 23-25, 1722), **TxU** (nos. 85, Dec. 15, 1715; 118, Mar. 1, 1716; 288, Mar. 12, 1717; 467, Jan. 17, 1718).

802. St. James's journal, with memoirs of literature. Nos. 1-56, May 3, 1722–May 18, 1723. w.
    CtY (July 19, Dec. 22, 27, 1722; Jan. 3–May 18, 1723), **DLC, TxU**.

803. St. James's magazine. R. Lloyd. 1762-64. m.
    CtY (v. 1-4, Sept. 1762–June 1764), **DLC** (v. 1-3, Sept. 1762–Feb. 1764), **IU** (v. 1-3), **PPH**.

804. St. James's magazine. 1774. m.
    WH (v. 1, Feb.–Dec. 1774, with supplement).

804a. St. James's post. 1715-34(?). t. w.
    CtY (inc., "a good file").

Salisbury and Winchester journal. *See* Salisbury journal; or, Weekly advertiser.

805. Salisbury journal; or, Weekly advertiser. *Continued as* Salisbury journal (from June 11, 1750); *as* Salisbury and Winchester journal (from Dec. 7, 1772). Salisbury, 1738+. w.
CtY (v. 12, nos. 441, 442, 446, June 30, July 7, Aug. 4, 1746; v. 44, nos. 2117, 2157, Jan. 4, Oct. 11, 1779; v. 45, no. 2197, July 17, 1780; v. 59, no. 2924, June 23, 1794), **WH** (v. 39, nos. 1898-99, 1901-03, Oct. 17–Nov. 21, 1774; v. 41, nos. 2002-10, Oct. 21–Dec. 16, 1776; v. 42, nos. 2015, 2020, 2024, 2027, 2032-34, 2036, 2062, Jan. 20–Dec. 15, 1777; v. 43, nos. 2066, 2068, 2070-78, 2080, 2112, 2116, Jan. 12–Dec. 28, 1778).

806. Satellite; or, Repository of literature. Carlisle and Newcastle, 1798-1800.
CtY (nos. 1-6, Nov. 10, 1798–June 1800).

807. Saunders' news-letter. *Continued as* Saunders' news-letter and daily advertiser (from Jan. 1, 1784). Dublin, 1755+. Possibly a continuation of no. 1353.
WH (no. 8815, June 23, 1785).

808. Scarborough miscellany. Scarborough, 1732-34.
DLC (1734).

Scientific magazine and freemasons repository. *See* Freemason's magazine.

810. Scotch intelligencer; or, The weekely newes from Scotland and the court. 1643.
CtY (Oct. 17, 1643).

811. Scotchman. 1772. w.
CtY (Jan. 21–June 6, 1772).

Scotch memoirs. *See* Scots memoirs.

Scots courant. *See* Edinburgh courant.

812. Scots magazine. Edinburgh, Jan. 1739+. m.
CSt, CtY, CU, DLC, ICN, ICU, IU, MB, MBB (1759, 1793, 1795), **MH, MHi** (1751-57, inc.), **MnU** (v. 1-26, 28), **NcU** (v. 40, 1778), **NjP** (v. 1, 3, 6-13, 15-19, 22, 24, 30, 32-35, 37, 39-42, 44-45, 47-51, 1739-89), **NN** (v. 1-39, 1739-77), **NNC, TxU** (v. 1-56, 58-62, 1739-1800), **WH**.

813. Scots memoirs, by way of dialogue. *Continued as* Scotch memoirs (from no. 2). 1683.
TxU (nos. 1-3, Feb. 20–Mar. 23, 1683; 4-5, n. d. [1683]).

Scots postman; or, New Edinburgh gazette. *See* Edinburgh gazette.

Scots scourge. *See* British antidote to Caledonian poison.

814. Scots spy; or, Critical observer. Edinburgh, 1776. w.
    NN (v. 1, no. 11, May 17, 1776).
815. Scots town and country magazine. Edinburgh, 1778-79. s. m.
    MB (v. 1-2, Dec. 22, 1778–Dec. 1779).
816. Scottish dove. George Smith. 1643-46.
    TxU (nos. 11, 27, 29, 36, 39, 41, 46, Dec. 29, 1643–Aug. 30, 1644).
817. Scottish mercury, relating the weekly intelligence from Scotland and the court. 1643.
    CtY (Oct. 13, 1643).
818. Scottish register; or, General view of history, politics, and literature. Edinburgh, 1794-95(?). q.
    CtY (nos. 1-6, Jan. 1794–June 1795), MdBP (nos. 1, 2, 4, 1794-95).
819. Scourge, in vindication of the Church of England. T. Lewis. 1717. w.
    DLC (nos. 1-43, Feb. 4–Nov. 25, 1717), NNC (rep. 1720).
820. Scourge. Nos. 1-81, Nov. 28, 1752–June 2, 1753. t. w.
    DLC.
821. Selector. 1799-1800. s. m.
    CtY (May 5, 1799–Dec. 28, 1800).
822. Senator; or, Clarendon's parliamentary chronicle. 1790+. w.
    DLC, MB, MH (v. 1-8, 1790-94), NN (v. 1-8, inc., Nov. 25, 1790–July 5, 1794), NNC (v. 1-15, Nov. 25, 1790–May 20, 1796), WH.
823. Sentimental magazine; or, General assemblage of science, taste, etc. 1773-77.
    CtY (v. 1-4, Mar. 1773–Aug. 1776), DLC (v. 1-5, 1773-77), NN (v. 3, 1775), NNC (v. 2, 1774).
824. Sentimental and masonic magazine. Dublin, 1792-95.
    CSt (v. 4, Jan.–June 1794), MB (v. 2-3, Jan.–Dec. 1793).
825. Severall proceedings in Parliament. *Continued as* General proceedings of state affairs (from Apr. 28, 1653); *as* Severall proceedings of state affairs (from Sept. 28, 1654); *as* Perfect proceedings of state affairs (from Feb. 22, 1655). Henry Scobell and Henry Walker. 1649-55.
    CtY (nos. 5, 23, 28, 50, 57-58, 64, Nov. 2, 1649–Dec. 19, 1650), DLC (12 nos., Dec. 1653–Aug. 1654), ICN (no. 26, Mar. 21-28, 1650), ICU (nos. 26, 33, 44, 53, Mar. 18–Oct. 3, 1650), MnU (nos. 2-156, Oct. 9, 1649–Sept. 23, 1652).

Shift shifted. *See* Robin's last shift.

Smith's currant intelligence. *See* Currant intelligence (J. Smith).

826. Smith's Protestant intelligence, domestick and foreign. 1681.
  MnU (nos. 7-8, 11-13, 16-18, 20-22, Feb. 18–Apr. 14, 1681), **TxU** (nos. 1-12, Feb. 1–Apr. 14, 1681).

827. Snotty-nose gazette. 1679.
  CSH (no. 1, Nov. 24, 1679).

Society of antiquaries of Scotland. Transactions. *See* Archaeologia Scotica.

827a. Some speciall passages from London, Westmister [*sic*], Yorke, Hull, Ireland and other parts. No. 1, June 2, 1642.
  MnU.

828. Some speciall passages from Westminster, Hull, Yorke, and other parts. 1642.
  TxU (no. 8, July 12, 1642).

829. South Briton. 1763.
  CtY (no. 1, rep. in Political controversy, May 2, 1763).

830. Sowerby's English botany. *Ed.* James Sowerby. 1790+. m.
  ICU (v. 2), **MH**.

831. Speciall passages and certain informations from several places. *Printed for* H. Blunden. 1642-43. w.
  CtY (nos. 32, 34, 38, 39, Mar. 21–May 9, 1643), **ICN** (nos. 13-14, Nov. 8-15, 1642), **TxU** (nos. 5, 27, 28, 33, 34, 35, 37, Sept. 13, 1642–Apr. 25, 1643).

832. Spectator. Steele, Addison, etc. Nos. 1-555, Mar. 1, 1711–Dec. 6, 1712; nos. 556-635, June 18–Dec. 20, 1714. d. (1711-12); s. w. (1714).
  CSH, CtY (nos. 1-554), **ICN** (nos. 1-555), **ICS** (inc.), **IU, MB, MH, MnU, NIC** (nos. 1-42), **NN** (nos. 1-621, inc.), **TxU** (nos. 1-555; also rep. 1712).

833. Spectator. 1753-54. s. w.
  TxU (nos. 1-19, Nov. 3, 1753–Jan. 5, 1754).

835. Speculator. N. Drake, etc. 1790. s. w.
  CtY (nos. 1-26, Mar. 27–June 22, 1790, rep. Dublin, 1791), **DLC** (nos. 1-26), **RPB** (rep. 1791).

836. Spendthrift. Henry Fox, Lord Holland(?). 1766.
  CtY (nos. 1-20, Mar. 29–Aug. 9, 1766).

837. Spinster: in defense of the woollen manufacturers. Steele. No. 1, Dec. 19, 1719.
  CtY (rep. in Town talk ..., 1789), **IU** (rep. in Town talk ..., 1790), **MB** (rep. 1790), **MBB** (rep. 1790), **TxU.**

838. Spirit of the public journals. 1797+. a.
 CtY, ICN, MB, MH, NN, NNC (v. 1, rep. 1802; v. 2-3, rep. 1805; v. 4 +, orig. issues), WH.

839. Spirit of the times. 1790. w.
 MB (nos. 2, 3, 7, 8, 1790).

840. Spiritual magazine. 1761-84. Merged with Gospel magazine; or, Treasury of divine knowledge (1784).
 CtY (v. 1, 2 inc., 1761-62).

841. Sporting magazine; or, Monthly calendar of the transactions of the turf, the chase, etc. 1792+. m.
 DLC, MH (lacking v. 1, 3, 7, 12-15), NN, PU (v. 1-2, 1792-93; 7, 1795-96; 13-16, 1798-1800).

842. Spy upon the Spectator. 1711.
 NNC.

842a. Stamford mercury. *Continued as* Howgrave's Stamford mercury (from 1722, with new numbering); *as* Stamford mercury (from 1736); *as* Lincoln, Rutland and Stamford mercury (from 1784). Stamford and Lincoln, 1713+. w.
 CtY (Jan. 24, 1794+).

843. Star and evening advertiser. *Continued as* Stuart's star (from Apr.[?], 1789); *as* Morning star (from July[?], 1789); *as* Star (from Aug.[?], 1789). 1788+. d.
 CtY (Dec. 17, 1788; Jan. 1, 17, 20, 23, Feb. 10, Mar. 11, Apr. 3, 22, July 8-11, Aug. 13, 1789; Jan. 14, 18, Oct. 5, Dec. 14, 19, 1792; Jan. 8, 28, 31, Feb. 1, 2, 1793), DLC (Oct. 9–Dec. 31, 1794), NN (July 14, 1795), WH (nos. 162-63, 165-76, 181-88, 191, 199, Nov. 7–Dec. 20, 1788; 217, 223-25, 228-29, 234-37, 241-42, 245-47, Jan. 10–Feb. 14, 1789).

Stuart's star. *See* Star and evening advertiser.

844. Student; or, The Oxford monthly miscellany. *Continued as* Student; or, The Oxford and Cambridge monthly miscellany (from no. 6). Oxford, 1750-51. m.
 CtY, DLC, IU, MB, MH, NN, NNC, RPB (v. 2, 1751), TxAG (v. 1, 1750).

845. Sun. 1792+. d.
 CtY (Aug. 4-13, Sept. 8-20, Oct. 11-13, 16, 17, 20-23, 31–Nov. 6, 8-18, Dec. 11, 1794; Aug. 1-3, 1795; Oct. 14, 1797; Sept. 21, 22, 26-29, 1798; Oct. 14-16, 18, 24, 28-31, Nov. 4, 6, 8, 11, 29, 1799; 1800+), DLC (Oct. 1, 1792+), NN (Nov. 9, Dec. 13, 1796; Jan. 5, 12, 1798; Oct. 14–Nov. 29, 1799; Jan. 1–Nov. 14, 1800).

846. Sussex weekly advertiser. Lewes, 1746+.
 CtY (June 30, 1755), WH (no. 1182, Feb. 20, 1769).

847. Swedish intelligencer. Nathaniel Butter and Nicholas Bourne. 1632-35.
    CtY (pts. 1-4, 6, 1632-34; pt. 1, 1632, newly revised and corrected; pt. 3, 2nd ed.), NN (1632), NNC.

848. Swinney's Birmingham and Stafford chronicle. Birmingham, 1766(?)+.
    WH (v. 9, no. 49, Dec. 14, 1775).

849. Sylph. Deptford and London, nos. 1-40, Sept. 22, 1795--Apr. 30, 1796. s. w.
    CtY, PPL.

850. Tatler. Steele, Addison, etc. Nos. 1-271, Apr. 12, 1709–Jan. 2, 1711. t. w. The following "continuations" of the Tatler appeared during the early part of 1711: (1) one sold by John Baker, of which only two numbers—272, Jan. 4, and 273, Jan. 6—seem to be known; (2) a continuation published by John Morphew, which began on Jan. 6 with a double number, 272-273, and continued tri-weekly until no. 330, May 19; and (3) the Tatler of William Harrison. This last began on Jan. 13 with no. 1, published by Mrs. A. Baldwin, and ran semi-weekly until no. 6 as a rival publication to Morphew's. On Feb. 3, however, in consequence of a quarrel with his printer, Harrison shifted to Morphew, took over Morphew's numbering, and continued to publish through Morphew to the end of the series; so that from no. 285, Feb. 3, to no. 330, May 19, Harrison's continuation and Morphew's were one and the same paper. As reprinted in volume form Harrison's Tatler included nos. 1-6, printed for Mrs. Baldwin, and nos. 285-330, printed for Morphew, the whole renumbered 1-52.
    CtY (nos. 1-330), ICN (nos. 1-271), ICS (nos. 1-271, lacking nos. 7, 28, 35, 42, 50, 59, 69, 81, 103, 138, 156, 170, 202, 211; also Baker's continuation, no. 272, and the Morphew-Harrison continuation, nos. 272-79, 282-98; also rep. of Harrison's continuation), ICU (nos. 1-271; also Baker's continuation, nos. 272 and 273, and the Morphew-Harrison continuation, nos. 272-290, 293-330; also James Watson's Edinburgh rep., nos. 1 [Steele's no. 130]-142 [Steele's no. 271], Feb. 13-1710–Jan. 9, 1711), IU (nos. 1-271), MH, NN (nos. 1-302), TxU (nos. 1-271; also nos. 272-73 [Baker] and nos. 274-330 [Morphew-Harrison]; also 1710 rep.).

851. Tatler, by Donald MacStaff of the North. Robert Hepburn. Edinburgh, 1711.
    TxU (nos. 4-24, Jan. 24–Apr. 4, 1711).

852. Tatler. 1753-54.
    NN (nos. 1-4, 1753-54).

853. Telegraph. 1794-97(?).
    TxU (Sept. 28, 1794).

854. Templar; or, Monthly register of legal and constitutional knowledge. 1788-89. m.
    NN (v. 1, Feb.–July 1788).

855. Terrae filius. N. Amhurst. Oxford, nos. 1-50, Jan. 11–July 6, 1721; rep. as Terrae filius; or, The secret history of the University of Oxford in several essays, 1726. s. w.
    CtY (rep. 1726), CU (rep.), ICU (rep.), IU (rep.), MB (rep.), MnU (rep.), TxU (rep.).

856. Test. Henry Fox, Lord Holland. Nos. 1-35, Nov. 6, 1756–July 9, 1757. w.
    CSH (no. 24, Apr. 23, 1757), CtY, DLC, ICU, IU, MH, MnU, NN, WH.

857. Test-paper. *Continued as* Weekly test-paper (from no. 2). Nos. 1-3(?), 1688.
    CSH.

858. Theatre. Steele. Nos. 1-28, Jan. 2–Apr. 5, 1720. s. w.
    CtY (also rep. 1791), MB, MH (rep. 1791), TxU (nos. 7-12, 20-21).

859. Theatrical guardian. 1791. w.
    MB (nos. 1-6, Mar. 5–Apr. 9, 1791), MH (nos. 1-5).

860. Theatrical register. 1769.
    MH.

861. Theatrical register. York, 1788.
    DLC (nos. 1-18), MH (nos. 1-8).

862. Theatrical review for 1757. 1758.
    CSH, IU, MB, PPL.

863. Theatrical review; or, A new companion to the playhouse. 1772.
    CSH, MH.

864. Theatrical review; or, Annals of the drama. 1763. m.
    DLC, ICU, MB (Jan. 1763), MH (v. 1, Jan.–June 1763).

865. Theological miscellany, and review of books on religious subjects. *Ed.* C. de Coetlogon. 1784-89. m.
    CtY (v. 1-5, 1784-88).

866. Theological repository. J. Priestley, etc. 1769-88.
    CtY, CU (v. 1, rep. 1773; v. 2, 1770; v. 3, 1771), ICN, MB (v. 1-3), MH.

867. Theosophical transactions of the Philadelphian society. 1697.
　　CSH (nos. 1-2, Mar.–Apr. 1697).

868. Thespian magazine, and literary repository. V. 1-3, 1792-94. m.
　　CSH, CtY (v. 1-2, June 1792–Dec. 1793), DLC, MB, MBB, MH, MiU, PU (v. 1).

869. Thistle. Edinburgh, nos. 1-105, Feb. 13, 1734–Feb. 11, 1736. w.
　　CtY, TxAG (nos. 1-7, 9-11, 14-15, 19-20, 41-42, 51-54, 57-58, 61).

870. Tickler. 1747-48. ir.
　　MH (nos. 1-7, 2nd ed. 1748).

871. Tickler. 1770. w.
　　CtY (nos. 1-5, 7-8, Oct. 20–Dec. 8, 1770).

　　Times. *See* Daily universal register.

872. Tomahawk; or, Censor-general. 1795-96. d.
　　CtY (nos. 1-113, Oct. 27, 1795–Mar. 7, 1796), DLC (nos. 1-113), MH (inc.), NN (nos. 1-75, 77-85, 100).

873. Topographer for the year . . . , containing a variety of original articles. *Continued as* Topographical miscellanies (from 1792). *Ed.* Sir E. Brydges and S. Shaw. 1789-92(?). m.
　　CtY (v. 1-4, Apr. 1789–Jan. 1791), ICN (1789-91), MB (v. 1-5, 1789–June 1791; 1792), NN (v. 1-4).

　　Topographical miscellanies. *See* Topographer for the year. . . .

874. Town and country magazine; or, Universal repository of knowledge, instruction and entertainment. 1769-96. m.
　　CSH (Sept. 1777), CtY (v. 1-24, Jan. 1769–Dec. 1791), DLC, MB (1769-84), MBB, MdBP (v. 1-9, 1769-77), MH (v. 1-22, 1769-90), MHi (v. 1, 4, 6, 15, 16, 17, inc.), MiU (v. 6, 1774), N (v. 1-21, 1769-89, lacking v. 4, 10), NjP (v. 1-9, 1769-77), NN (v. 1-24), NNC (v. 1-23), PPH (v. 1, 1769), PU (v. 4, 1772), WH (v. 2-6, 9, 11-12).

875. Town and country weekly magazine. Dublin, 1785-86. w.
　　DLC (v. 1, nos. 4, 6, 8, 16, 19, 24, 27, 29; v. 2, nos. 1-3, May 7, 1785–Jan. 21, 1786).

876. Town-talk. Steele. Nos. 1-9, Dec. 17, 1715–Feb. 13, 1716. w.
　　CtY (reps. 1789, 1790), IU (rep. 1790), MB (rep. 1790), MBB (rep. 1790), TxU (no. 5; also reps. 1716, 1789).

877. Traiteur. 1780-81. w.
 MiU (nos. 1-20, Nov. 18, 1780–Mar. 31, 1781).

878. Tribune. *Ed.* Patrick Delany. Dublin, nos. 1-21, 1729.
 CtY, NNC (London rep.).

879. Tribune. J. Thelwall. 1795-96. w.
 CtY (Mar. 14, 1795–Oct. 2, 1796), DLC, NN (Mar. 14–Sept. 23, 1795).

880. Trifler. 1762.
 CtY (rep. in Political controversy, 1762-63).

881. Trifler. R. Oliphant, J. H. Allen, etc. Nos. 1-43, May 31, 1788–Mar. 21, 1789. w.
 CtY, ICN, ICU, IU, MB, MH, NIC (nos. 1-41), NN.

882. Trimmer. 1762.
 CtY (rep. in Political controversy, 1762-63).

883. True and impartial account of the remarkable incidents . . . happening in city and country. 1688.
 CtY (nos. 9-11, July 28–Aug. 25, 1688).

884. True Briton. Philip, Duke of Wharton. Nos. 1-74, June 3, 1723–Feb. 17, 1724. s. w.
 CtY, ICU (nos. 1-73), IU, MBB (nos. 1-37), MnU, NIC, NNC, PPL, TxAG (nos. 1-43, nos. 1-32 rep.), TxU, WH.

885. True Briton. 1792+. d.
 CtY (nos. 1255-1566, Jan. 2–Dec. 30, 1797).

886. True Briton; in which the state, constitution and interest of Great Britain will be considered. 1751-53. w.
 CtY (v. 1, Jan. 2–June 19, 1751), NNC (v. 2, June 26–Dec. 25, 1751), WH (nos. 1-25, Jan. 2–June 19, 1751).

887. True character of Mercurius urbanicus & rusticus. *Continued as* City and countrey mercury: for the help of trade and dealing both in countrey and city (from no. 2); *as* Mercury, publishing advertisements of all sorts: as of persons run away, lost or spirited; horses, or other things lost or stoln (from no. 14). Nos. 1-33(?), June 10–Oct. 24, 1667.
 CSH (nos. 1-33), DLC (nos. 1-20).

888. True diurnall of the last weeks passages in Parliament. *Continued as* Continuation of the true diurnall of passages in Parliament (from no. 2, Jan. 17-24, 1642). *Printed for* H. Blunden. Jan. 17–Mar. 21(?), 1642. w. *Cf.* Times literary supplement, Dec. 4, 1924, p. 823, and Apr. 9, 1925, p. 253, and no. 126a, above.
 ICN (no. 6, Feb. 14-21), TxU (nos. 1-2, 4-8, Jan. 17–Mar. 7).

True diurnall; or, A continued relation of Irish occurrances. *See* Ireland's true diurnall.

889. True diurnal occurrences; or, Proceedings in the Parliament this last weeke. 1642.
    ICN (no. 3, Jan. 31).

890. True diurnal occurrances; or, The heads of the proceedings in both houses in Parliament. 1642.
    ICN (Feb. 7).

890a. True diurnall; or, The passages in Parliament. 1642.
    ICN (no. 2, Jan. 24).

True domestick intelligence. *See* Domestick intelligence . . . (Thompson).

891. True informer. Henry Walley. 1643-45.
    CSH (1643), **TxU** (no. 42, Aug. 17, 1644).

891a. True informer; or, Monthly mercury, being the certain inteligence of Mercurius militaris, or the armies scout. No. 1, Oct. 7–Nov. 8, 1648. Contains nos. 1-4 of Mercurius militaris, of which it is apparently a monthly edition. *Cf.* no. 1638.
    IWS (no. 1).

892. True intelligence from the head-quarters. 1650.
    CtY (no. 3, Aug. 7, 1650).

True news; or, Mercurius Anglicus. *See* Mercurius Anglicus; or, The weekly occurrences faithfully transmitted.

893. True patriot, and the history of our own times. 1745-46. w.
    CtY (nos. 1-32, Nov. 5, 1745–June 10, 1746, photographs).

894. True Protestant (domestick) intelligence. 1680. Published during the suspension of Protestant domestick intelligence. *See also* Domestick intelligence (B. Harris).
    NN (nos. 1-7, Apr. 23–May 14, 1680), **TxU** (nos. 1-7), **WH** (nos. 4-7).

895. True Protestant mercury; or, Occurrences foreign and domestick. *Printed for* L. Curtiss. 1680-82. s. w.
    CSH (1681), **MnU** (nos. 7, 11-12, 14, 16-17, 19, 21-27, 29-50, 52-63, 64-108, 110-19, 121-27, Jan. 15, 1681–Mar. 25, 1682), **NN** (May 5, 16, Sept. 27, 1681; May 20, 24, 31, 1682), **TxU** (nos. 1-188, Dec. 28, 1680–Oct. 25, 1682).

896. True Protestant mercury; or, Occurrences foreign and domestick. *Continued as* Impartial Protestant mercury . . . (from no. 5). *Published by* R. Janeway. 1681-82. s. w.

CSH (1682), CtY (nos. 8, May 19, 1681; 34, 38-115, Aug. 19, 1681–May 30, 1682), MnU (nos. 1-96, lacking nos. 2, 34, 67, Apr. 27, 1681–Mar. 24, 1681/2), NN (May 16, Sept. 27, 1681).

897. Trysorfa Ysprydol. Mold, 1799+.
ICN (v. 1, nos. 1, Apr. 1799; 4, Jan. 1800; also reps.).

898. Tunbridge miscellany. Tunbridge, 1713(?)-39(?).
CtY (1713, 1733, 1737-39), ICU (1713).

899. Tuner. 1754.
CtY.

900. Universal advertiser; or, A collection of essays moral, political, etc. Dublin, 1754.
CtY, ICU, IU.

901. Universal catalogue. 1772-74.
DLC.

902. Universal historical bibliotheque; or, An account of most of the considerable books printed in all languages. . . . Jan.–Mar. 1687. m.
CtY (Jan.), DLC, MH (lacking March), PPL (Jan., Feb.).

903. Universal intelligence. 1688-89.
CSH, CtY (no. 8, Jan. 3, 1689).

903a. Universal London morning advertiser. *Continued as* Penny London morning advertiser (from Jan. 9, 1744); *as* Penny London post; or, The morning advertiser (from Aug. 15, 1744); *as* London morning penny post (from May 6, 1751). J. Nicholson. 1743-51. t. w. *Cf.* no. 1527.
TxU (no. 1358, Dec. 21, 1750).

904. Universal magazine and review; or, Repository of literature. Dublin, 1789-92(?). m.
CtY (v. 2, 1789, lacking some plates), MB (v. 1, Jan.–June 1789).

905. Universal magazine of knowledge and pleasure. 1747+. m.
CSH (v. 56-57, 1775), CtY (v. 1-21, 1747-57; 23-98, 1758-96; 100-06, 1797-1800), DLC, ICU (v. 1-40, June 1747-1767; v. 42+, 1768+), MB (1747-94), MBB (inc.), MH (v. 38 inc., 1766; 54-107, 1766-1800), MHi (1754-78, inc.), MiU (v. 2-37, 1748-65), N (v. 34-81, 1764-87), NcU (v. 74, 1784), NIC, NN, NNC (1747+, lacking v. 11, 27, 38-39, 50-51, 58, 64, 94, 100, 105), PPH (v. 14, 1754; 34, 1764), PPL (v. 2+, 1747+), TxU (v. 1-21, 1747-58), WH (1747-94, lacking about 42 v.).

906. Universal masquerade. 1742.
MH (v. 2, 1742).

907. Universal museum; or, Gentleman's and ladies polite maga-

zine of history, politics and literature. *Continued as* Universal museum and complete magazine of knowledge and pleasure (from 1764). 1762-70. m.
CtY (v. 1-5, Jan. 1762–Dec. 1766), **MH** (Jan.–June, Aug.–Oct. 1765), **NIC** (1769), **NN** (v. 1-2, 1762-63; n. s., v. 2-3, no. 6, Jan. 1766–June 1768; v. 4-5, 1769-70), **TxU** (v. 1-3, 1762-64).

908. Universal spectator, and weekly journal. Henry Baker. 1728-46. w.
CtY (Jan. 30, Mar. 20, May 29, Aug. 21, Oct. 9, 1731; Jan. 20–Mar. 17, Apr. 7, May 5-12, June 16-23, July 7-21, Aug. 4-11, 25, Sept. 15–Oct. 6, Nov. 10-24, Dec. 8-15, 1733; Apr. 26, May 3, Oct. 11, 1735; also 2nd ed., 1747), **DLC**, **ICU** (3rd ed., 1756), **TxU** (1736), **WH** (nos. 97, 101, 104, 107, Aug. 15–Oct. 24, 1730; 138, 149, May 29, Oct. 23, 1731; 169-190, 193-221, Jan. 1–Dec. 30, 1732; 222-23, 226-27, 229-34, 236, 239-40, 242-49, 251-61, 264-65, 267-71, Jan. 6–Dec. 15, 1733; 273-75, 277-78, 284-89, 293-95, 299-311, 313-15, Dec. 29, 1733–Oct. 19, 1734; 325-27, 329-31, 333-41, 344-48, 351, 355, 358-60, 372, Dec. 28, 1734–Nov. 22, 1735; 392-411, 414-22, June 5–Nov. 6, 1736; 431-44, 446-70, 472-82, Jan. 8–Dec. 31, 1737; 483-89, 491-92, 496, 499-503, 505-07, Jan. 7–June 24, 1738, reps.; 535-46, 548-74, Jan. 6–Oct. 6, 1739; 576-89, 591-94, 597-610, 612, 614-19, Oct. 20, 1739–Aug. 16, 1740; 622-91, Sept. 6, 1740–Jan. 2, 1742).

909. Universal spy; or, The royal oak journal reviv'd. 1732. w.
TxAG (nos. 1-3, 5-8, 10, 12, Apr. 29–Sept. 22, 1732).

910. Useful transactions in philosophy. W. King. 1709.
CtY (pts. 1-3, Jan.–Sept. 1709).

912. Visions of Sir Heister Ryley, with other entertainments. Charles Povey(?). Nos. 1-80, Aug. 21, 1710–Feb. 20, 1711. t. w.
CtY, ICN, ICU, IU, MH, MnU, NN, NNC, TxAG, TxU.

913. Vocal magazine. 1778.
CtY (nos. 1-9, 1778), **DLC** (nos. 1-9), **NIC** (nos. 1-9), **NN** (nos. 1-9, words only).

914. Vocal magazine. James Sibbald. Edinburgh, 1797-99. m.
MH.

Walker's Hibernian magazine. *See* Hibernian magazine.

915. Wanderer. John Fox and Daniel Hanchet. Nos. 1-26, Feb. 9–Aug. 1, 1717. w.
CtY (rep. 1718).

916. Watchman. S. T. Coleridge. Bristol, nos. 1-10, Mar. 1–May 13, 1796. w.
CtY, DLC (nos. 1-5, Mar. 1–Apr. 2, 1796), **MH.**

916a. Weekly accompt; or, Perfect diurnall of some passages in both Houses of Parliament and from other parts of this kingdome. No. 1, June 10, 1643.
CtY.

916b. Weekly account. *Continued as* Perfect weekly account (from no. 18, May 5, 1647). Sept. 6, 1643–June 28, 1647.
TxU (Nov. 20, 1644; July 2, 1645; Feb. 19, July 28, Sept. 3, 1646).

917. Weekly advertisements of things lost and stollen, with catalogue of books newly come forth. 1669. w.
CSH (nos. 1-2, Jan. 1669).

918. Weekly amusement; or, An useful and agreeable miscellany of literary entertainments. 1763-67. w.
CtY (Dec. 24, 1763–Dec. 26, 1767), ICU (Jan. 5, 1765–Dec. 26, 1766), TxU (Aug. 4–Dec. 29, 1764).

919. Weekly amusement; or, The universal magazine. 1734-35. w.
CtY (nos. 1-15, Nov. 9, 1734–Feb. 15, 1735; 31-45, June 7–Sept. 13, 1735), ICU (v. 1-3, Nov. 1734–Sept. 1735), WH (v. 1, no. 1–v. 3, no. 45, Nov. 9, 1734–Sept. 13, 1735).

920. Weekly amusement; or, Universal magazine; containing essays . . . from the Craftsman, Fog, the Grub-Street journal, Prompter, and other weekly papers. Dublin, 1735. w.
CSH (no. 1, 1735), CtY (nos. 1-2, 1735).

921. Weekly comedy; or, The humours of a coffee-house. Edward Ward. 1707-08. w.
MH (nos. 1-14, Aug. 13–Nov. 14, 1707).

922. Weekly discoverer stripp'd naked. B. Harris. 1681. w.
TxU (nos. 1-5, Feb. 16–Mar. 16, 1681).

923. Weekly discovery of the mystery of iniquity, in the rise, growth, methods and ends of the unnatural rebellion in England. 1681. w.
CSH (nos. 1-8, 11-30, Feb. 5–Aug. 27, 1681), CtY (nos. 1-30), DLC, MH (nos. 1-30), NN (Apr. 30–July 2, 16–Aug. 6, 1681).

924. Weekly entertainer; or, Agreeable and instructive repository. Sherborne, 1784+. w. *Cf.* no. 937.
DLC (1798-99).

925. Weekly essay; or, Middlesex journal. 1737-38. w.
CtY (nos. 1-19, Nov. 5, 1737–Mar. 11, 1738).

926. Weekly intelligencer of the Commonwealth. Richard Collings(?). July 23, 1650–Sept. 25, 1655. w.
CtY (no. 131, Aug. 9, 1653).

927. Weekly journal; or, British gazetteer, being the freshest advices foreign and domestick. *Continued as* Read's weekly journal; or, British gazetteer (from Aug. 15, 1730); *as* London spy and Read's weekly journal (from May 9, 1761). George Read. 1715-61. w.

CtY (Apr. 16, June 25, July 23, Aug. 20, 27, 31, 1715; Jan. 17, 1719–Dec. 31, 1720; Aug. 12, 1721; Jan. 19, Apr. 6, 1723; June 12, 1731–Dec. 30, 1732; July 18–Dec. 20, 1761), **DLC** (nos. 471-692, Mar. 30, 1734–Dec. 10, 1737), **MH** (Mar. 29, Apr. 12, 1718; Nov. 14, 1719; Jan. 9–Feb. 27, Mar. 12–Apr. 9, 23–May 7, June 11, Sept. 10–Oct. 22, Nov. 26, Dec. 31, 1720; Jan. 21, 1721), **NN** (May 7, July 30, Oct. 22, 1715; Sept. 10, 1720; Jan. 4–Feb. 15, Mar. 1-22, Apr. 5–Aug. 2, 23, Sept. 13-20, Oct. 4, 18, Nov. 1, 22–Dec. 27, 1729; Mar. 21, 1730; Jan. 2–Dec. 25, 1731; Jan. 1–Apr. 1, 1732), **TxU** (Mar. 10, May 12, 1716).

928. Weekly journal; or, Saturday's post, with fresh advices foreign and domestick. *Continued as* Mist's weekly journal (from May 1, 1725, with new numbering); *as* Fog's weekly journal (from Sept. 28, 1728, with new numbering). N. Mist. Dec. 15, 1716–Oct. 22, 1737. w. Portions reprinted in A collection of miscellany letters selected out of Mist's weekly journal, 1722, and in Select letters taken from Fog's weekly journal, 1732.

CtY (Jan. 30, 1720–Oct. 19, 1723; Jan. 11–Dec. 26, 1724; Jan. 2–Apr. 24, 1725; June 25–Oct. 29, 1726; Jan. 14, 1727–Sept. 14, 1728; Sept. 28, 1728–Dec. 27, 1729; Jan. 3–Dec. 26, 1730; Jan. 2, 1731–Dec. 30, 1732; Feb. 10, July 14, Oct. 27, 1733; Jan. 5, 1734–Dec. 25, 1736; also Select letters), **DLC** (Select letters), **ICU** (Collection and Select letters), **MB** (1716-25, 1728, 1729), **MnU** (Select letters), **NN** (Apr. 16, 1720; May 29, 1736), **PPL** (Collection and Select letters), **TxAG** (July 7, 1733–Jan. 4, 1735, inc.; also Select letters), **TxU** (Feb. 9, 1716/7–Dec. 28, 1723, almost complete; Jan. 2–Apr. 24, 1725; scattering numbers between May 1, 1725 and Dec. 28, 1728; Jan. 4–Mar. 22, 1729; also Collection).

928a. Weekly journal with fresh advices foreign and domestick. Robert Mawson. 1715. w.

TxU (nos. 42, Oct. 22, 1715; 46, Nov. 19, 1715; also Supplement to the Weekly journal, Nov. 16, 1715).

929. Weekly magazine; or, Gentleman and lady's polite companion. 1760. w.

CSH (nos. 1-4).

930. Weekly magazine and historical register. Dublin, 1793. w.

DLC (v. 1, no. 4, inc., n. d.; v. 1, no. 6, Mar. 9, 1793).

931. Weekly magazine and literary review. 1758. w.
   CtY (nos. 1-16, Apr. 15–July 29, 1758).

932. Weekly magazine; or, Edinburgh amusement. *Continued as* Edinburgh magazine; or, Literary amusement (from Dec. 30, 1779); *as* Edinburgh weekly magazine (from July 3, 1783). *Ed.* Walter Ruddiman. Edinburgh, 1768-84. w.
   CtY (v. 1-14, July 7, 1768–Dec. 26, 1771; 16-23, Apr. 2, 1772–Mar. 24, 1774; 30-60, Dec. 7, 1775–June 17, 1784), **DLC** (v. 1, July 7–Sept. 29, 1768; 27, Dec. 30, 1774–Mar. 23, 1775; 29-32, July 27, 1775–Apr. 11, 1776; 33, June 27–Sept. 19, 1776), **NN** (v. 10, Oct. 4–Dec. 20, 1770; 14-15, Oct. 17, 1771–Mar. 19, 1772; 19-20, Jan. 1–Apr. 29, 1773; 31-33, Feb. 15–July 25, 1776, inc.), **PU** (v. 34, Oct.–Dec. 1776), **WH** (v. 1-20, July 7, 1768–June 24, 1773; 23-28, Dec. 30, 1773–June 22, 1775).

933. Weekly medley; or, The gentleman's recreation. 1718-20. w.
   TxU (nos. 1-27, July 26, 1718–Jan. 24, 1719, lacking no. 23).

934. Weekly memorials for the ingenious; or, An account of books lately set forth in several languages, with other accounts relating to arts and sciences. *Published by* Henry Faithorne and John Kersey. Nos. 1-50, Jan. 16, 1682–Jan. 15, 1683 (with two issues of no. 9). w.
   CSH, CtY, DLC, ICN, ICU (lacking nos. 15, 19, 20), **IU, IWS, MH, MHi, NjP, NIC** (no. 44), **NNC, PPL.**

935. Weekly memorials for the ingenious; or, An account of books lately set forth in several languages, with other accounts relating to arts and sciences. *Published by* R. Chiswell, etc. Nos. 1-29, Mar. 20–Sept. 25, 1682. w. The text of no. 1 of this periodical is the same as that of no. 10 of the preceding; nos. 2-29 constitute an independent periodical.
   CSH (nos. 1-7, 10-29), **NjP.**

936. Weekly memorials; or, An account of books lately set forth, with other accounts relating to learning. 1688. w.
   CSH (no. 1, Jan. 19, 1688).

   Weekly miscellany, giving an account of the religion, morality, and learning of the present times. . . . *See* Miscellany. . . .

936a. Weekly miscellany of instruction and entertainment. *Continued as* Phoenix; or, Weekly miscellany improv'd (from 1792); *as* Asylum; or, Weekly miscellany (from 1794). Glasgow, 1789-96. w.
   NN (v. 3-4, July 10, 1793–July 2, 1794).

937. Weekly miscellany; or, Instructive entertainer. Sherborne, 1773-83. w. *Cf.* no. 924.
   CtY (v. 1-5, [1773-75]).

938. Weekly museum. 1788(?)-95(?). w.
   NNC (v. 7, nos. 348-88, Jan. 10–Dec. 5, 1795).

   Weekly observator. *See* Mercurius reformatus; or, The new observator.

939. Weekly oracle; or, Universal library. 1734-37. w.
   CtY (nos. 1-2, 7-14, 16-23, 25-53, 56-58, Dec. 7, 1734–Jan. 16, 1736).

940. Weekly packet. 1712-21. w.
   MH (nos. 90-443, lacking nos. 172, 315, 316, 319, 328, 329, 332, 336, 337, 432), TxU (nos. 179, Dec. 10, 1715; 451, Feb. 25, 1721).

941. Weekly pacquet of advice from Geneva. 1681. w.
   TxU (nos. 1-2, May 20-26, 1681).

942. Weekly pacquet of advice from Geneva. 1683. w.
   CSH (nos. 1-6, 1683).

943. Weekly pacquet of advice from Germany; or, The history of the reformation of religion there. 1679-80. w.
   NNC (nos. 1-16, Sept. 3–Dec. 17, 1679).

   Weekly pacquet of advice from Rome. *See* Pacquet of advice from Rome.

   Weekly post. *See* Faithful post.

944. Weekly post. D. Border(?). 1659-60. w.
   CtY (nos. 32-33, Dec. 13-20, 1659; 35, Jan. 3, 1660), MnU (no. 42, Feb. 21, 1660).

945. Weekly register; or, Universal journal. 1730-34(?). w.
   CtY (May 22, June 5, 1731; Jan. 6, 1733).

946. Weekly remarks and political reflections upon the most material news, foreign and domestick. 1715-16. w.
   TxU (nos. 1-11, Dec. 3, 1715–Feb. 11, 1716).

947. Weekly review of the affairs of France, purg'd from the errors and partiality of news-writers and petty-statesmen, of all sides. *Continued as* Review of the affairs of France . . . (from no. 8, Apr. 1, 1704); *as* Review of the affairs of France, with some observations on transactions at home (from v. 2, no. 1, Feb. 27, 1705); *as* Review of the state of the English nation (from v. 3, no. 1, Jan. 1, 1706); *as* Review of the state of the British nation (from v. 4, no. 12, Mar. 8, 1707). Daniel Defoe. V. 1-9, Feb. 19, 1704–June 11, 1713. w.; s. w. (from

v. 1, no. 7); t. w. (from v. 3, no. 1, Jan. 1, 1706). There were two important supplements: (1) A supplementary journal to the advice from the Scandal. Club (with no. 2 entitled: A supplement to the advice from the Scandal. Club), nos. 1-5, Sept. 1704–Jan. 1705; and (2) The little review; or, An inquisition of scandal: consisting in answers of questions and doubts, remarks, observation and reflection, nos. 1-23, June 6–Aug. 22, 1705. The first appeared monthly; the second semi-weekly.

CSH (v. 4, no. 6, Feb. 22, 1706; v. 6, nos. 30, 87, 148, June 11, Oct. 25, 1709, Mar. 18, 1710; v. 7, nos. 1, 8, 10, 14, 20, 47, 49, 52, 56, 61, 64-65, 67, 70-72, 74-76, 79, 80, 85, 87, 96-99, 101-02, 106-12, 114-16, 121, 123-24, 126-28, 130-31, 133-35, 137, Mar. 28, 1710–Feb. 8, 1711), **CtY** (v. 1-3, Feb. 19, 1704–Feb. 6, 1706; v. 5, no. 124, Jan. 11, 1709; v. 6-7, 1709-1711), **IWS** (v. 1-8, lacking v. 8, nos. 142, 159-61; v. 6, Edinburgh rep.; also Supplementary journal . . . and Little review, both complete), **MH** (v. 1-2, Feb. 19, 1704–Dec. 27, 1705), **TxU** (v. 1-4, 6-7; 1-4, 6, Edinburgh rep.; also Supplementary journal . . . , nos. 1-5, Oct. 1704–Jan. 1705).

Weekly test-paper. *See* Test-paper.

948. Weekly visions of the late popish plot. T. Benskin. 1681.
NN (nos. 1-3, 5-7, Apr.–June, 1681), **TxU** (nos. 1-7, n. d. [impr. 1681]).

Weekly Worcester journal. *See* Worcester postman.

Western county magazine. *See* County magazine.

Westminster gazette. *See* English gazette.

949. Westminster journal and London miscellany. 1782-96. w.
IU (1782, 1784-87, 1789-90, 1794-96, inc.).

950. Westminster journal; or, New weekly miscellany. 1741+. w.
CtY (nos. 643, 644, 691, 709, 729, May 4, 1754–Dec. 27, 1755), **NN** Oct. 27, 1744).

951. Westminster magazine; or, The pantheon of taste. V. 1-13, 1773-85. m.
CtY (v. 1-10, 1773-82; 12-13, 1784-85), **DLC** (v. 4, 6, 8 inc., 10), **MB** (v. 11), **MH** (v. 5, 12 inc.), **MHi** (Jan. 1779; July 1783), **NjP** (v. 1), **NN** (v. 4-7, 8 inc., 9 inc., 10 inc., 11 inc.), **NNC** (v. 1-9, 11), **PPL**, **PU** (v. 9-10), **WH** (v. 1, 5-6, 11 inc., 13).

952. Westminster projects. 1648.
CSH (nos. 5-6).

953. What d'ye call it. 1733. w.
CtY (no. 2, Dec. 1, 1733).

955. Whig examiner. Addison. Nos. 1-5, Sept. 14–Oct. 12, 1710. w.
    CtY (rep. 1712), DLC, ICU (rep. 1789), IU (reps. 1712, 1789), MH (Sept. 14–Oct. 5, 1710), NIC, NNC, PPL, TxU (rep. 1789).

956. Whisperer. *Ed.* William Moore. Nos. 1-100, Feb. 17, 1770–Jan. 11, 1772. w.
    CtY, DLC, ICU (nos. 3-38, Mar. 28–Apr. 11, 1770), IU (Feb. 17–June 30, 1770), MH, NN, NNC (nos. 1-8, Feb. 17–Apr. 7, 1770), TxU (no. 12, May 5, 1770), WH.

957. Whitehall evening-post. 1718-1800(?). t. w.
    CtY (1720, 1722, 1733-34, 1736, 1746-48, 1754-55, 1765-80, inc.), IEK (1723, 1726-31, a good file), MB (Feb. 28–Sept. 2, 1721), NN (nos. 359-62, 364-65, 371, 376, 389-90, 410, 421, 465, 506-07, 509-10, 525, 527-29, 531-33, 546, 547, Dec. 29, 1720–Mar. 13, 1722; May 21, 1737), TxU (nos. 383, 506, 525, 529, 630, Feb. 25, 1721–Sept. 22, 1722; also suppl. to no. 525, Jan. 22, 1722).

958. Whitehall evening-post; or, London intelligencer. 1746+. t. w.
    CtY (1747, 1748, inc.), TxU (Aug. 6, 1755; May 26, 1756; Jan. 24, Oct. 23, 1760; Jan. 8, 11, 1763).

960. Wit's magazine; or, Library of Momus. *Ed.* Thomas Holcroft. 1784-85. m.
    CSH, CtY (v. 1-2, Feb. 1784–Apr. 1785), DLC (v. 1-2, 1784-85), ICN, ICU, MH (v. 1-2, Jan. 1784–May 1785).

961. Woman's almanack. 1731.
    PPL.

962. Wonderful and lamentable newes. . . . 1624.
    NN (Oct. 11, 1624, rep.).

963. Wonderful magazine and marvellous chronicle; or, New weekly entertainer. 1793-94. w.
    NN (v. 1-2, 4-5, n. d.), WH.

Worcester journal. *See* Worcester postman.

964. Worcester postman. *Continued as* Worcester post; or, Western journal (from 1722); *as* Weekly Worcester journal (from 1725), *as* Worcester journal (from 1748); *as* Berrow's Worcester journal (from 1753). Worcester, 1709+.
    TxU (no. 247, Mar. 19, 1714).

965. Works of the learned. J. de la Crose. 1691-92. m.
    CtY (Jan.–Feb. 1692), DLC (v. 1, Aug. 1691–Apr. 1692), ICN (v. 1, nos. 8-10, Aug.–Oct. 1691).

966. World. Edward Moore, assisted by Horace Walpole, Chesterfield, R. O. Cambridge, and others. Nos. 1-209, Jan. 4, 1753–Dec. 30, 1756. w.
CSt (nos. 1-52), CtY (also rep. 1767, and A world extraordinary, n. d.), DLC, ICN, MH (lacking no. 208), NN, NNC (also reps. 1763, 1793, 1794), PP, PPAP, PU (Jan. 4, 1753–Apr. 22, 1756), TxU (rep. 1755-57), WH.

967. World: fashionable advertiser. *Continued as* World (from no. 272, Nov. 27, 1787). Nos. 1-2342, Jan. 1, 1787–June 30, 1794. d.
CtY (May 29, 1789; May 11, 13-15, 1790; May 7, 1792).

968. York chronicle and weekly advertiser. *Continued as* Etherington's York chronicle (from Jan. 1774); *as* Etherington's York chronicle and northern flying post (from Jan. [?] 1777); *as* York chronicle and general advertiser (from Feb. 1777). York, 1772+. w.
CtY (Dec. 18, 1772–Dec. 21, 1773).

969. Young gentleman's and lady's magazine. V. 1-2, 1799-1800. m.
CtY, DLC, MB.

970. Young gentleman's magazine; or, Monthly repository of science, moral and entertaining matter. 1777.
CtY (v. 1, Jan.–June 1777).

II. BRITISH PERIODICALS, 1620-1800, NOT FOUND IN AMERICAN LIBRARIES

Difficulties in numbering have caused a few items which were added after the index had been made and the bibliography put in type to be entered slightly out of alphabetical order.

1001. Aberdeen intelligencer. Aberdeen, Oct. 3, 1752–Feb. 22, 1757. w. Incorporated with the Aberdeen journal, 1757.

1002. Aberdeen's journal. *Continued as* Aberdeen journal (from no. 9). Aberdeen, 1748+. w. Absorbed Aberdeen intelligencer, 1757.

1003. Aberdeen magazine, literary chronicle, and review. Aberdeen, 1788-91. f. (to Dec. 30, 1790); m. (June–Nov. 1791).

1004. Aberdeen magazine; or, Universal repository. Aberdeen, 1796-98. m.

1006. Abstract and brief chronicle of the time. 1782.

1007. Account of the chief occurrences of Ireland. W. Bladen. Dublin, no. [5], Mar. 13-19, 1660.

1008. Acta Germanica; or, The memoires of Germany. 1742.

1009. Actor. 1789.

1010. Advertiser. Greenock, 1799+.

1010a. Advice from Parnassus, by Trojano Boccalini . . . with observations, reflections, and notes. No. 1, Mar. 1727. m.

1011. Adviser. 1762.

1012. Advocate. No. 1, Feb. 17, 1725.

1013. African Association proceedings. 1790.

1014. Agreeable companion. 1745.

1015. Agreeable miscellany; or, Something to please every man's taste. Kendal, 1745. f.

1015a. Albion and evening advertiser. No. 106, Jan. 9, 1800.

1016. All-alive and merry; or, The London daily post. 1741-43.

1017. Alston miscellany. Aldstone, 1799+.

1018. Amsterdam slip. 1697.

1019. Anatomist. 1747.
1019a. Anbury's weekly journal. Dublin, 1727.
1020. Ancient and modern library. 1714.
1021. Annual anthology. Bristol and London, 1799-1800.
1022. Anomaliae. Whitby, 1797-98.
1023. Anti-aulicus. No. 1, Feb. 6, 1644.
1024. Anti-Gallican and anti-levelling songster, being a selection of curious political songs. 1793.
1024a. Arbroath magazine. Arbroath, 1799.
Archer's Bath chronicle. *See* Bath chronicle and weekly gazette.
1026. Armies intelligencer. No. 1, Aug. 5, 1651.
1027. Armies modest intelligencer. *Continued as* Armies weekly intelligencer (from no. 4, Feb. 15, 1649). 1649. w.
1028. Armies painfull-messenger. No. 1, Aug. 2, 1649.
1029. Armies post. No. 1, July 8, 1647.
Armies scout. *See* Faithful scout. 1651-55.
Armies weekly intelligencer. 1649. *See* Armies modest intelligencer.
1030. Army list. 1800. m.
1030a. Asiatic researches: or, Transactions of the Society, instituted in Bengal, for inquiring into the history and antiquities, the arts, sciences and literature of Asia. 1799+.
1031. Association papers, for 1793. 1793(?).
1032. Associator. 1792.
Astrological observator. *See* Infallible astrologer.
1034. Athenian news; or, Dunton's oracle. 1710.
1035. Athenian spy. 1704.
1035a. Athlone herald. Athlone, 1785+.
1035b. Athlone sentinel. Athlone, 1798+.
1036. Aurora, and universal advertiser. 1781.
1037. Aurora; or, The dawn of genuine truth. 1799-1800.
1038. Aylesbury journal. Aylesbury, 1762.
1039. Ayre's Sunday London gazette. 1795.
1040. Baker's news; or, The Whitehall journal. No. 1, May 24, 1722. w.

1041. Balm of Gilead; or, The healer of divisions. 1714.

1042. Batchelor; or, Speculations of Jeoffrey Wagstaffe, Esq. 1766-68. w.

1043. Bath advertiser. *Continued as* Bath chronicle (from 1760). Stephen Martin. Bath, 1755+.

Bath and Bristol chronicle. *See* Bath chronicle and weekly gazette.

1043a. Bath and Bristol magazine. Bath(?), 1776.

1044. Bath and west of England Agricultural Society. Correspondence. 1780+.

Bath chronicle. 1760. *See* Bath advertiser.

Bath chronicle. 1770. *See* Bath chronicle and weekly gazette.

1044a. Bath chronicle and weekly gazette. *Continued as* Pope's Bath chronicle (from Nov. 1761); *as* Archer's Bath chronicle (from Aug. 1768); *as* Bath and Bristol chronicle (from Sept. 1768); *as* Bath chronicle (from Sept. 1770). Bath, 1760+.

1044b. Bath courant. Gye and Salmon. Bath, 1773-(?).

1044c. Bath gazette. Bath, 1778.

Bath herald. *See* Bath herald and general advertiser.

1045. Bath herald and general advertiser. *Absorbed* Bath register and general advertiser (in 1793); *continued as* Bath herald and register (from 1793); *as* Bath herald (from 1800). Meyler. Bath, 1792+.

Bath herald and register. *See* Bath herald and general advertiser.

1046. Bath miscellany for the year. . . . Bath, 1741.

1046a. Bath register and general advertiser. J. Johnson. Bath, 1792-93. See also Bath herald and general advertiser.

1046b. Bee and Sketchley's weekly advertiser. Bristol, 1777.

1046c. Bee. 1715.

1047. Belfast mercury; or, Freeman's chronicle. Belfast, 1784-86.

1049. Best and most perfect intelligencer. No. 1, Aug. 8, 1650.

1049a. Bibliotheca biblica. 1717. m.

1049b. Bibliotheca curiosa. 1708.

1050. Bibliotheca universalis. Edinburgh, 1688.

1051. Bingley's journal; or, The universal gazette. 1770-75.
1052. Birch. Oxford, 1795-96.
1052a. Birmingham journal. Birmingham, 1732(?).
1053. Birmingham register; or, Entertaining museum. Birmingham, 1764-65.
1056. Bonner and Middleton's Bristol journal. Bristol, 1774+.
1057. Bon-ton magazine. 1791-93.
1057b. Boston weekly journal. Boston, 1731-39.
1058. Bouquet; or, Blossoms of fancy. 1795(?)-96.
1059. Brice's weekly journal. A. Brice. Exeter, 1725-31(?).
1059a. Brighton guide. Brighton, 1797(?).
1060. Bristol and Bath magazine. Bristol, 1782-83.
1060a. Bristol, Bath, and Somersetshire journal. Bristol, no. 68, 1743.
1061. Bristol chronicle; or, Universal mercantile register [slight changes of title]. *Printed by* John Grabham and William Pine. Bristol, 1760-61.

Bristol journal. *See* F. Farley's Bristol journal *and* Sam Farley's Bristol post man.

1062. Bristol journal extraordinary. Bristol, Apr. 8, 1776.
1062a. Bristol mirror. Bristol, 1773.
1062b. Bristol mercury, and universal advertiser. Bulgin and Rosser. Bristol, 1790+.
1062c. Bristol mercury. Bristol, 1747(?)-49.
1062d. Bristol mercury from Holland, France and Spain. Bristol, 1715-16(?).
1063. Bristol oracle, and country intelligencer. *Continued under different titles such as* Bristol oracle and country advertiser, Bristol oracle and weekly miscellany, *and* Oracle county advertiser. Andrew Hooke. Bristol, 1743(?)-49.
1064. Bristol post-boy. *Printed and sold by* W. Bonny. Bristol, no. 91, Aug. 12, 1704-1712.
1065. Bristol postman. Bristol, 1712-25. w.
1065a. Bristol times. Bristol, 1735.

1065b. Bristol weekly intelligencer. *Printed by* E. Ward. Bristol, 1749-58(?).

1066. Bristol weekly mercury. Bristol, 1715-16.

1067. Britaines remembrancer. 1644.

1068. Britain's genius; or, The weekly correspondent. 1718.

1069. Britanicus vapulans. *Possibly continued as* Mercurius urbanus (from no. 2, Nov. 9, 1643). 1643.

1070. British censor. 1738.

1071. British chronicle. *Printed by* James Palmer. Kelso, 1783(?)+. w.

1072. British chronicle; or, Pugh's Hereford journal. Hereford, v. 3, 1773+.

1072a. British courant; or, Preston journal. Preston, 1745-(?).

1074. British harlequin. 1720.

1074a. British intelligencer; or, Universal advertiser. No. 10, May 23, 1743.

1075. British merchant; or, A review of the trade of Great Britain. 1719.

1076. British mercury. 1710-12.

1077. British mercury, . . . to which is now added The priests of Apollo. 1787-88.

1078. British miscellany. 1779-(?).

1079. British observator. 1733-34.

1080. British physician. 1716.

British spy; or, Derby postman. *See* Derby postman.

1080a. British spy; or, New universal London weekly journal. Nos. 234-35, Aug. 14-21, 1756.

1081. British spy; or, Weekly journal. 1725.

1082. British theatre. 1800+.

1083. Briton. Newark, 1793.

1084. Burnisher. 1800+. w.

1084a. Bury and Norwich post. P. Gedge. Bury St. Edmunds, 1782(?)+.

1085. Busy body. 1742.

1086. Busy body. Oliver Goldsmith and others. 1759.

1087. Busy body. 1787.

1088. Busy body. V. 2, 1789.
1089. Cabinet. 1792.
1090. Cabinet magazine; or, Literary olio. 1796-97.
1091. Caledonian chronicle. Edinburgh, 1792-93.
1092. Caledonian gazetteer. Edinburgh, 1776. t. w.
1093. Caledonian magazine and review. Perth, Mar. 1783. f.
1094. Caledonian magazine; or, Aberdeen repository. *Ed.* A. Leighton. Aberdeen, Oct. 6, 1786–Oct. 5, 1787. f.
1095. Caledonian magazine; or, Aberdeen repository. *Ed.* Andrew Shirreffs. Aberdeen, v. 1-5, Jan. 1788–Dec. 1790. m.
1095a. Cambridge chronicle. Cambridge, 1744.
1095b. Cambridge chronicle and journal. Cambridge, no. 376, Jan. 6, 1770-1792(?).
1096. Cambridge journal. Cambridge, 1746-60.
1096a. Carey's Waterford packet. Waterford, 1791.
1097. Casket; or, Hesperian magazine. Cork, 1797-98.
1098. Casuist. 1719-20. w.
1099. Cavalier's diurnal. 1644.
1100. Censor; or, Mustermaster-General of all the newspapers. No. 2, Apr. 6, 1726. w.
1101. Censor; or, The citizens journal; by Frank Somebody, Esq. James Esdall. Dublin, v. 1, nos. 1-27, June 3, 1749–May 5, 1750. w.
1102. Certain passages of every dayes intelligence. May 19 and July 20, 1654.
1103. Certain passages of every day's intelligence. No. 1, Sept. 7, 1655.
1104. Character of Mercurius politicus. 1650.
1105. Chester chronicle. Chester, 1775-92(?).
1105a. Chester courant. Chester, 1730-33.
1106. Chester weekly journal. Chester, no. 174, Sept. 3, 1724. Perhaps the same as no. 1107.
1107. Chester weekly journal. William Cooke. Chester, 1725(?). See no. 1106.
1108. Chiefe heads of each dayes proceedings in Parliament. No. 1, May 8-15, 1644.

1109. Chit-chat. Steele(?). 1716. w.
1110. Christian history; or, A general account of the progress of the gospel in England, Wales, Scotland, and America, so far as the Rev. Mr. Whitefield, his fellow-labourers, and assistants are concerned. 1740-(?).
1111. Christian priest. 1720.
1112. Christian's amusement. 1740-41. w.
1113. Christian's magazine; or, Gospel repository. 1790-92.
1114. Church-man. No. 1, Oct. 29, 1718.
1114a. Churchman; or, Loyalist's weekly journal. 1726-27.
1114b. Churchman; or, Loyalist's weekly journal. 1719-20.
1115. Church Missionary Society report. 1795+.
1115a. Cirencester flying post and weekly miscellany. Cirencester, nos. 42-164, Oct. 5, 1741–Feb. 6, 1744.
1116. Cirencester post; or, Gloucestershire mercury. Cirencester, 1719(?)-1720(?).
1117. Citizen. *Published by* N. Mist. 1716. s. w.
1118. Citizen. *Published by* J. Roberts. 1727.
1119. Citizen. Edinburgh, 1764.
1120. Citizen. 1788. w.
1121. Citizen; or, The weekly conversation of a society of London merchants on trade and other publick affairs. 1739. w.
1122. Citties weekly post. 1645-46.
1124. City mercury: from the office at the Royal Exchange. 1680.
1125. City mercury; or, Advertisements concerning trade. 1675-76.
1126. City mercury, published (gratis) every Monday for the promotion of trade. Thomas Howkins. 1692-94 (?).

City scout. *See* Heads of some notes of the citie scout.

1127. Civic sermons to the people. Dundee, 1792.
1127a. Clare journal. Ennis, 1778+.
1128. Clerical review; or, Impartial report of sermons. Edinburgh, 1800. w.
1129. Club. 1723.

1129a. Coffee-house mercury; containing all the remarkable events that have happened. *Printed by* J. Astwood. Nov. 4, 1690.

1129b. Coffee-house morning post. Apr. 28, 1729.

1130. Colchester spie. 1648.

Collins's weekly journal. *See* Loyal observator revived; or, Gaylard's journal.

1131. Comical observer. No. 1, Nov. 7, 1704.

1132. Comick magazine; or, Compleat library of mirth. 1796.

1133. Commentator. 1720. s. w.

1133a. Compendio mercuriale. Feb. 24-29, 1691.

1134. Compleat courtier; or, The morals of Tacitus. 1700.

1134a. Compleat linguist; or, An universal grammar of all the considerable tongues in being. No. 6, for the months March, April, and May, 1720.

1135. Complete magazine. 1764.

1136. Comptroller. No. 1, Sept. 20, 1759.

1137. Condoler, 1709.

1138. Conjurer. Edinburgh, no. 11, Jan. 16, 1736.

1138a. Connaught gazette. Loughrea, 1797.

1138b. Connaught mercury; or, Universal register. Loughrea, no. 64, May 24, 1770.

1139. Constitutional chronicle. Bristol. 1780-82. w.

1140. Constitutional guardian. 1770.

1141. Constitutional letters. Edinburgh, 1792.

1142. Constitutional magazine; or, Complete treasure of politics and literature. 1768-69.

1142a. Continuation of certain speciall and remarkable passages, informed to the Parliament, from the army and otherwise from divers parts of the kingdome. Nos. 1-13, July 17–Sept. 17, 1647.

1143. Continuation of certaine speciall and remarkable passages. *Printed for* Marke Wallace and later for John White. No. 1, Oct. 14, 1642.

1143a. Continuation of certaine speciall and remarkable passages from both Houses of Parliament and other parts of the kingdome. *Printed for* John White. 3 nos., Nov. 11-24, 1642.

1143b. Continuation of certaine speciall and remarkable passages from both Houses of Parliament and other parts of the kingdome. *Printed for* I. Coule. Nov. 24, 1642.

1144. Continuation of our weekly news from the 30 of December to the 5 of January, printed for Mercurius Britannicus [Thomas Archer(?)]. No. 2, Jan. 5, 1625-26. Imperial and Spanish newes, printed by Mercurius Britannicus, 1626, may be part of this journal. *Cf.* Nichols, Literary anecdotes, IV, 39.

Continuation of remarkable passages. *See* Remarkable passages.

1146. Continuation of the true diurnall. No. 1, Aug. 15, 1642.

1147. Continuation of the true diurnall occurrences in Parliament. Edinburgh, 1642.

1147a. Continuation of the weekly occurrences in Parliament. May 16-23, 1642.

1148. Continuation of true and special passages. *Printed for* William Cook. No. 1, Sept. 29, 1642.

1149. Continued heads of perfect passages. 1649.

1150. Controller, being a sequel to the Examiner. J. Morphew. 1714-15. w.

1151. Convivial magazine and polite intelligencer. 1775.

1152. Corante; or, News from Italy, Germany, Hungaria, Polonia, France and Dutchland. Adrian Clarke. The Hague, Aug. 10, 1621.

[Coranto]. M. H. *See* Newes from the Low Countries.

1153. [Corantos of various titles]. *Printed by* George Veseler. Amsterdam, 1620-21.

1154. [Corantos of various titles]. Nathaniel Butter, alone or in collaboration with one or more of the following: Thomas Archer, Nicholas Bourne, Bartholomew Downes, and William Sheffard. 1621-32.

1155. [Corantos of various titles]. Broer Jonson. Amsterdam, 1621.

1156. [Corantos of various titles]. Thomas Archer, alone or with either Nicholas Bourne or Bartholomew Downes. 1622.

1157. [Corantos of various titles]. Nath. Newbery, alone or with William Sheffard. 1622.

1157a. Cork news letter. Cork, 1723-25.

1157b. Cork advertiser; or, Commercial advertiser. Cork, 1799.
1157c. Cork chronicle; or, Free intelligencer. Cork, 1764-68.
1157d. Cork chronicle; or, Universal register. Cork, 1764.
1157e. Cork courier. Cork, 1794.
1157f. Cork evening post. *Printed by* P. and G. Bagnell. Cork, 1755-74. s. w.
1157g. Cork gazette. Cork, 1793-94.
1157h. Cork gazetteer; or, General advertiser. Cork, 1789-97.
1157i. Cork general advertiser. Cork, 1776-78.
1157j. Cork herald; or, Munster advertiser. Cork, 1798.
1157k. Cork journal. Cork, 1778.
1157l. Cork packet. Cork, 1793.
1157m. Cork weekly journal. Cork, 1779-80.
1158. Cornucopia. 1766.
1159. Correspondence française; ou, Tableau de l'Europe. *Continued as* Correspondence politique; ou, Tableau de l'Europe (from 1793). *Ed.* J. G. Peltier. 1793-94. t. w.

Correspondence politique; ou, Tableau de l'Europe. *See* Correspondence française; ou, Tableau de l'Europe.

1160. Correspondent. 1731.
1161. Cosmopolitan. Oxford, 1788-(?). f.
1162. Cottager. No. 1, Mar. 17, 1761.
1163. Countrey foot-post. *Continued as* Countrey messenger (from no. 2). No. 1, Oct. 2, 1644.

Countrey messenger. *See* Countrey foot-post.

1164. Country common sense. Gloucester, 1739.
1165. Country gentleman. J. Roberts. 1726. s. w.
1165a. Country gentleman. *Printed by* G. Faulkner. Dublin, 1726.
1166. Country gentleman's courant; or, Universal intelligence. No. 1, Oct. 12, 1706-07.
1167. Country messenger; or, The faithful foot post. No. 1, Sept. 20, 1644.
1167a. Country oracle. *Published by* T. Cooper. 1741. w.
1168. County chronicle. 1788+.

1168a. County gentleman's courant. *Published by* Morphey. 1685.
1168c. County journal. Dublin, 1735.
1168d. Courier de Londres [in French]. (?)-1792(?). s. w.
1169. Courier politique et littéraire; or, French evening post. No. 17, Feb. 27, 1778.
1169a. Course of the exchange. 1720-55.
1169b. Court spy; including The Christian's gazette, and The lame post. John Dunton, 1713.
1170. Covent Garden chronicle. 1768.
1171. Covent Garden journal. 1749. m.
1171a. Covent Garden monthly recorder. 1792.
1172. Covent Garden magazine; or, The amorous repository. 1773.
1172a. Coventry mercury. Noah Rollason. Coventry, no. 2728 Apr. 16, 1792+. w.
1172b. Coventry, Birmingham, and Worcester chronicle. Coventry, v. 6, no. 289, Sept. 23, 1762-1763(?).
1173. Craftsman; or, Say's weekly journal. No. 649, Jan. 5, 1771+.
1176. Critical memoirs of the times. 1769.
1176a. Cruttwell's Sherborne journal. *Continued as* Sherborne journal (from ?); *as* Dorchester and Sherborne journal and western advertiser (from ?). Sherborne, 1764+.
1177. Cry from the wilderness. 1712.
1178. Culler. Glasgow, nos. 1-20, 1795. w.
1179. Cumberland chronicle. Whitehaven, 1776-78.
1180. Cumberland pacquet and Ware's Whitehaven advertiser. Whitehaven, 1775(?)+.
1181. Curiosity; or, Gentlemen and ladies repository. Lynn Regis, 1740.
1181a. Current domestick and foreign intelligence. *Printed by* George Croom. 1682.
1182. Curry-comb. Dublin, 1755.
1183. Daily benefactor. 1715.
1183a. Daily communicant. *Published by* P. Gilbourne. 1698.
1184. Daily intelligencer of court, city, and country. 1643.
1185. Daily oracle. M. Smith. Nos. 1-17, 1715. d. (to no. 10); t. w.

1186. Daily packet; or, The new London daily post. No. 1, Jan. 20, 1721.
1187. Daily proceedigs [*sic*]. No. 1, June 17, 1653.
1187a. Dalton's Dublin impartial news-letter. *Printed by* S. Dalton. Dublin, 1734.
1188. Dawks's news-letter. Nos. 277-513, Mar. 26, 1698–Nov. 16, 1706.
1189. Declaration collected out of the journals of both houses of Parliament. No. 1, Dec. 6, 1648.
1190. Delights for the ingenious; or, A monthly entertainment for the curious of both sexes. 1711.
1191. Democritus ridens; or, Comus and Momus. 1681.
1191a. Dependent free-thinker. J. Roberts. 1720.
1191b. Derby herald; or, Derby, Nottingham, & Leicester advertiser. *Published by* Charles Sambroke Ordoyno. Derby, 1792.
1192. Derby mercury. *Continued as* Drewry's Derby mercury (from 1769?). *Printed by* S. Drewry. Derby, 1732+. w.
1193. Derby postman. *Continued as* British spy; or, Derby postman (from 1726). *Printed by* S. Hodgkinson. Derby, 1719-31(?).
1193a. Derbyshire journal. Derby(?), 1738(?)–(?).
1194. Derrick's leisure hour. 1769.
Derry journal. *See* Londonderry journal.
1195. Detector. 1780.
1196. Detector. Salisbury, 1786-87.
1197. Detector. Dublin, nos. 1-36, Jan. 30–May 20, 1800.
1198. Devil. 1755.
1199. Diarie; or, An exact journall. No. 1, July 17, 1647.
1200. Diary. No. 1, Sept. 29, 1651.
1200a. Diary; or, An exact journall of the proceedings of the treaty betwixt the Parliament and the army. Nos. 1-2, July 17-29, 1647.
1200b. Dickson's news letter. *Printed for* C. Dickson. Dublin, 1727.
1201. Director. 1720-21.

1202. Diurnall and particula [sic] of the last weekes daily occurrents from his Majesty, in severall places. 1642.

1202a. Diurnall occurrences; or, Proceedings in the Parliament the last weeke. Nos. 1-3, Jan. 17-31, 1642.

1203. Diutinus Britanicus. *Continued as* Mercurius diutinus (not Britanicus) (from no. 3). 1646-47.

1203a. Diverting post. *Printed by* A. Rhames. Dublin, no. 5, Oct. 1, 1709.

1204. Diverting post. *Printed by* A. Rhames. Dublin, nos. 2-6, Oct. 18–Nov. 22, 1725. w.

1205. Doctor. 1718. s. w.

1205a. Doncaster journal. E. Sanderson. Doncaster, (?)-1792(?). w.

Dorchester and Sherborne journal and western advertiser. *See* Cruttwell's Sherborne journal.

1206. Dramatic review; or, Mirror of the stage. 1795.

1207. Dreamer. 1754.

Drewry's Derby mercury. *See* Derby mercury.

1207a. Drogheda newsletter. Drogheda, 1769 or 1770(?).

1207b. Drogheda journal; or, Meath and Louth advertiser. Drogheda, v. 15, no. 1378, Dec. 13, 1778-1797(?).

1208. Drumfries [sic] mercury. Dumfries, 1721. w.

1208b. Dublin castle. *Printed by* Edward Waters. Dublin, 1708.

1208c. Dublin chronicle. Dublin, v. 3, no. 204, Oct. 7, 1762.

1209. Dublin courant. *Printed by* A. Reilly. Dublin, nos. 1-613, Apr. 24, 1744–Mar. 24, 1750. s. w.

1209a. Dublin courant. *Printed by* Oliver Nelson. Dublin, 1740-49(?).

1210. Dublin courant, containing news both foreign and domestick. Dublin, nos. 245-997, Sept. 27, 1718–Dec. 11, 1725. s. w.

1211. Dublin courier. *Printed by* James Potts. Dublin, nos. 201-1423, Jan. 7, 1760–Dec. 30, 1766. s. w.

1212. Dublin daily advertiser. *Printed for* James Hamilton and Co., by Ebenezer Rider. Dublin, v. 1, nos. 8-50, Oct. 14–Dec. 2, 1736. d.

1213. Dublin evening packet. *Printed by* Alex McCullock. Dublin, v. 1-2, 1770-71.

1214. Dublin evening-post. *Printed by* S. Powell. Dublin, v. 1, no. 1, June 10, 1732+.

Dublin evening post. *See* Independent Irishman.

1214a. Dublin gazette. Dublin, 1689(?).

1215. Dublin gazette. *Printed by* Edw. Sandys. Dublin, no. 129, July 16, 1706+. s. w.

1215a. Dublin gazette; or, Weekly courant. *Printed by* Thomas Hume. Dublin, 1703(?)-28(?).

Dublin impartial news-letter. *See* Walsh's Dublin weekly impartial news-letter.

1216. Dublin intelligence. *Printed by* Andrew Crook. Dublin, nos. 4-152, Oct. 21, 1690–Oct. 14, 1693.

1216a. Dublin intelligence, published by authority. *Printed by* John Ray. Dublin, 1690.

1216b. Dublin intelligence. *Published by* R. Thornton. Dublin, 1691.

1216c. Dublin intelligence. *Printed by* James Carson. Dublin, 1724.

1217. Dublin intelligence, containing a full and impartial account of the foreign and domestick news. *Printed by* Francis Dickson (to 1712); *by* R. Dickson and G. Needham (to 1725). Dublin, nos. 491-2455, Aug. 10, 1708–Dec. 28, 1725. s. w.

1218. Dublin intelligencer. *Printed by* James Hoey. Dublin, June 17, 1756.

1218a. Dublin literary journal. Dublin, no. 1, Oct. 1734.

1218b. Dublin journal, with advices foreign and domestick. *Printed by* Edward Waters. Dublin, 1729.

1218c. Dublin joker. Dublin, 1753.

1219. Dublin magazine. Dublin, 1798-1800.

1219a. Dublin mercury. Dublin, no. 1, Jan. 1723.

1219b. Dublin mercury. *Printed by* S. Powell. Dublin, 1704-06.

1220. Dublin mercury. *Printed by* Thomas Bacon. Dublin, nos. 2-71, Jan. 26–Sept. 25, 1742. s. w.

1221. Dublin mercury. *Printed by* James Hoey, Jr. Dublin, nos. 1-1006, Mar. 18, 1766–Apr. 1, 1773. s. w.

1222. Dublin mercury, containing a full and impartial account of the foreign and domestick news. *Printed for* A. Thiboust. Dublin, 1722(?)-24. Also supplements. 1723-24.

1222b. Dublin packet. *Printed by* James Hoey. Dublin, 1730.

1222c. Dublin post boy. *Printed by* James Carson. Dublin, 1729-30.

1223. Dublin post-boy. *Printed by* James Hoey. Dublin, July 25-Aug. 30, 1734. w.

1224. Dublin post-man, containing foreign and domestick news. *Printed by* G. Needham. Dublin, nos. 34-737, Dec. 14, 1724-Dec. 20, 1725. s. w.

1224a. Dublin Society. Transactions. Dublin, 1800+.

1224b. Dublin Society's weekly observations. Dublin, nos. 1-52, Jan. 4, 1737-Apr. 4, 1738(?).

1225. Dublin spectator. Dublin, v. 1, no. 38, June 1, 1768.

1225a. Dublin spy. Dublin, 1753-54.

1226. Dublin weekly intelligence, containing a full and impartial account, of the foreign and domestick news. *Printed by* E. Waters. Dublin, 1710.

1227. Dublin weekly journal. *Printed by* James Carson. Dublin, 1725-33(?).

1227a. Dublin weekly journal. Dublin, v. 10, no. 7, Feb. 14, 1795.

1228. Dublin weekly magazine. Dublin, 1778.

1229. Dumfries weekly journal. *Ed.* Provost Jackson. Dumfries, 1777-1800(?). w.

1230. Dumfries weekly magazine. Dumfries, v. 1-18, Mar. 16, 1773-June 24, 1777. w.

1231. Dundee magazine and journal of the times. Dundee, Jan 1799+. m.

1232. Dundee mail. Dundee, 1798.

1232a. Dundee register of merchants and trades . . . for the year 1782. Dundee, 1782.

1233. Dundee repository of political and miscellaneous information. Dundee, Feb. 15, 1793-Feb. 21, 1794.

1234. Dundee weekly magazine; or, A history of the present times. Dundee, Aug. 11, 1775-1778. w.

1235. Dungannon weekly magazine. Dungannon, 1800.

1235a. Durham courant. Durham, (?)-1736(?).

1236. Dutch intelligencer. No. 1, Sept. 8, 1652.

1237. Dutch prophet; or, The devil of a conjuror. No. 1, Dec. 3, 1700. w.
1238. Dutch spy. No. 1, Mar. 25, 1652.
1239. East India examiner. 1766.
1240. East India observer. 1766.
1240a. Echo; or, Impartial repeater. J. Roberts. 1721. w.
1241. Eclipses; or, Luminaries involved in darkness: an universal repository for enigmatical . . . questions. Newmarket, 1795.
1242. Edinburgh clerical review; or, Weekly report of the different sermons preached every Sunday by the established clergy of Edinburgh. Edinburgh, 1799.
1243. Edinburgh courant. Daniel Defoe. Edinburgh, 1710.
1244. Edinburgh courant revived. Edinburgh, 1707.
1245. Edinburgh eighth-day magazine. Edinburgh, 1779-80.
1246. Edinburgh evening post. Edinburgh, 1780-81.
1247. Edinburgh flying post. Edinburgh, 1707.
1248. Edinburgh flying post. Edinburgh, 1708-10(?). t. w.
1249. Edinburgh gazette. Edinburgh, 1680-(?).
1250. Edinburgh gazette. Edinburgh, 1780.
1251. Edinburgh gazette; or, Scot's postman. Edinburgh, 1714-15.
1252. Edinburgh gazetteer. Edinburgh, 1792-93.
1253. Edinburgh herald. *Continued as* Edinburgh herald and chronicle (from Jan. 2, 1797). t. w.
1254. Edinburgh magazine. Edinburgh, 1757-62.
1255. Edinburgh monthly intelligencer. Edinburgh, no. 10 (first no.), 1792-(?).
1256. Edinburgh museum; or, North-British miscellany. Edinburgh, v. 1-2, Jan. 1763–Dec. 1764. m.
1257. Edinburgh repository for polite literature. Edinburgh, 1792.
1258. Edinburgh repository; or, Fortnight's magazine. Edinburgh, 1774.

Edinburgh weekly journal, 1757(?)-75(?). *See* Weekly journal (no. 2128).

1259. Edinburgh weekly journal. Edinburgh, 1798+.

E. Johnson's British gazette. *See* British gazette and Sunday monitor.

1259a. England an unlucky soil for Popery. No. 1, Jan. 10, 1689.

1259b. England's monitor; or, The history of separation. No. 1, Mar. 30, 1682.

1259c. Edward Waters' Dublin intelligence. Dublin, 1708.

1259d. Elixir. Nos. 8-21, Jan. 26–Mar. 2, 1706.

1260. England's remembrancer. No. 1, Jan. 14, 1646.

1261. Englands remembrancer of London's integritie. No. 1, Jan. 19, 1647.

1262. English and French journal. No. 25, Aug. 15, 1723. English and French in parallel columns.

1263. English courant. 1695.

1264. English examiner. 1715.

1264a. English Gusman; or, Captain Hilton's memoirs. No. 1, Jan. 27, 1683.

1265. English intelligence. Thomas Burrell. 1679-(?).

1266. English Lucian; or, Weekly discoveries of the witty intrigues, comical passages and remarkable transactions in town and country. 1698. w.

1267. English lyceum. 1787-88.

1268. English magazine, and commercial repository. 1796-97.

1269. Englishman. 1733-(?). s. w.

1270. Englishman. 1737(?)-40(?). w.

1271. Englishman. 1762+.

1272. Englishman's journal. 1722.

1273. English Martial. 1699.

1274. English post. 1641(?).

1275. English post. 1700-08.

1276. English post, giving an authentick account of the transactions of the world, foreign and domestick. *Continued as* English post; with news foreign and domestick (from no. 28, Dec. 16, 1700). Nos. 1-383(?), 1700-03. t. w.

1277. English spy; or, The weekly observator. No. 1, Aug. 18, 1699.

1277a. Enniss chronicle and Clare advertiser. Ennis, 1783-1800(?).

1278. Entertainer. 1745.
1279. Entertaining correspondent. 1739.
1280. Entertaining correspondent; or, Curious relations. 1783.
1281. Epitome of the weekly news. 1679.

Esdall's news-letter. *See* General news-letter.

1284. Essex mercury; or, Colchester weekly journal. Colchester, no. 173, July 3, 1736.
1284a. État present de l'Europe, suivant les gazettes et autres avis d'Angleterre, France, Hollande, &c. Guy Miege. No. 1, Sept. 25, 1682.
1285. European repertory. (?)-1800.
1285a. Evangelical magazine; or, Christian library. Newcastle-upon-Tyne, 1777-78.
1286. Evening chronicle. *Printed by* F. Ross. Dublin, no. 50, March 31, 1784.
1286a. Evening courant. No. 5, July 26, 1711.
1287. Evening entertainment. Nos. 3-4, Jan. 27-30, 1727.

Evening general post. *See* General post.

1288. Evening herald; or, General advertiser. *Published by* R. Bett and Co. Dublin, nos. 19-587. May 17, 1786–Dec. 31, 1789.
1289. Evening journal. 1727-28.

Evening post; or, The new Edinburgh gazette. *See* New Edinburgh gazette.

1290. Evening weekly pacquet. No. 9, Mar. 3, 1716.
1290a. Every man's journal. Dublin, nos. 1-5, 1765.
1290b. Exact account of the daily proceedings in Parliament. No. 56, Jan. 13, 1660.
1291. Exact and true diurnall. No. 1, Aug. 15, 1642.
1291a. Exact coranto. 1642.
1292. Exact diurnal. 1644.
1293. Examiner. No. 1, Sept. 14, 1715.
1294. Exchange evening post. 1721.

Exeter evening post; or, The west country advertiser. [Subtitle changed several times.] *See* Exeter mercury; or, West-country advertiser.

1296. Exeter gazette. S. Woolmer. Exeter, (?)-1792(?). w.
Exeter journal (Farley). *See* Farley's Exeter journal.
1296a. Exeter journal. E. Grigg. Exeter, (?)-1792(?). w.
1296b. Exeter mercury; or, West-country advertiser. *Continued as* Exeter evening post; or, The west country advertiser (from no. 98, July 11, 1765); *as* Exeter evening post; or, The Plymouth and Cornish courant (from no. 99, July 18, 1765); *as* Exeter evening post; or, Plymouth and Cornish advertiser (from no. 211, Sept. 18, 1767); *as* Trewman's Exeter evening post; or, Plymouth and Cornish advertiser (from no. 293, Apr. 28, 1769); *as* Trewman's Exeter flying post; or, Plymouth and Cornish advertiser (from no. 380, Dec. 28, 1770). Exeter, no. 1, Sept. 2, 1763+.
1297. Exeter mercury; or, Weekly intelligence. S. Farley. Exeter, 1714-25(?).
1297a. Exeter mercury; or, West country advertiser. W. Andrews and R. Trewman. Exeter, 1763-(?).
1297b. Exeter post boy. Exeter, 1711.
1298. Exhortation to the inhabitants of the south parish of Glasgow, and the hearers in the college kirk. Glasgow, v. 1-2, Sept. 26, 1750–Apr. 10, 1751.
1298a. Express and evening chronicle. No. 439, July 6-8, 1797.
1298b. Express and the London herald. *Printed by* T. Smith. No. 1324, Aug. 27-29, 1799. Perhaps a continuation of no. 1298a.
1299. Exshaw's magazine. Dublin, 1741-93.
1300. Fairy tatler. No. 9, Feb. 3, 1722.
1301. Faithful collections. 1715.
1302. Faithfull scout. *Continued as* National scout (from no. [?], July 16, 1659); *as* Loyall scout (from no. [12], July 22, 1659). 1659-60.
1303. Faithful mercury, imparting news foreign and domestick, 1669.
1305. Faithful scout. *Continued as* Armies scout (from no. 115, Apr. 30, 1653?); *as* Faithful scout (from no. 115 [*sic*], June 10, 1653). 1651-55.
1306. Fall of Britain. 1776-77. w.
1306a. Family library. (?)-1791(?).

1307. Farley's Bath Journal. Bath, 1756. w.
1307a. Farley's Bristol advertiser. *Printed by* Felix Farley & Co. Bristol, 1744(?)-46. Published alternately every other week with Felix Farley's Bristol journal.

Farley's Bristol journal. *See* F. Farley's Bristol journal.

Farley's Bristol news-paper. *See* Sam Farley's Bristol post man.

1308. Farley's Exeter journal. Exeter, 1722(?)-28. w.
1308a. Farrago. 1792.
1309. Fashionable magazine; or, Lady and gentleman's recorder of new fashions. 1786.
1310. Fashions of London and Paris. 1795-1800.
1311. Fast. 1757.
1313. Faulkner's Dublin post boy, being the most impartial advices both foreign and domestick. *Printed by* George Faulkner. Dublin, 1725-32(?).
1314. Felix Farley's Bristol journal. Felix Farley. Bristol, 1752+.
1315. Female guardian. 1787.
1316. Female mentor. 1793-98.

Ferrar's Limerick chronicle. *See* Limerick chronicle, 1768+.

1316a. F. Farley's Bristol journal. *Continued as* Farley's Bristol journal (from Jan. 16, 1748); *as* Bristol journal (from 1749); *as* Sarah Farley's Bristol journal (from 1777). Bristol, no. 17, Mar. 24, 1744-1793. Till 1746 published alternately, every other week, with Farley's Bristol advertiser.
1317. First decade of useful observations. No. 1, June 28, 1649.
1318. Flowers of Parnassus; or, Lady's miscellany. 1736.
1319. Flying eagle. 1652-53.
1320. Flying post. No. 1, May 10, 1644.
1321. Flying post. Dublin, 1722-24.
1321a. Flying post. *Printed by* Edward Waters. Dublin, 1729.
1322. Flying post. Dublin, 1744.
1322a. Flying post and medley. Daniel Defoe. July 27–August 21, 1714. t. w.
1323. Flying-post from Paris and Amsterdam. 1695-96. s. w.

1323a. Flying post man; or, The Dublin post man. *Printed by* Nicholas Hussey. Dublin, 1729.

1323b. Flying post; or, The post master. Dublin, 1699-1709.

1324. Flying post; or, The post-master. *Printed by* F. Dickson and S. Powell. Dublin, 1705-10.

1325. Flying-post; or, The post-master's news. Dublin, 1709-10.

1326. Flying-post; or, The weekly medley. *Continued as* Weekly medley (from Aug. 2, 1729); *as* Weekly medley and literary journal (from Nov. 1, 1729). 1728-30. w.

1327. Foreign and domestick news; with the pacquet boat from Holland and Flanders. No. 14, July 1, 1695.

1328. Foreign medical review. 1779.

1329. Foreign post, with domestick news. 1697.

1331. Freeholder. No. 7, Jan. 13, 1716.

1333. Freeholder and weekly packet. Edinburgh, 1716.

1334. French intelligencer. 1651.

1335. French occurrences. 1652.

1336. Friend. 1755. w.

1337. Friend. 1760. s. w.

1339. Friend, a weekly essay. 1796.

1340. Friendly couriere. 1711.

1341. Gazette. *Continued as* Norwich gazette; or, The loyal packet (from ?). Norwich, 1706(?)-47.

1342. Gazette-à-la-mode; or, Tom Brown's ghost. 1709.

1343. Gazette de Guernsey. St. Peter Port(?), 1791+.

1344. Gazette de l'Île de Jersey. St. Hélier(?). 1786+.

1345. Geirgrawn. Chester, 1796.

1346. General account. No. 1, Mar. 31, 1645.

1346a. General advertiser. *Printed by* A. McCulloch. Dublin, 1754.

1347. General advertiser. *Continued as* Gore's general advertiser (from ?). Liverpool, v. 12, 1777+.

1348. General Baptist magazine. 1798-1800.

1348a. General correspondent. Dublin, 1740.

1349. General evening post. *Printed by* J. Cavendish (to May

29, 1784); *by* John Fleming. Dublin, v. [1], no. 107–v. 4, no. 510, Jan. 3, 1782–July 31, 1784.

1350. General history of the principal discoveries and improvements in useful arts. Defoe. 1726-27. m.

1351. General magazine; or, Epitome of useful knowledge. 1793.

1352. General news from all parts of Christendom. No. 1, May 6, 1646.

1353. General news-letter. Dublin. *Probably continued as* Esdall's news-letter (from 1746). Dublin, 1744-55. s. w. *Cf.* no. 807.

1354. General post. 1711-(?).

1355. General post. No. 1, Jan. 15, 1716.

1356. General post. *Continued as* Evening general post (from no. 13). No. 1, Mar. 15, 1716-(?).

1357. General post office advertiser. Dublin, 1739(?)-41.

1358. General postscript. 1709.

1359. General remark on trade. *Printed by* R. Everingham. No. 9, Nov. 20, 1705. Perhaps continued as General remark on trade, set forth by Mr. Povey.

1360. General remark on trade, set forth by Mr. Povey, undertaker of the traders exchange-house in Hatton Garden. *Continued us* General remark on trade: with an extract of foreign news, and observations on publick affairs (from no. 214); *as* General remark on trade: with curious observations done by the ingenious (from no. 240). *Printed by* Matthew Jenour. Nos. 213-50, July 7–Oct. 1, 1707. t. w. *Cf.* no. 1359.

1361. General review of foreign literature. 1775.

1362. Generous advertiser; or, Weekly information of trade and business. 1707. s. w. [*sic*]

1363. Generous London morning advertiser. *Continued as* Rayner's London morning advertiser (from 1742). 1742.

1365. Genius of Kent; or, Country magazine. Canterbury and Margate, 1792-95. m.

1367. Gentleman and lady's museum. 1777.

1368. Gentleman and lady's pocket register; or, Fortnigt's [*sic*] intelligencer. Edinburgh, 1780.

1369. Gentleman's journal for the war. 1693.

1369a. Gentleman's magazine and monthly oracle. *Printed by* J. Ilive. 1736-38(?). *Cf.* Athenæum, Oct. 26, 1889, p. 560.

1370. Gentleman's musical magazine. 1788.

1371. Geographical intelligence for the better understanding of foreign news. No. 1, June 19, 1689.

1372. Geographical magazine; or, The universe displayed. Dublin, 1790-92.

1372b. George Swiney's Corke journal. Cork, 1754-69.

1373. Glasgow advertiser. *Continued as* Glasgow advertiser and evening intelligencer (from ?); *as* Glasgow advertiser (from 1794). Glasgow, 1783+.

1373a. Glasgow advertiser. *Continued as* Glasgow advertiser and herald (from ?); *as* Glasgow herald (from ?). Glasgow, 1777-(?). s. w.

1374. Glasgow courant, containing the occurrences both at home and abroad. *Continued as* West country intelligence (from no. 3). Glasgow, no. 1, Nov. 14, 1715-16.

Glasgow herald. *See* Glasgow advertiser.

1375. Glasgow journal. Glasgow, 1729+.

1376. Glasgow magazine. Glasgow, 1770. f.

1377. Glasgow mercury. Glasgow, v. 1-20, Jan. 8, 1778–Sept. 27, 1796. w.

1378. Glasgow museum; or, Weekly instructor. Glasgow, Jan. 11–July 10, 1773. w.

1379. Glasgow united magazine. Glasgow, 1773.

1380. Glasgow universal magazine of knowledge and pleasure. Glasgow, Aug. 13, 1772–Feb. 1773. w.

1381. Glasgow weekly chronicle. Glasgow, 1766.

1382. Glasgow weekly history relating to the history of the gospel at home and abroad. Glasgow, 1743.

1383. Gleaner. Dublin, 1793.

1384. Gleaner. Edinburgh, 1795.

1384a. Gloucester gazette. Gloucester, 1788+.

1384b. Gloucester gazette; and South Wales, Worcester and Wiltshire general advertiser. Gloucester, v. 2, no. 100, July 8, 1784-1796(?).

1385. Goggin's Ulster magazine, a weekly journal. S. Goggin. Monaghan(?), 1798(?)-99(?).

1386. Good news for England. 1645.

Gore's general advertiser. *See* General advertiser.

1387. Grand diurnall of the passages in Parliament. No. 1, Nov. 28, 1642.

1390. Great Britain's painful messenger. No. 1, Aug. 16, 1649.

1390a. Great news from Ireland, being motives of encouragement for the officers and soldiers who shall serve in the present war in Ireland. No. 1, Apr. 11, 1689.

1391. Greenwich observatory. Astronomical observations made at the royal observatory. 1750+.

1392. Grouler; or, Diogenes robb'd of his tub. 1711.

1393. Grumbler, by Squire Gizzard. 1715. w.; s. w.

1393a. Guide into the knowledge of publick affairs. 1728.

Haerlem courant. *See* Paris gazette.

1394. Halfpenny London journal; or, The British oracle. No. 10, Jan. 10, 1725.

1394a. Hampshire chronicle; or, Portsmouth, Winchester, and Southampton gazette. Southampton; Portsmouth (from 1780), 1778-85.

1394b. Hampshire telegraph and Sussex chronicle, and general advertiser for Hants, Sussex, Surrey, Dorset, and Wilts. Portsmouth, 1799+.

1395. Hampshire journal. J. Robbins. Winchester, (?)-1792(?). w.

1396. Hanover journal. 1720.

Harding's Dublin impartial news letter. *See* Harding's weekly impartial news letter.

1397. Harding's weekly impartial news letter. *Probably continued as* Harding's Dublin impartial news letter (from 1724). Dublin, 1723-25. s. w. [*sic*]

1398. Harlem currant. No. 2, Feb. 19, 1689.

1399. Harlem's courant. Haarlem, no. 1, May 28, 1695. A translation.

1399a. Harrop's Manchester mercury. *Continued as* Harrop's Manchester mercury and general advertiser (from no. 9). Manchester, no. 1, Mar. 3, 1752-64(?).

1399b. Harp of Erin. Cork, 1798.

1399c. Harrison's Derby journal. *Continued as* Harrison's Derby & Nottingham journal; or, Midland advertiser (from Nov.[?], 1776). *Printed and published by* James Harrison. Derby, no. 1, Aug. 2, 1776-1781(?).

1400. Heads of a diarie. 1648-49.

1400a. Heads of all the proceedings in both Houses of Parliament. *Printed for* J. Smith and A. Coe. May 23-30, 1642.

1401. Heads of chiefe passages in Parliament. *Continued as* Kingdoms weekly account of heads (from no. 4). 1648.

1402. Heads of some notes of the citie scout. *Continued as* City scout (from no. 11). 1645.

1404. Heaven and Hell magazine. 1790-91.

1405. Help to history; or, A short memorial of the most material matters. 1711-14.

1406. Heraclitus ridens: a discourse between Jest and Earnest concerning the times. *Sold by* W. Boreham. 1718.

1407. Heraclitus ridens, in a dialogue between Jest and Earnest, concerning the times. 1703-04.

1407a. Herald of literature; or, A review of the most considerable publications that will be made in the course of the ensuing winter. 1784.

1407b. Herald. (?)-1792(?). d.

1407c. Herald. Clonmel, 1800.

1407d. Hereford journal. Hereford, 1713-(?).

1408. Hermit. 1715.

1409. Hermit, by way of short essays upon several subjects. 1711-12.

1409a. Hibernian chronicle. *Printed by* William Flynn. Cork, 1768+.

1410. Hibernian journal. Dublin, v. 3, 1773+.

1410a. Hibernian morning post; or, Literary chronicle. Cork, 1776.

1413. Highland and agricultural society of Scotland. Transactions. 1799+.

1414. Highland gentleman's magazine. Edinburgh, 1751.

1415. Historian. 1712.

1416. Historical account of books and transactions in the learned world. 1688.
1416a. Historical and political mercury. 1759.
1417. Historical list of all horse matches . . . with a list also of the principal cock matches. J. Cheny. 1729-49.
1418. Historical list of horse matches. B. Walker. 1770-71.
1419. Historical list of horse matches . . . cock-matches. R. Heber. 1753-69.
1420. Historical, political, and literary register for 1769. 1770(?).
1421. Historical register; or, Edinburgh monthly intelligencer. *Continued as* Universal monthly intelligencer (from 1792). Edinburgh, 1791-92.
1422. History of cradle-convulsions, vulgarly black and white fits; or, Monthly observations on the weekly bills of mortality. No. 1, Sept. 1701.
1423. Hive; a hebdomadal selection of literary tracts. 1789.
1425. Honest true Briton. 1724.
1426. Hue and crie after Mercurius elencticus, Britannicus, melancholicus, and aulicus. 1651.
1427. Hull advertiser. Hull, 1794+.
1428. Hull packet. Hull, 1787+.
1431. Humorist's magazine. 1787-(?).
1433. Humours of the age; or, Dean Swift's evening post. 1738.
1434. Hunter's Dublin chronicle; or, Universal journal for the year 1762. Dublin, v. 3, no. 204, Oct. 7, [1762].
1435. Hypocrite unmasked. 1780. w.
1435a. Idler. *Printed by* George Bennett. Cork, no. 1, Feb. 1, 1714.
1436. Impartial intelligencer. No. 2, July 12, 1653.
Impartial occurrences foreign and domestick. *See* Pue's occurrences.
1437. Impartial review; or, Literary journal. No. 1, Nov. 1, 1759.
Impartial scout. *See* Scout.
1438. Important Protestant mercury. No. 66, Dec. 9, 1681.
1439. Independent chronicle; and universal advertiser. Dublin, no. 1, Mar. 1, 1777.

1440. Independent chronicle; or, The freeholders evening post. W. Bingley. No. 1, Sept. 29, 1769-(?). t. w.
1441. Independent Irishman. *Continued as* Dublin evening post (from 1771?). Dublin, 1770-71.
1442. Independent London journal. 1735-36. w.
1444. Infallible astrologer. *Continued as* Astrological observator (from no. 16, Feb. 17, 1701); *as* Jesting astrologer (from no. 17). 1700-01. w.
1445. Informator rusticus; or, The country intelligencer. No. 1, Nov. 3, 1643.
1446. Inquisitor. No. 1, June 26, 1711.
1447. Inquisitor. 1724.
1448. Inquisitor, containing a full answer to the Hyp-doctor. 1731.
1448a. Inspector. Dublin, 1748.
1449. Instructor. 1715.
1450. Instructor. 1724. w.
1451. Intelligence. J. Macock. 1666.
1452. Intelligence domestick and foreign. B. Harris. 1695.
1453. Intelligence of the civil war in France. No. 1, May 17, 1652.
1454. Investigator. No. 321, 1754.
1456. Invisible spy. 1759.
1457. Ipswich gazette. Ipswich, 1720(?)-37. w.
1459. Ipswich magazine. Ipswich, 1799.
1460. Irish courant; or, The weekly packet of advice from Ireland. No. 1, April 4, 1690.
1461. Irish mercury, monethly communicating all true intelligence within the dominion of Ireland. Cork; rep. London, 1650.
1462. Irish monthly mercury. Cork; rep. London, no. 1, Feb. 6, 1650.
1463. Januaries account, giving a full and true relation of the remarkable passages of that month. *Printed for* Richard Harper. Jan. 1645.
1465. Jester's magazine; or, The monthly merrymaker. 1765-66.

Jesting astrologer. *See* Infallible astrologer.

1466. Jesuit. 1783.
1467. Jesuita vapulans; or, A whip for the fool's back, and a gag for his foul mouth. 1681.
1468. Jesuite. 1719.
1469. Jockey's intelligencer; or, Weekly advertisements of horses and second-hand coaches to be bought or sold. 1683.
1470. Jones's evening news-letter. No. 1, Oct. 29, 1716. t. w.
1471. Jordan's parliamentary journal for the year 1793. 1794(?).
1472. Jos. Bliss's Exeter post-boy. Exeter, no. 211, May 4, 1711. Perhaps continued as Protestant mercury (cf. no. 1910).
1473. Journal Britannique. Matthew Maty. 1750-55.
1474. Journall of Parliament. 1648.
1475. Journal of a learned and political club. 1738.
1476. Jovial mercury. 1693.
1477. Juvenile library: the juvenile encyclopædia. 1800+.
1478. Juvenile magazine. 1788.
1479. Juvenile olio. 1796.
1480. Kelso mail. Kelso, 1797+.
1480a. Kendal courant. Kendal, 1731.
1480b. Kendal weekly mercury. Kendal, no. 427, Mar. 5, 1742. w.
1480c. Kentish herald. Canterbury(?), 1792.
1481. Kentish post; or, The Canterbury news letter. Canterbury, 1717-68(?). s. w.
1481a. Kerry evening post. Tralee, 1774.
1482. Kingdome's weekly post. 1643-44.
1483. Kingdom's faithful and impartial scout. No. 1, Feb. 9, 1649.
1484. Kingdom's faithful post. 1649.
1485. Kingdoms intelligencer of the affairs now in agitation in Scotland, England, and Ireland. . . . Edinburgh, Oct. 30, 1661-1668(?). w. Started as a rep. of the London paper by that name, but apparently continued independently after 1663.

Kingdoms weekly account of heads. *See* Heads of chiefe passages in Parliament.

1486. Kingdom's weekly post. 1645.

1487. Kingdom's weekly post. No. 1, Jan. 5, 1648.
1488. Knight-errant. 1729. w.
Lacedemonian mercury. *See* London mercury. 1692.
1489. Ladies journal. 1727. w.
1489a. Ladies' magazine. No. 1, Oct. 1759.
1490. Ladies mercury. No. 1, Feb. 18, 1693.
1491. Lady and gentleman's scientifical repository. Newark, 1782-84.
1492. Lady's curiosity; or, Weekly Apollo. 1752.
1493. Lady's drawing-room. 1744.
1494. Lady's magazine; or, Polite companion for the fair sex. 1760-63.
1496. Lady's musical magazine; or, Monthly repository of new vocal music. 1788. m.
1497. Lady's new and elegant pocket magazine. 1795.
1498. Lady's weekly magazine, published under the direction of Mrs. Penelope Pry. 1747.
1499. Lantern. Dublin, nos. 1-6, Feb. 26–Mar. 9, 1799. t. w.
1500. Latest remarkable truths. 1642.
1501. Laughing mercury; or, True and perfect news from the Antipodes. 1652.
Laughing mercury. *See* Mercurius Democritus, 1652-53.
1502. Lawyer's magazine. 1773.
1503. Leeds mercury. Leeds, 1718-20(?). *Cf.* no. 366.
1504a. Leicester chronicle. J. Ireland. Leicester, (?)-1792(?). w.
1504b. Leicester herald. Richard Phillips. Leicester, 1790-95(?).
1505. Letters of the critical club. Edinburgh, 1738. m.
1506. Limerick chronicle. Ferrar. Limerick, 1768+. s. w.
1507. Limerick chronicle. *Continued as* Watson's Limerick chronicle (from no. 3061, Jan. 11, 1794); *as* Limerick chronicle (from 1795). Andrew Watson. Limerick, v. 23, no. 2260, Apr. 26, 1790-1796(?).
1507a. Limerick herald. Limerick, 1787.
1507b. Limerick herald and Munster advertiser. *Printed by* Robert Law. Limerick, 1788-89.

1507c. Limerick journal. *Printed by* Edward Flynn. Limerick, 1787-91(?).

1507d. Limerick magazine. Limerick, 1752.

1508. Limerick weekly magazine; or, Miscellaneous repository. Limerick, 1790.

1508a. Lincoln gazette; or, Weekly intelligencer. Lincoln, 1729.

1508b. Linx Brittanicus. 1648.

1510. Literary mirror. Montrose, 1793+.

1511. Literary miscellany. 1756-57.

1512. Literary museum; a weekly magazine. Belfast, 1793. w.

1512a. Literary review. 1794-95.

1513. Little-Compton scourge; or, The anti-courant. *Printed for* J. Franklin. Boston, Aug. 10, 1721.

1514. Liverpool advertiser, Liverpool, 1756-(?).

1515. Liverpool courant. Liverpool, no. 18, July 18, 1712(?).

1515a. Liverpool general advertiser. Liverpool, no. 1, Dec. 27, 1765-92(?).

1515b. Liverpool phœnix. R. Ferguson. Liverpool, (?)-1792(?). w.

1516. Liverpool trade list. Liverpool, 1798+.

1516a. Liverpool weekly herald. H. Hodgson. Liverpool, (?)-1792(?). w.

1517. Lloyd's list. 1762+.

1519. Lloyd's news. 1696.

1520. Loiterer; or, Universal essayist. 1796.

1521. London daily advertiser and literary gazette. 1751-53.

1521a. London crier. 1733.

1521b. Londonderry journal and general advertiser. *Continued as* Londonderry journal, and Donegal and Tyrone advertiser (from v. 21, 1793?). Londonderry, no. 1, June 3, 1772-1800(?).

1521c. London chronicle. Dublin, 1758.

1522. London gazetteer. 1749(?)-51(?).

1522a. London herald and evening post. Nos. 400-02, Feb. 9-16, 1799.

1522b. London journal and country craftsman. Nos. 34-46, Dec. 24, 1743-Mar. 17, 1744.

1523. London mercury. No. 20, June 13, 1682.
1524. London mercury. *Continued as* Lacedemonian mercury (from no. 9). Thomas Brown. 1692.
1525. London mercury; or, Great Britain's weekly journal. No. 1, Mar. 14, 1719.

London mercury; or, Great Britain's weekly journal (1721). *See* Penny weekly journal; or, Saturday's entertainment.

1525a. London mercury; or, Mercure de Londres. No. 1, June 3, 1696.
1526. London mercury, published for the promoting of trade. 1695-97.
1527. London morning penny advertiser. *Continued as* London morning advertiser (from no. 47, May 5, 1742). J. Nicholson. 1742-43. *Cf.* no. 903a.
1528. London news letter. 1695-96.
1529. London post. 1646-47.
1529a. London post. Nos. 18-43, Apr. 6–June 6, 1705.
1530. London post. 1715-16.
1531. London post. No. 1, Mar. 31, 1716.
1532. London post. 1722.
1532a. London postman; or, A supplement to the Dublin intelligence. *Printed by* J. Carson. Dublin, nos. 25-50, Mar. 21, 1722–May 21, 1724.
1533. London post; or, Tradesman's intelligencer. No. 48, July 19, 1717.

London post, with intelligence foreign and domestick. *See* London slip of news, both foreign and domestick.

1534. London post, with the best account of the whole week's news, foreign and domestick; with room left to write into the country without the charge of double postage. No. 1, Jan. 15, 1716.
1535. London post; with the newest intelligence, both foreign and domestick. No. 1, May 17, 1697.
1536. London price current. Nos. 700-1228, 1789-99.
1537. London recorder. 1783+. Amalgamated with Sunday reformer and universal register in 1796.
1538. London review. (?)-1800.
1539. London's diurnall. 1660.

1540. London slip of news, both foreign and domestick. *Continued as* London post, with intelligence foreign and domestick (from no. 2). 1699-1705.
1541. London spy reviv'd. 1736-38(?). t. w.
1542. London terrae filius. 1707-08.
1542a. Looking-glass for the Mirror. Dublin, no. 1, July 1751. *Cf.* no. 1676a.
1542b. Lord's Munster herald or general advertiser. Cashel, 1788.
1543. Loyal intelligencer. No. 73, Jan. 30, 1654.
1544. Loyal intelligencer. 1678.
1544a. Loyal intelligencer; or, Lincoln, Rutland, Leicester, Cambridge and Stamford advertiser. Stamford, no. 65, June 10, 1794.

Loyall scout. *See* Faithfull scout, 1659-60.

1545. Loyal messenger. No. 1, Aug. 10, 1653.
1546. Loyal messenger; or, Newes from Whitehall. No. 4, Apr. 10, 1654.
1547. Loyal observator. No. 1, Jan. 12, 1704.
1548. Loyal observator revived; or, Gaylards journal. *Continued as* Collins's weekly journal (from no. 27). 1722-23.
1549. Loyal post; with foreign and inland intelligence. No. 1, Nov. 23, 1705.
1550. Loyal scout. No. 1, Dec. 26, 1659.
1550a. Luckman and Sketchley's Coventry gazette and Birmingham chronicle. Coventry, no. 233, Sept. 10, 1761-1763(?). w.
1551. Ludlow post-man; or, The weekly journal. Ludlow, 1719-20.
1552. Lynx. 1796.
1553. Magazine a la mode; or, Fashionable miscellany. 1777.
1554. Magazin de l'Île de Jersey. St. Hélier(?), 1784.
1555. Magazin du monde politique, galant et littéraire; or, The gentleman and lady's magazine ... in French and English. 1776.
1556. Magee's weekly packet; or, Hope's lottery journal, of news, politics and literature. Dublin, 1777-93.
1556a. Magazine of ants; or, Pismire journal. James Murray. Newcastle-upon-Tyne, 1777.
1557. Magazine of female fashions of London and Paris. 1798.

1558. Magazine of magazines, composed from original pieces. 1750-51.
1559. Magic and conjuring magazine and wonderful chronicle. 1795.
1560. Maidstone journal. Maidstone, 1737.
1561. Maidstone journal. Maidstone, 1786(?)+. w.
1562. Maidstone mercury. Maidstone, 1725.
1562a. Manchester chronicle. *Published by* Charles Wheeler. Manchester, (?)-1792(?). Perhaps continued as Wheeler's Manchester guardian.
1562b. Manchester chronicle; or, Anderton's universal advertiser. Manchester, June 1762-(?). w.
1563. Manchester gazette. Manchester, 1730-60.
1563a. Manchester gazette. Manchester, no. 1, Mar. 1795.
1564. Manchester herald. Manchester, 1792-93.
1564a. Manchester journal. *Printed by* J. Schofield and M. Turnbull. Manchester, no. 1, Mar. 2, 1754-56. w.

Manchester magazine. *See* Whitworth's Manchester gazette.

1565. Manchester mercury and Harrop's general advertiser. Manchester, no. 774, Mar. 4, 1766+.
1566. Manchester weekly journal. Roger Adams. Manchester, 1719(?)-25(?).
1567. Man in the moon. No. 1, Apr. 26, 1660.
1568. Man in the moon. No. 1, Aug. 20, 1660.
1569. Man in the moon. 1663.
1570. Manufacturer; or, The British trade truly stated. D. Defoe, etc. 1719. f.
1570a. Martin Burke's Connaught journal. Galway, 1769(?)-79.
1570b. Marlborough journal. Marlborough, 1771-74.
1571. Martin Nonsence his collections. No. 1, Nov. 27, 1648.
1571a. Masonic mirror. Edinburgh, 1797.
1572. Masquerade. Southampton, 1798.
1573. Mathematical companion. 1798+.
1574. Mathematical magazine. G. Witchell, T. Moss, etc. 1761(?).
1575. McDonnel's Dublin weekly journal. Dublin, 1785(?)-95.
1576. McKenzie's loyal magazine. Dublin, 1800.

1577. Medical communications. 1784-90.
1578. Medical extracts. 1796-97.
1579. Medical magazine. 1774.
1580. Medicina curiosa; or, A variety of new communications in physick, chirurgery. . . . 1684.
1581. Meditator. 1798.
1582. Medley. No. 1, July 7, 1715.
1582a. Medley. Cork, 1738.
1583. Medley. Newcastle-upon-Tyne, 1766.
1584. Medley. 1797.
1585. Medley; or, Daily tatler. 1715.
1586. Memoires littéraires de la Grande Bretagne. Deyverdun and Gibbon. 1768-69.
1587. Merchant's magazine; or, Factor's guide. 1743.
1588. Merchant's remembrancer. James Whiston. 1681. Perhaps continued as Whiston's merchant's weekly remembrancer.
1589. Mercure anglois. Robert White and Nicholas Bourne. 1644-46.
1590. Mercure anglois. 1648.
1591. Mercure de France. 1800+.
1593. Mercurio volpone; or, The fox. 1648.
1594. Mercurius academicus. 1645-46.
1597. Mercurius Anglicus; or, A post from the north. 1644.
1598. Mercurius Anglicus. 1650.
1599. Mercurius aulico-mastix; or, The whipping mercury. *Printed by* G. Bishop. No. 1, Apr. 12, 1644.
1599a. Mercurius aulicus, communicating intelligence from all parts of the kingdome, especially from Westminster and the headquarters. Nos. 2-4, August 1648. w.
1600. Mercurius aulicus. Nos. 1-2, Mar. 20-27, 1654.
1601. Mercurius aulicus. *Printed for* G. Horton. No. 12, June 25, 1660.
1601a. Mercurius aulicus (for King Charls II). Nos. 1-3, Aug. 21–Sept. 4, 1649.
1602. Mercurius belonius. Nos. 1-4, Feb. 4–Mar. 3, 1652.

1602b. Mercurius Britanicus, communicating the affaires of great Britaine, for the better information of the people *Printed by* G. Bishop. Nos. 27-29, Mar. 18–Apr. 1, 1644. w. A counterfeit.

1603. Mercurius Britanicus; or, A collection of such real and faithful intelligence as can be gathered from England and in Scotland concerning the present transactions in them both. Edinburgh, 1659-60.

1603a. Mercurius Britanicus representing the affaires of Great Britaine to the city and kingdome. *Printed by* B. W. Nos. 1-3, June 24–July 8, 1647. w.

1603b. Mercurius Britannicus, impartially communicating to the people, the faithful proceedings of the Lord General and his councel of officers, the most remarkable passages at sea, between the English and Dutch fleets, and the most choicest and notable occurrences from Holland, France, Spain, Denmark, Sweden, and the King of Scots. *Printed for* G. Horton. Nos. 2-10, May 23–June 20, 1653. w.

1604. Mercurius Britannicus, communicating his most impartial intelligence from all parts. . . . *Printed by* J. Cottrel and J. Moxon. Nos. 1-23, July 26–Dec. 28, 1652. w.

1605. Mercurius Britannicus. 1653.

1606. Mercurius Britannicus. 1689.

1607. Mercurius Britannicus; or, The London intelligencer turned solicitor. No. 1, Nov. 11, 1690.

1608. Mercurius Brittanicus, communicating his most remarkable intelligence unto the kingdome. No. 1, Apr. 7, 1648.

1609. Mercurius Caledonius. 1648.

1610. Mercurius Cambro-Britannicus; British mercury, or Welsh diurnal. No. 1, Oct. 30, 1643.

1610a. Mercurius Cambro-Britannicus; or, News from Wales. 1652.

Mercurius Cambro-Britannus, the British mercury, or the Welch Diurnall. No. 1, Oct. 28, 1643. *See* Welch mercury.

1611. Mercurius candidus. 1646.

1612. Mercurius candidus. 1647.

1613. Mercurius Carolinus. 1649.

1614. Mercurius cinicus. No. 1, Aug. 11, 1652.

1615. Mercurius civicus. 1660.

1616. Mercurius civicus. No. 241, May 12, 1680.
1617. Mercurius civicus; or, An account of affairs domestick and foreign. 1679.
1618. Mercurius civicus; or, The cities intelligencer. 1660.
1619. Mercurius classicus. 1653.
1620. Mercurius Democritus. *Continued as* Laughing mercury (from no. 22); *as* Mercurius Democritus (from Nov. 3, 1653). 1652-53.
1621. Mercurius Democritus. No. 82, Jan. 25, 1654.
1622. Mercurius Democritus. John Crouch. No. 1, May 22, 1661.
1622a. Mercurius Democritus, communicating faithfully. . . . No. 2, Apr. 26–May 3, 1659.
1623. Mercurius Democritus in querpo. No. 9, June 14, 1660.
1624. Mercurius diabolicus; or, Hell's intelligencer. 1647.
    Mercurius diutinus. *See* Diutinus Britanicus.
    Mercurius elencticus. *See* Mercurius pragmaticus revived.
1625. Mercurius eruditorum; or, News from the learned world. 1691.
1627. Mercurius helonicus. 1650.
1628. Mercurius Heraclitus; or, The weeping philosopher. No. 1, June 28, 1652.
1629. Mercurius Hibernicus. 1645.
1629a. Mercurius Hibernicus. *Printed for* Samuel Dancer. Dublin, nos. 1-15, 1663.
1630. Mercurius honestus. No. 1, Mar. 21, 1660.
1631. Mercurius Hybernicus. No. 1, Sept. 6, 1649.
1632. Mercurius icommaticus. No. 5, July 8, 1651.
1633. Mercurius jocosus. No. 1, July 21, 1654.
1634. Mercurius Latinus. 1746.
1635. Mercurius mastix, faithfully lashing all scouts, mercuries, posts, and others. No. 1, Aug. 27, 1652.
1635a. Mercurius melancholicus for King Charls II. John Taylor. May 24-31, 1649.
1636. Mercurius meretrix. 1658.
1637. Mercurius militans. No. 1, Nov. 14, 1648.
1638. Mercurius militaris. Nos. 1-5, Oct. 10–Nov. 21, 1648. *Cf.* no. 891a.

1638a. Mercurius militaris; or, Times only truth-teller. *Continued as* Metropolitan nuncio (from June 6, 1649). John Hackluyt. 1649.

1638b. Mercurius nullus; or, The invisible nuncio. No. 1, Mar. 13, 1654.

1639. Mercurius Oxoniensis; or, The Oxford intelligencer. 1707.

1640. Mercurius pacificus. 1648.

1641. Mercurius pacificus. No. 1, May 25, 1649.

1642. Mercurius pacificus. 1650.

1643. Mercurius philo-monarchicus. 1649.

1644. Mercurius phreniticus. 1652.

1645. Mercurius populi; or, Newes declaring plain truth to the people. No. 1, Nov. 11, 1647.

1646. Mercurius pragmaticus. No. 1, May 25, 1652.

1647. Mercurius pragmaticus. No. 1, July 6, 1652.

1648. Mercurius pragmaticus. No. 1, May 25, 1653.

1649. Mercurius pragmaticus. No. 1, June 8, 1653.

1649a. Mercurius pragmaticus. June 20, 1659.

1649b. Mercurius pragmaticus. *Printed for* H. Marsh. No. 1, Aug. 30–Sept. 6, 1659.

1650. Mercurius pragmaticus revived. *Continued as* Mercurius elencticus (from no. 2); *as* Mercurius scommaticus (from no. 3). 1651.

1651. Mercurius problematicus. 1644.

1652. Mercurius radamanthus. No. 1, June 27, 1653.

1653. Mercurius rusticus. No. 1, Nov. 3, 1643.

1654. Mercurius rusticus. No. 1, Nov. 12, 1647.

1654b. Mercurius rusticus; or, A countrey messenger. George Wither. No. 1, Oct. 26, 1643.

Mercurius scommaticus. *See* Mercurius pragmaticus revived.

1655. Mercurius Scoticus; or, A true character of affairs in England, Scotland, Ireland, and other forraign parts. Leith, 1651.

1655a. Mercurius Scoticus; or, The royal messenger. Eliz. Alkin. No. 2, Sept. 23-30, 1651.

1656. Mercurius somniosus. 1644.

Mercurius urbanus. *See* Britanicus vapulans.

1657. Mercurius vapulans; or, Naworth stript and whipt. 1644.

1658. Mercurius vapulans; or, The whipping of poor British mercury, by Mercurius urbanus, younger brother to Aulicus. No. 1, Nov. 2, 1643.

1659. Mercurius verax. 1649.

1660. Mercurius veridicus. No. 1, June 12, 1660.

1661. Mercurius veridicus, communicating the best and truest intelligence from all parts of England. No. 1, Jan. 7, 1681.

1662. Mercurius veridicus; or, True informations. 1645-46.

1663. Mercurius zeteticus. 1652.

1663a. Mercury; or, Advertisements concerning trade. 1668.

1663b. Mercury of England, giving an account of all publick events, with historical observations. No. 6, Aug. 25, 1704.

1664. Mercury; or, Advertisements concerning trade. No. 119, Feb. 21, 1677.

1665. Mercury; or, The northern reformer. Edinburgh. 1717.

1666. Merlinus phanaticus. No. 1, May 23, 1660.

1666a. Merry Andrew; or, British Harlequin. 1720.

1667. Merry mercury; or, The farce of fools. 1700.

1668. Methodist monitor. 1796.

Metropolitan nuncio. *See* Mercurius militaris; or, Times only truth-teller.

1670. Microcosm. 1757.

1671. Microscope; or, Minute observer. Belfast, 1799-1800.

1672. Military actions of Europe, collected weekly for the Tuesday's post. No. 1, Oct. 20, 1646.

1673. Military magazine. 1793.

1674. Military scribe. No. 1, Feb. 26, 1644.

1675. Minerva magazine. Dublin, 1793.

1676. Miniature. 1784.

1676a. Mirror. Dublin, 1750-51.

1677. Mirrour. 1719. w.

1678. Mirrour. 1733.

1679. Mirrour. 1759.
1680. Miscellanea curiosa. 1708.
1681. Miscellaneæ curiosæ; or, Entertainments for the ingenious of both sexes. York, 1734-35. q.
1682. Miscellany. 1711.
1683. Miscellany. 1715.
1684. Miscellany. Bishop Horne. 1768.
1685. Miscellany numbers. Edinburgh, nos. 1-29, 1712.
1686. Mock press; or, The encounter of Harry Lungs and Jasper Hem. 1681.
1688. Moderate informer. No. 1, May 19, 1659.
1689. Moderate informer of all occurrences at home and abroad. No. 1, May 12, 1659.
1690. Moderate intelligence. No. 1, May 24, 1649.
1692. Moderate intelligencer. 1653-54.
1693. Moderate intelligencer. 1682.
1694. Moderate mercury. No. 1, June 21, 1649.
1695. Moderate messenger. No. 1, Feb. 3, 1646.
1696. Moderate messenger. No. 22, Feb. 23, 1647.
1696a. Moderate messenger. No. 15, Aug. 6, 1649.
1697. Moderate messenger. No. 1, Feb. 7, 1653.
1698. Moderate messenger. No. 1, Feb. 27, 1653.
1699. Moderate occurrences. No. 1, Apr. 5, 1653.
1700. Moderate publisher. No. 1, Oct. 7, 1653.
1701. Moderator. 1692.
1702. Moderator. 1705.
1703. Moderator. J. Peele. 1721. t. w.
1704. Moderator. 1762.
1705. Moderator. No. 1, Nov. 19, 1763.
1705a. Modern characters. 1753.
1706. Moderne intelligencer. No. 1, Aug. 19, 1647.
1707. Moderne intelligencer. 1650.
1707a. Modern intelligencer. No. 5, Sept. 3, 1651.
1708. Modern monitor. 1770. s. w.

1709. Monethly intelligencer. No. 1, Jan. 1, 1660.
1710. Monitor. 1713.
1711. Monitor. Bristol, 1790.
1712. Monitor; or, Green-room laid open. *Continued as* Theatrical monitor; or, Stage management and green room laid open (from no. 2, Oct. 24, 1767). 1767-68. w.
1713. Monstrous magazine. Dublin, 1770.
1714. Monthly account. 1645.
1714a. Monthly account of the present state of affairs, &c. No. 3, Mar. 1700.
1715. Monthly advices from Parnassus. 1722. m.
1716. Monthly amusement. 1709.
1717. Monthly and critical review. 1756.
1718. Monthly collector of elegant anecdotes and other curiosities of literature. 1798.
1719. Monthly communications; being a collection of tracts on all subjects. 1793.
1720. Monthly intelligence, relating the affaires of the people called Quakers. No. 1, Aug.–Sept., 1662.
1721. Monthly London journal . . . by Cato Junr. No. 2, Nov. 22, 1722. m.
1722. Monthly magazine. Chelmsford, 1800.
1723. Monthly melody; or, Polite amusement for gentlemen and ladies. . . . 1760.
1724. Monthly miscellany; consisting of news, history, philosophy, poetry, music. 1692.
1725. Monthly miscellany; or, Irish review and register. Cork, 1796-97.
1726. Monthly miscellany; or, Memoirs for the curious. 1707-10.
1727. Monthly packet of advice from Parnassus, establish'd by Apollo's express authority and sent to England. 1723.
1728. Monthly preceptor. 1800+. m.
1729. Monthly record of literature. V. 4, 1767.
1730. Monthly recorder of all true occurrences both foreign and domestick. 1681-82.
1731. Monthly remembrancer; or, An historical and chronological diary of the . . . affairs of Europe. 1730.

1732. Monthly transactions. 1709. m.

1732a. Monthly weather-paper. Feb. 27, 1711.

1733. Moral and entertaining magazine; or, Literary miscellany of instruction and amusement. 1777-79. m.

1733a. Morsel from the wolf in bloudy sheep's clothing. Dublin, 1753.

1735. Munster journal. A. Welsh. Limerick, v. 23, no. 80, Oct. 5, 1761–v. 40, June 5, 1777.

1735b. Munster packet; or, General advertiser. Waterford, 1788.

1736. Muscovite. 1714. w.

1737. Musical companion; or, Songster's magazine. 1777.

1738. Musical magazine. 1760.

National scout. *See* Faithfull scout. 1659-60.

1739. Naturalist's pocket magazine. 1790-(?).

1740. Naval magazine; or, Maritime miscellany; containing voyages. . . . 1799.

1741. Needham's post-man; containing foreign and domestick news. *Printed by* G. Needham; by Richard Dickson (no. 27). Dublin, nos. 3-27, May 29–Sept. 17, 1724. t. w.

1742. Nettle. Dublin, 1751.

1742a. Newark herald. D. Holt. Newark, (?)-1792(?). w.

1743. Newcastle advertiser. *Published by* Matthew Brown. Newcastle-upon-Tyne, no. 1, Oct. 18, 1788+.

1743a. Newcastle gazette. Newcastle-upon-Tyne, 1744-55.

1744. Newcastle gazette; or, Northern courant. Newcastle-upon-Tyne. 1710.

1744a. Newcastle intelligencer. Newcastle-upon-Tyne, 1755-59.

1745. Newcastle magazine. Newcastle-upon-Tyne, 1785-86.

1745a. Newcastle mercury. R. Akenhead. Newcastle-upon-Tyne, 1722.

1746. Newcastle weekly magazine. Newcastle-upon-Tyne, 1776.

1747. New Christian uses upon the weekly true passages and proceedings. No. 1, Oct. 7, 1643.

1748. New Edinburgh gazette. *Continued as* Evening post; or, The new Edinburgh gazette (from 1711?). Edinburgh, 1710-12.

1749. Newes from the Low Countries. *Printed by* M. H. Altmore [Alkmaar(?)], July 29, 1621.
1750. Newes; or, The ful particulars of the last fight. No. 1, Aug. 12, 1653.
1751. New evening post. *Printed by* L. Walker. Dublin, v. 1, nos. 1-25, Oct. 15–Dec. 10, 1782. s. w.
1752. New express. 1700.
1753. New hackney coach companion. 1779(?).
1754. New magazine. *Continued as* Strabane magazine (from 1800). D. M'Anaw. Strabane, 1799-1800.
1755. New morning post; or, General advertiser. No. 0010 [*sic*], Nov. 14, 1776.
1756. New news-book; or, Occurrences foreign and domestic impartially related. 1681.
1757. New news, strange news, true news, and upon the matter no news. No. 1, June 15, 1648.
1757a. New observator. 1691.
1758. New observator. 1704.
1759. New observator on the present times. No. 1, Jan. 1, 1701.
1759a. New present state of England. R. Baldwin. V. 1-2, 1753.
1760. New print magazine; being a collection of picturesque views. 1795.
1761. New Scots spy; or, Critical observer. Edinburgh, nos. 1-12, Aug. 29, 1777–Nov. 14, 1777. w.
1762. News from Germany. 1642.
1763. News journal, in English and French. No. 1, Feb. 28, 1723.
1764. News letter. *Printed by* J. Ray *for* R. Thornton. Dublin, 1685-86.
1765. News letter. No. 1, Jan. 7, 1716.
1766. New spiritual magazine; or, Evangelical treasury of experimental religion. 1783-85.
1767. New state of Europe, both as to publick transactions and learning. 1701.
1768. New state of Europe; or, A true account of public transactions and learning. 1701.
1769. New tea-table miscellany. 1741.
1770. New universal magazine. 1775.

1771. New universal magazine of knowledge, pleasure and amusement; or, Gentleman's grand imperial museum. V. 2, 1788.

1772. New weekly miscellany. 1741.

1772a. Nicholas Hussey's weekly post; or, The Dublin impartial intelligence. Dublin, 1728.

1774a. Night post. No. 68, Jan. 1, 1712.

1775. Nonsense of common sense. 1737-38.

1776. Noon gazette and daily spy. 1781-82.

1777. Norfolk chronicle; or, Norwich gazette. Norwich, 1769(?)+. w.

1778. Norfolk poetical miscellany. Norwich, 1744.

1778a. Northampton journal. J. Pasham. Northampton, 1721(?).

1779. Northampton miscellany; or, Monthly amusements calculated for the diversion of the country and the profit of the printer. Northampton, 1721.

1779a. Northamptonshire journal. Northampton(?), (?)-1741(?).

1780. North British miscellany; or, Dundee amusement. Dundee, v. 1-2, June, 1778–June, 1780. f.

1780a. North country journal; or, The impartial intelligencer. Newcastle-upon-Tyne, 1785.

1780b. North country journal; or, The impartial intelligencer. Newcastle-upon-Tyne, 1734-39.

1781. Northern Atlantis; or, York spy. York(?), 1713.

1782. Northern gazette; literary chronicle, and review. Aberdeen, Apr. 6, 1787–Dec. 27, 1787. w.

1783. Northern star. *Printed by* John Rabb. Belfast, 1792-97.

1784. North tatler. Edinburgh, no. 1, April 1, 1710.

1784a. Norwich courant; or, Weekly packet. Norwich, 1714-(?).

Norwich gazette. 1706(?)-47. *See* Gazette.

1785. Norwich gazette. Norwich, 1761-64.

1785a. Norwich gazette; or, Henry Crossgrove's news. Norwich, 1721-(?).

1785b. Norwich journal. Norwich, 1723.

1786. Norwich mercury. Norwich, 1725+.

1787. Norwich post. Norwich, 1701(?)-09. w.

1788. Norwich post man. Norwich, 1706-09. w.

1788a. Norwich weekly mercury; or, Protestant packet. Norwich. 1721.

1789. Nose. 1800. m.

1790. Nottingham chronicle. *Published by* George Burbage. Nottingham. 1772-75.

1790a. Nottingham courant. *Continued as* Nottingham journal (from 1769). *Published by* George Ayscough (to 1769); then by Samuel Creswell; then by Creswell and George Burbage (from 1775); then by Burbage (from 1786). Nottingham, 1732+.

Nottingham journal. *See* Nottingham courant.

1791. Nottingham mercury; or, A general review of the affairs of Europe. Nottingham, 1715-20. w.

1792. Nottingham post. Nottingham, no. 42, July 18, 1711.

1793. Nottingham post. *Printed and published by* John Collyer. Nottingham, no. 1, 1716.

1793a. Nottingham weekly courant. Nottingham, no. 1, Nov. 27, 1710.

1794. Nouvelles ordinaires de Londres. William Du Gard (to 1660); Samuel Brown (from 1660). 1650-66(?).

1795. Novel reader. 1800.

1795a. Observations historical, political, and philosophical upon Aristotle's first book of political government. No. 1, Apr. 11, 1654.

1795b. Observations upon the most remarkable occurrences in our weekly news. No. 1, May 31, 1693.

1796. Observator. 1718.

1797. Observator. 1724.

1798. Observator, being a sequel to the Englishman. 1714(?).

1799. Observator; or, A dialogue between a countryman and a landwart schoolmaster concerning the proceedings of the Parliament in England in relation to Scots affairs. Edinburgh, no. 1 [n. d.]-no. 9, July 23, 1705; no. 10, May 25, 1706. ir.

1800. Observator reformed. No. 1, Sept. 10, 1704.

1801. Observator, with a summary of intelligence. 1654.

1802. Observer. Glasgow, 1785.

1803. Observer; or, A delineation of the times. Edinburgh, no. 1, Sept. 28, 1793.
1804. Occasional courant: religious qualifications for civil employments candidly consider'd. 1717.
1805. Occasional historian. 1730-32.
1806. Occasional paper. 1726.
1807. Occasional paper. 1740.
1808. Occasional paper upon the subject of religion, and the church establishment. 1735-36.
1809. Occasional respondent. Cambridge, no. 1, Apr. 12, 1764.
1810. Occasional writer. No. 1, June 26, 1762.
1811. Occasionalist. 1768.
1812. Occurrences from Ireland. No. 3, Apr. 22, 1642.
1813. Occurrences of certain speciall and remarkable passages. 1644-46.
1814a. Old British spy. No. 2255, Jan. 4, 1783–1792(?). w.
1815. Old English journal. 1743-46. w.
1816. Old English journal; or, National gazette. 1751.
1817. Old Englishman, and anti-Jacobin examiner. Nos. 1-14, Dec. 5, 1798–Feb. 10, 1799. s. w.
1818. Old post-master. 1696.
1819. Olio. 1792.
1820. Olio; or, Anything Arian magazine. Dublin, 1800.
1821. Oracle. No. 1, Aug. 1, 1715.

Oracle county advertiser. *See* Bristol oracle, and country intelligencer.

1822. Oracle; or, Sunday gazette. *Printed by* J. Henshall. Dublin, v. 2, no. 3, Oct. 22, 1797.
1822a. Orange intelligence. *Printed by* George Croom. 1688.
1823. Orator's miscellany. J. Henley. 1731.
1824. Original London post; or, Heathcote's intelligence. 1718-(?).
1824a. Original star, and grand weekly advertiser. No. 5, May 7, 1788.

Original York journal. *See* York mercury.

1825. Orphan. No. 1, Mar. 21, 1716.

1826. Oxford gazette, and Reading mercury. *Continued as* Reading mercury and Oxford gazette (from 1767). Reading, no. 420, Nov. 26, 1753+. w.
1827. Oxford mercury and Midland County chronicle. Oxford, 1795.
1828. Packet of letters, No. 1, June 26, 1646.
1828a. Packet of letters from Sir Thomas Fairfax his quarters. . . . No. 1, Oct. 30, 1645.
1829. Pacquet-boat from Holland and Flanders. 1695.
1830. Pacquet of advice from France; or, The historical and political account of the French intrigues. 1691.
1830a. Pacquets of advice from Ireland, with the Irish courant. J. Hunt. 1690.
1832. Paris gazette. Edinburgh, 1708. Supplementary section entitled Haerlem courant.
1832a. Paris gazette, English'd. No. 17, Jan. 10, 1705.
1833. Parliamentary register. John Almon. 1774-(?). m.
1834. Parliament scout. 1643-45.
1835. Parliament's scout's discovery. No. 1, June 16, 1643.
1836. Parlour window. Dublin, 1795.
1837. Parrot. 1728. w.
1837a. Particular relation of the most remarkable occurrances from the united forces in the north. No. 3, June 10, 1644.
1837b. Passages concerning the King, the army, city, and kingdom. No. 1, Dec. 6, 1648.
1838. Passatempo Italico. 1795-96.
1839. Passenger. 1766.
1841. Patriot. No. 1, Mar. 6, 1720.
1842. Patriots' weekly chronicle. Edinburgh, 1794-96(?).
1844. Penny medley; or, Weekly entertainer. 1746.
1845. Penny post. No. 1, July 19, 1715.
1846. Penny post; or, Tradesman's select pacquet. No. 1, Mar. 13, 1717.
1847. Penny weekly journal; or, Saturday's entertainment. *Continued as* London mercury; or, Great Britain's weekly

journal (from no. 15, Feb. 11, 1721). Oct. 19, 1720-1721.

1848. Perfect account. No. 3, Jan. 29, 1651-1655.

1849. Perfect declaration of the proceedings in Parliament and true information from the armies. *Continued as* True informer: containing a perfect collection of the proceedings in Parliament (from no. 2). 1645-46.

1850. Perfect diary of passages of the King's army. No. 1, June 26, 1648.

1850a. Perfect diurnall of the passages in Parliament. *Printed for* Robert Williamson. Nos. 1-5, June 20–July 18, 1642. w.

1850b. Perfect diurnall; or, The proceedings in Parliament. No. 1, July 11-19, 1642.

1850c. Perfect diurnall; or, The proceedings in Parliament. *Printed for* John Thomas. No. 1, July 18-25, 1642.

1851. Perfect diurnall occurrences of certain military affairs. . . . *Continued as* Perfect diurnall; or, Occurrences of certain military affairs. . . . (from no. 2, May 15). *Printed for* F. Coles. Nos. 1-28, May 8–Oct. 30, 1654. w.

1851a. Perfect diurnall of passages in Parliament, wherein is communicated the chiefest intelligence from . . . the Lord Gen. Fairfax and his army. . . . *Printed by* Robert Wood. Nos. 1-2, July 16-23, 1649. w.

1851b. Perfect diurnall of some passages and proceedings of and in relation to the armies in England, Ireland, and Scotland. *Printed by* John Field. Nos. 138-40, Aug. 2-16, 1652. w. Distinct from no. 699.

1852. Perfect diurnall; or, The daily proceedings in the conventicle of the phanatiques. No. 1, March 19, 1660.

1852a. Perfect diurnal of the passages in Parliament. *Printed by* Andrew Coe, R. Austin, and John Clowes. 1642-43.

1852b. Perfect narrative of the whole proceedings of the High Court of Justice in the tryal of the King. John Playford. Nos. 1-3, Jan. 20-27, 1649.

1853. Perfect occurrences of every daies journall in Parliament. 1647-49.

1854. Perfect occurrences. 1653.

1855. Perfect occurrences. No. 1, Feb. 6, 1654.

1856. Perfect occurrences. No. 41, May 18, 1660.

1857. Perfect occurrences of both houses of Parliament. 1646.

1857a. Perfect occurrences of every dayes journall in Parliament, and other moderate intelligence. *Printed for* I. Coe and A. Coe, and later for Robert Ibbitson and John Clowes. Jan. 8, 1647–Oct. 12, 1649.
1858. Perfect passages of proceedings in Parliament. No. 2, Oct. 22, 1644.
1859. Perfect relation; or, Summary. Printed for Francis Coles. No. 1, Sept. 19-29, 1642.
1860. Perfect summarie of the chiefe passages in Parliament. No. 1, Feb. 19, 1648.
1861. Perfect summary. No. 1, July 26, 1647.
1862. Perfect summary. No. 1, Oct. 9, 1648.
1863. Perfect summary of exact passages. No. 1, Jan. 29, 1649. *See* Williams, History, p. 242.
1864. Periodical accounts of the United Brethren missions. 1790+.
1865. Peripatetic. 1793.
1866. Perth magazine of knowledge and pleasure. Perth, 1772-73. w.
1867. Phanatick intelligence. 1681.
1868. Phanatique intelligencer. No. 1, Mar. 24, 1660.
1869. Philosophical herald. 1795.
1870. Philosophical observator. No. 1, Jan. 22, 1695. w.
1872. Phœnix of Europe. No. 1, Jan. 16, 1646.
1873. Pianoforte magazine. 1796+. w.
1874. Pilgrim. No. 1, June 22, 1711.
1875. Pilgrim. Dublin, 1775.
1876. Plain dealer. 1717. w.
1878. Plain Scottish; or, News from Scotland. 1690.
1880. Play house journal. Dublin, 1749-50.
1881. Plymouth magazine. Plymouth, 1772.
1882. Plymouth weekly journal; or, General post. Plymouth, 1718-25.
1882a. Poetical entertainer. J. Morphew. Nos. 1-5, 1712-13.
1883. Poetical magazine. 1779.
1884. Poetical magazine; or, The muses monthly companion. 1764.
1885. Poetical observator. Printed by D. Edwards. 1702-03.

1885a. Poetical observator revived; to be continued monthly. 1703.
1886. Political history of Europe; with an account of new books. 1697.
1887. Political magazine. 1794.
1888. Political mercury. No. 1, Jan., 1727. m.
1889a. Political monitor. 1796.
1890. Political tatler. No. 1, Jan. 19, 1716.
1891. Political touchstone. 1782.
1892. Politick commentary upon the life of Caius July Caesar. No. 1, May 23, 1654.
1893. Politick spy; or, The weekly reflexions on the state and present dangers of Christendom. 1701. w.
1894. Politique informer. No. 1, Jan. 30, 1654.
1895. Polyhymnia. Glasgow, nos. 1-20, 1799.
1895a. Poor Robin's intelligence; or, News from city and country. *Printed for* W. Brown. Nos. 1-2, July 8-17, 1691.
Pope's Bath chronicle. *See* Bath chronicle and weekly gazette.
1896. Popish mass display'd; or, The superstitions and fopperies of the Roman church discovered. 1681.
1897. Porcupine. 1800+.
1898. Portsmouth gazette. Portsmouth, 1793+.
1899. Portsmouth telegraph. Portsmouth, 1799+.
1900. Post-boy. *Printed by* John Harding. Dublin, 1718-24.
1901. Post-man: and the historical account. *Printed by* Edw. Sandys; *by* Thos. Hume (from 1717). Dublin, nos. 19-331, Sept. 15, 1708–Jan. 9, 1723. w.
1902. Postmaster; or, The loyal mercury. A. Brice. Exeter, nos. 6-220, Sept. 2, 1720–Apr. 9, 1725.
1903. Practical reflexions, moral, satirical, etc. 1709.
1904. Prattler. No. 1, Dec. 30, 1740.
1904a. Prescott's Manchester journal. Manchester, no. 1, Mar. 23, 1771-1774. w.
1904b. Preston review and county advertiser. Preston, June 1, 1793-(?).
1904c. Preston journal. W. Smith. Preston, 1742(?).

1904d. Proceedings of the Parliament of Scotland. Edinburgh, no. 1, Apr. 18, 1693.
1905. Projector. No. 1, Feb. 6, 1721.
1906. Protestant advocate, with remarks upon popery, serious and comical. 1724. s. w.
1907. Protestant intelligence. No. 1, Jan. 1, 1724.
1907a. Protestant intelligence, with news foreign and domestick, by a society of gentlemen. Nos. 21-23, Feb. 13-27, 1725.
1909. Protestant medley; or, Weekly courant. W. Boreham. No. 1, Aug. 17, 1717-1720.
1910. Protestant mercury; or, The Exeter post-boy. Jos. Bliss. Exeter, no. 4, Oct. 7, 1715. *Cf.* no. 1472.
1911. Protestant packet. *Contrib. by* Steele (?). 1716.
1912. Protestant packet; or, British monitor. Newcastle-upon-Tyne, 1780-81.
1913. Protestant pacquet. No. 1, Jan. 21, 1716.
1914. Protestant's magazine. 1761.
1915. Protestant York courant. York, no. 224, Mar. 6 (and other numbers that year), 1749.
1916. Public advertiser; or, The theatrical chronicle. *Printed by* James Parker. Dublin, v. 1, nos. 67-68, Feb. 14-16, 1774.
1917. Public adviser. No. 1, May 26, 1657.
1918. Public journal. *Printed by* Peter Hoey. Dublin, no. 214, Feb. 27, 1771.
1919. Publick advertisements. Sir Roger L'Estrange. No. 1, June 25, 1666.
1920. Publick intelligencer. 1660.
1921. Public magazine. 1760. f.
1922. Public prompter, and Irish journal. *Printed by* Bart. Gorman. Dublin, v. 1, nos. 1-9, Nov. 1-22, 1765. s. w.
1923. Pue's occurrences. *Printed by* James Pue. Dublin, 1704-92. First published under the title Impartial occurrences foreign and domestick(?).
1924. Quotidian occurrences. 1642.
1925. Racing calendar. 1774-84. f.
1926. Rambler. No. 4, Mar. 19, 1712.

Rayner's London morning advertiser. *See* Generous London morning advertiser.

Reading mercury and Oxford gazette. *See* Oxford gazette and Reading mercury.

1928. Reasoner and free enquirer. No. 1, Oct. 17, 1761. w.
1929. Reconciler. Nos. 1-25, Apr. 30–June 22, 1713.
1930. Records of love; or, Weekly amusements for the fair. 1710. w.
1932. Reflector, reflecting human affairs. 1750.
1932a. Reformer. Edmund Burke. Dublin, nos. 1-13, Jan. 28, 1747/8–Apr. 21, 1748. w.
1933. Reformer. 1756. w.
1934. Regal rambler, for 1793. 1793(?).
1935. Rehearsal rehearsed; in a dialogue between Bayes and Johnson. No. 1, Sept. 27, 1706.

Reilly's weekly oracle. *See* Weekly oracle; or, universal library.

1936. Relationes extraordinariae. 1679.
1936a. Relation of the particulars of the reduction of the greatest part of the province of Munster in Ireland to the obedience of the commonwealth of England. . . . Matthew Simmons. No. 14, Dec.[?], 1649.
1937. Religious magazine; or, Christian's storehouse. Edinburgh, 1760.
1938. Remarkable occurrences. No. 1, Feb. 19, 1716.
1938a. Remarkable occurences from the High Court of Parliament. I. Smith and And. Coe. May 16-23, 1642.
1939. Remarkable occurrences of news. 1630.
1940. Remarkable passages. *Continued as* Continuation of remarkable passages (from Dec. 29, 1643). 1643-44.
1941. Remarkable passages; or, A perfect diurnall. No. 1, Sept. 12, 1642.
1942. Remembrancer. James Ralph. 1748-51.
1943. Remembrancer: essays and dissertations. Bath, 1771.
1944. Reporter; or, The general observer. 1797. f.
1945. Repository; containing various political, philosophical, . . . and miscellaneous articles. 1782-89.
1946. Repository; or, Library of fugitive pieces. Dublin, 1763.
1947. Reprisal. 1717. w.

1948. Restorer. No. 1, Aug. 17, 1711.
1949. Restorer. 1715.
1950. Re-tatler. 1709.
1951. Retrospector. 1754-55. w.
1952. Rhapsodist. 1757. w.
1953. Rhapsody. 1712.
1954. Rights of Irishmen; or, National evening star. *Printed by* R. M'Allister. Dublin, nos. 214-15, Mar. 21-23, 1793.
1954a. Robin Snap. Norwich, 1770. w.
1955. Royal diurnal. No. 1, July 31, 1648.
1956. Royal diurnall. No. 4, March 19, 1650.
1957. Royall diurnall. No. 1, Apr. 22, 1650.
1958. Royal Irish academy. Transactions. Dublin, 1787+.
1959. Royal magazine. 1788.
1960. Royal-oak journal. 1732.
1961. Royal Society of Edinburgh. Transactions. Edinburgh, 1788+.
1962. Royal Westminster journal. 1762-63.
1963. St. Ives mercury. *Printed by* William Dicey. St. Ives, 1719-20.
1964. St. Ives post. St. Ives, 1717-18.
1965. St. Ives post boy; or, The loyal packet. St. Ives, 1718-19. w.
1966. St. James's evening post. *Printed by* Corn. Carter. Dublin, 1719-25. w.
1967. St. James's weekly journal. 1717.
1968. St. James's weekly journal; or, Hanover postman. 1719.
1968a. Salisbury journal. Salisbury, no. 58, July 6, 1730. Possibly continued as no. 805.
1969. Salisbury post-man. Sam Farley. Salisbury, No. 1, Sept. 27, 1715.
1970. Salmon's mercury. *Continued as* Salmon's mercury and general advertiser (from no. 4); *as* Salmon's mercury; or, Entertaining repository (from no. 22). J. Salmon. Bath, 1777-81(?).
1971. Salopian journal and courier of Wales. Shrewsbury, 1794+.
1972. Sam Farley's Bristol post man. *Continued as* Farley's

Bristol news-paper (from 1725) ; *as* Sam Farley's Bristol newspaper (from 1737?) ; *as* Bristol journal (from 1749) ; *as* Sarah Farley's Bristol journal (from 1777). Bristol, 1715-93.

Sarah Farley's Bristol journal. *See* F. Farley's Bristol journal *and* Sam Farley's Bristol post man.

1974. Saturday's post. No. 1, Sept. 29, 1716.

1975. Schemer, for 1753. 1753(?).

1976. Schofield's Middlewich journal; or, General advertiser. Middlewich, 1756-57.

1977. Scientific receptacle; containing problems ... anagrams ... selected by T. Whiting. 1795+.

1978. Scotch mercury. No. 1, May 8, 1692.

1979. Scotch mercury, communicating the affairs of Scotland. No. 1, Oct. 5, 1643.

1980. Scots antiquarian miscellany. Glasgow, 1784.

1981. Scots chronicle. Edinburgh. 1796+.

1982. Scots courant. 1705.

1983. Scots farmer. Edinburgh, 1772.

1984. Scots observator. 1708.

1985. Scots weekly magazine; or, Grand repository. Edinburgh, no. 1, Oct. 3, 1775.

1985a. Scottish chronicle. Edinburgh, 1788.

1986. Scottish mercury, giving a true account of the daily proceedings and most remarkable occurrences in Scotland. 1692.

1987. Scourge. 1771.

1988. Scourge. 1780.

1989. Scout. *Continued as* Impartial scout (from no. 53, June 28, 1650). 1649-50.

1990. Scout of cockney. Edinburgh, 1661.

1991. Scrutator. 1764.

1992. Seasonable writer. No. 2, Sept. 15, 1727.

1993. Second character of Mercurius politicus. 1650.

1994. Secret mercury; or, The adventure of seven days. 1702.

1995. Selector. 1776-77.

1996. Senator. 1728.
1996a. Serio-jocular medley. Cork, 1738.
1996b. Several letters from Scotland, of the proceedings of the army. F. Neile. No. 1, July 8-15, 1651.
1996c. Several proceedings of Parliament. John Field. Nos. 1-21, July 4–Dec. 13, 1653.
1997. Serious thoughts; or, A golden chain of contemplations. 1710.
1997a. Shamroc. Waterford(?), 1799.
1997b. Sheffield advertiser. William Ward. Sheffield, (?)-1792(?). w.

Sheffield iris. *See* Sheffield register.

1997c. Sheffield register. *Continued as* Sheffield iris (from ?). Joseph Gales; later James Montgomery. Sheffield, no. 1, June 1787-92(?).
1997d. Shepherd. *Published by* N. Crook. Dublin, 1759.

Sherborne journal. *See* Cruttwell's Sherborne journal.

1998. Sherborne mercury; or, Weekly advertiser. *Continued as* Western flying-post; or, Sherborne and Yeovil mercury (from Jan. 30, 1749); *as* Western flying post or Sherborne and Yeovil mercury and general advertiser (from Sept. 23, 1765). Sherborne, 1737+.
1999. Shopkeeper and tradesman's assistant. 1773+.
2000. Shrewsbury chronicle. Shrewsbury, 1771(?)+.
2000a. Shuffler. 1727.
2000b. Shropshire journal. London, no. 73, Feb. 12, 1739.
2001. Silent monitor. 1711.
2001a. Silver court gazette. *Printed by* Richard Dickson. Dublin, 1726.
2002. Skeptic; or, Unbeliever. 1773.
2002a. Sligo journal. Sligo, 1800.
2002b. Sligo morning herald. Limerick, 1793.
2003. Social magazine; or, Monthly cabinet of wit. 1800.
2004. Soldier's pocket magazine. 1798.
2005. Society for the improvement of medical and chirurgical knowledge. Transactions. 1793-1800.

2006. Society for the encouragement of arts, manufacturers, and commerce. Transactions. 1783+.
2007. Some special and considerable passages from London, Westminster. . . . No. 1, Aug. 16, 1642.
2008. Special and considerable passages. No. 1, Aug. 16, 1642.

Speciall passages continued. *See* Wednesday's mercury.

2009. Special passages from divers parts. No. 2, Aug. 23, 1642.
2010. Spectator. W. Bond and George Sewel. 1715.
2011. Speculatist. Matthew Concanen. 1730.
2012. Speedy post, with more news from Hull. 1642.
2013. Spring-Garden journal. 1752. w.
2014. Spie, communicating intelligence from Oxford. 1644.
2015. Sportsmans and breeders vade mecum. York, 1786-97.
2016. Spy, 1720-21. w.
2017. Spy on the conjuror. 1725.
2018. Staffetta Italiana; or, The Italian post. Nos. 3-7, Jan. 2-30, 1729.
2019. Statesman; or, The constitutional advocate. 1761.
2020. Stockton bee. Stockton-on-Tees, 1793-95.
2021. Storm, being a periodical paper containing . . . no name . . . but such as are notoriously known to be of that exterminating banditti called Orange-men. [Dublin, 1798.]
2021a. Strabane journal; or, The general advertiser. Strabane, 1771-(?). w.

Strabane magazine. *See* New magazine.

2021b. Strabane news-letter. Strabane, 1788-(?).
2022. Strange and wonderful news from Norwich. 1681.
2023. Student. Liverpool, 1798.
2023a. Suffolk mercury; or, St. Edmunds Bury post. Bury St. Edmunds. No. 43, Feb. 3, 1717-1731(?).
2023b. Sunday chronicle. 1788-90.
2023c. Sunday reformer and universal register. 1793-95.
2024. Sunday London gazette. 1783+.
2024a. Sunday observer. (?)-1792(?). w.

2024b. Sunday reformer and universal register. *Amalgamated with* London recorder (in 1796). 1793-96.

2024c. Supplement. No. 1, Jan. 19, 1708-1712(?).

2024d. Supplement, by way of postscript to the Weekly journal, and other weekly accounts. No. 1, Jan. 4, 1716.

2025. Supplement to the Dublin impartial news-letter. *Printed by* Samuel Dalton. Dublin, Sept. 12, 1734.

2026. Surprise. Oxford, 1711.

2027. Surprize. No. 4, Sept. 6, 1711.

2028. Sylphid. 1799.

2030. Tatler reviv'd. 1727-28.

2031. Tatler revived. 1750.

2032. Tatling harlot. 1709.

2033. Tea-table. *Attributed to* Steele. 1716.

2034. Tea table. Eliza Haywood. 1724. s. w.

2035. Tell-tale. 1709.

2036. Tell-tale, being a conversation piece on the fears of popery. 1734.

2036a. Tell-tale, No. 1, 1783 (or 1784).

2037. Templar. 1731.

2038. Templar and literary gazette. 1773. s. w.

2038a. Temple—Oge intelligencer. *Printed by* S. Powell. Dublin, 1728.

2039. Terrae filius. Oxford. 1763. d.

2040. Terrae-filius. No. 11, Mar. 17, 1764.

2041. Terrae-filius. J. Scott(?). Nos. 1-3, Mar. 15-29, 1764. w.

2041a. Terrae filius. Nos. 1-5, Mar. 16–Apr. 6, 1764.

2042. Theatrical magazine. 1800(?). m.

Theatrical monitor. *See* Monitor; or, Green-room laid open.

2044. Theme; or, Scoto-Presbyter. 1652.

2045. Thespian telegraph. 1796.

2046. Titt for tatt. 1710.

2047. Topics of the day. 1764.

2048. Torch; or, A light to enlighten the nations of Europe in their way towards peace and happiness. [Dublin, 1798].

2049. Torch; or, Glasgow museum. Glasgow, 1796.
2050. Tory tatler. 1710-11. t. w.
2050a. Town and country magazine and Irish miscellany. Dublin, 1784-85.
2051. Town spy. 1704.
2052. Trance; or, News from hell, brought fresh to town, by Mercurius Acheronticus. No. 1, Dec. 11, 1648.
2053. Traveller. 1731.
2054. Travellers magazine; or, Gentleman and lady's agreeable companion. 1749.
2055. Treaty traverst. No. 1, Sept. 26, 1648.

Trewman's Exeter evening post. *See* Exeter mercury; or, West-country advertiser.

Trewman's Exeter flying post. *See* Exeter mercury; or, West-country advertiser.

2055a. Trifler; by Timothy Scribbler, Esq. *Printed for* J. Peele. No. 6, Nov. 28, 1722.
2056. Trifler. Edinburgh, 1795-96. w.
2056a. Trifler. Dublin, Jan. 1754.
2057. True and perfect diurnal. No. 1, Dec. 27, 1652.
2058. True and perfect diurnall of all chiefe passages in Lancashire. No. 1, July 19, 1642.
2059. True and perfect diurnall of the passages in Parliament. No. 11, Sept. 6, 1642.
2060. True and perfect Dutch diurnall. 1653-54.
2062. True and perfect journal of the warres in England. 1644.
2062a. True British courant; or, Preston journal. Preston, 1745-(?).
2063. True collection of weekly passages. 1645.

True informer. 1645-46. *See* Perfect declaration.

2064. True informer: of the actions of the army in England, Scotland, and Ireland. *Printed for* F. N. No. 1, Aug. 28, 1651.
2066. True informer: comprizing several proceedings of state affairs, in England, Scotland and Ireland. *Continued as* True and perfect informer: comprizing several proceedings of the armies (from no. [3]). *Printed by* T. Lock. Nos. [2]-[3], Jan. 13-20, 1654.

2068. True newes from our navie now at sea. 1642.
2069a. True Protestant domestic intelligence. S. Crouch. No. 1, July 9, 1679-(?).
2070. True Protestant mercury; or, An impartial history of the times. No. 1, Dec. 6, 1689.
2070a. True Protestant mercury. No. 2, Jan. 10, 1689(?). Perhaps an issue of no. 2070.
2071. Trysorfa Gwybodaeth. Carmarthen, 1770.
2072. Tuesdaies journall. No. 1, July 1, 1649.
2073. Tuesdaies journal of perfect passages in Parliament. No. 1, July 23, 1649.
2073a. Tuner. Paul Hiffernan. Dublin, 1754-55.
2074. Tuner. No. 1, Dec. 9, 1769.
2074a. Ulster miscellany. Belfast(?), 1753.
2075. Union star. [Dublin, 1798].
2075a. Universal advertiser. *Published by* M. Williamson. Dublin, 1731-66.
2076. Universal chronicle; or, Weekly gazette. John Newbery. 1758-60.
2077. Universal intelligence. 1679.
2078. Universal intelligence. 1681.
2078a. Universal intelligence. John Wallis. 1688-89.
2079. Universal intelligence; or, General collection of advertisements. 1707.
2080. Universal intelligencer. No. 12, Feb. 13, 1689.
2081. Universalists' miscellany; or, Philanthropist's museum: intended chiefly as an antidote against the Antichristian doctrine of endless misery. 1797+.
2082. Universal journal. 1723-24.
2083. Universal journal. *Printed by* Halhed Garland. Dublin, no. 174, Feb. 17, 1746.
2084. Universal journalist. Dublin: printed for the Spectator Club, June 1, 1768.
2085. Universal librarian. 1751.
2086. Universal magazine and review. Dublin, 1789-92.
2088. Universal mercury. J. Roberts. 1726. m.

Universal monthly intelligencer. *See* Historical register; or, Edinburgh monthly intelligencer.

2089. Universal museum; or, The entertaining repository, for gentlemen and ladies. Coventry, 1765.

2090. Universal politician. 1796.

2091. Universal review; or, A critical commentary on the literary productions of these kingdoms. 1760.

2093. Universal spy; or, London weekly magazine. 1739.

2094. Universal visitor and memorialist, for the year 1756. Christopher Smart, Samuel Johnson, etc. 1756. m.

2094a. Universal weekly journal. 1739.

2095. Unsuspected observer. 1792.

2096. Urbanicus and Rusticus; or, The city and country mercury. 1691.

2097. Useful intelligencer. No. 39, July 10, 1711. s. w.

2097a. Useful intelligencer for promoting trade. Nos. 7-10, Jan. 1-11, 1712.

2098. Verity; or, Facts and queries. Glasgow, 1785.

2099. Visiter. 1723-24. w.; s. w.

2099a. Vocal magazine. 1781.

2100. Volunteer evening post. *Printed by* W. Bulmer. Dublin, nos. 1-357, Nov. 11, 1783–Feb. 18, 1786. t. w.

2101. Volunteers journal; or, Irish herald. *Printed by* William Corbett. Dublin, nos. 2-170, Oct. 15, 1783–Nov. 10, 1784. s. w.

2102. Votes of both Houses. No. 1, June 20, 1660.

2103. Votes of the House of Commons in Ireland. Dublin; rep. London, 1692.

2103a. Waies of literature. 1714.

2104. Walsh's Dublin weekly impartial news-letter. *Printed by* Thomas Walsh. Dublin, 1729(?).

2105. Wandering spy; or, The merry observator. 1729.

2106. Wandering spy; or, The way of the world enquired into. No. 1, June 9, 1705.

2107. Wandering whore. 1660.

2108. Warranted tidings from Ireland. 1641.

2108a. Warwick and Staffordshire journal. London, nos. 13-149, Nov. 12, 1737–June 18, 1740.

2108b. Waterford chronicle. Waterford, 1765+.

2108c. Waterford flying post. Waterford, 1729.

2109. Waterford herald. Waterford, no. 567, Sept. 16, 1794-1796. t. w.

2109a. Waterford journal. Waterford, 1765.

Watson's Limerick chronicle. *See* Limerick chronicle.

2110. Weaver; or, The state of our home manufacture considered. No. 1, Nov. 23, 1719.

2111. Wednesday packet. Edinburgh, 1798+.

2112. Wednesday's journal; being an auxiliary pacquet to the Saturday's post. 1717.

2113. Wednesday's mercury; or, Speciall passages and certain informations from severall places. *Continued as* Special passages continued (from no. 2, July 22); *as* Wednesday's mercury; or, The speciall passages and certain informations from severall parts of the kingdome (from no. 4, Aug. 2). *Printed by* T. P. and M. S. No. 1, July 19, 1643.

2114. Weekly abstract: presenting to the eye the most remarkable passages throughout the most noted parts of Christendome. Nos. 1-3, June 3-19, 1654.

2114a. Weekly accompt of certain special and remarkable passages from both Houses of Parliament and other parts of the kingdome. *Printed for* B. Alsop. No. 1, July 27–Aug. 3, 1643.

2114b. Weekly account, faithfully representing, the most remarkable passages in Parliament; and proceedings of the armies. *Printed by* E. Alsop. No. 1, May 25–June 1, 1659.

2115. Weekly account, on the establishment of a free state. No. 1, May 25, 1659.

2116. Weekly advertisement of books. 1680.

2116a. Weekly amusement. No. 1, 1784.

2117. Weekly character; being the character of a pope. 1679.

2118. Weekly comedy. 1699.

2118a. Weekly courant. Nottingham, 1722.

2119. Weekly entertainment. 1700.
2120. Weekly history; or, An account of the most remarkable passages relating to the present progress of the Gospel. 1741-42.
2121. Weekly information. No. 1, July 20, 1657.
2122. Weekly intelligence. 1642.
2123. Weekly intelligence. No. 1, May 10, 1659.
2124. Weekly intelligence; or, News from city and country. 1679.
2125. Weekly intelligencer of the commonwealth. No. 1, May 10, 1659.
2126. Weekly intelligencer of the commonwealth. No. 1, July 26, 1659.
2127. Weekly journal. *Printed for* Robert Harrison. 1714-15.
2128. Weekly journal. Edinburgh, 1757(?)-75(?).
2128a. Weekly journal. Manchester, 1719.
2129. Weekly journal from London. Edinburgh, no. 4, May 30, 1688.
2130. Weekly journal; or, General post. 1720.
2131. Weekly magazine and literary review. Dublin, 1779.

Weekly medley. *See* Flying-post; or, The weekly medley.

2132. Weekly memorial; or, Political observations on England's benefits by the war with France. 1692.
2133. Weekly mercury; or, The Protestant's packet. Norwich, 1721-23.
2134. Weekly mirror. Edinburgh, 1780-81. w.
2135. Weekly miscellany. No. 3, Feb. 22, 1701.
2136. Weekly miscellany. *Printed by* S. Powell for Edward Exshaw. Dublin, v. 1, nos. 1-52, Jan. 10, 1734–Jan. 4, 1735. w.
2137. Weekly miscellany for the improvement of husbandry, trade, arts, and sciences. R. Bradley. 1727-40(?).
2138. Weekly news from forraigne parts beyond the seas. 1644.
2139. Weekly news-letter. 1695.
2140. Weekly newspaper. Dundee, 1778. w.
2141. Weekly observator. 1716.
2142. Weekly oracle; or, Universal library. *Continued as* Reilly's weekly oracle (from v. 2, no. 1, Mar. 2, 1736). *Printed by* R. Reilly. Dublin, v. 1, no. 1-v. 2, no. 53, May 3, 1735–Aug. 31, 1736.

2143. Weekly packet. 1743(?)-44.
2143a. Weekly packet, with the price courant. Mar. 22, 1718.
2144. Weekly post; or, A just account of all the principal news, both foreign and domestic. No. 1, Dec. 1, 1711.
2145. Weekly post master. 1645.
2146. Weekly register. 1798+.
2147. Weekly remarks on the transactions abroad. Nos. 1-5, Mar. 25–May 13, 1691. ir.
2148. Weekly remembrancer. 1702.
2149. Weekly repository for 1792. 1792(?).
2150. Weekly review. *Ed.* James Tytler. Edinburgh, 1780.
2151. Weekly review; or, Literary journal. 1799.
2152. Weekly review; or, The Wednesday's post. No. 1, Aug. 14, 1717.
2153. Weekly survey of the world; or, The gentleman's solid recreation. No. 1, Oct. 29. 1696.
2153a. Weekly Worcester journal. Worcester, no. 144, Mar. 28, 1712.
2155. Weepers; or, Characters of the diurnals. 1652(?).
2156. Welch mercury, communicating remarkable intelligences and true newes to awle the whole kingdome. *Continued as* Mercurius Cambro-Britannus, the British mercury, or the Welch diurnall (from no. 4). *Printed by* W. Ley and G. Lindsey; *by* Bernard Alsop (from no. 4). No. 1, Oct. 28, 1643-1644.

West country intelligence. *See* Glasgow courant, containing the occurrences both at home and abroad.

Western flying-post. *See* Sherborne mercury; or, Weekly advertiser.

2157. Western informer. No. 1, Mar. 7, 1646.
2158. West Indian monthly packet of intelligence. No. 1, Nov. 30, 1745.
2158a. Westmeath journal. Mullingar, 1783+.
2158b. Westminster gazette; or, Constitutional evening post. Nos. 116-24, Aug. 14–30, 1777.
2159. Westminster magazine. 1750.
2159a. Wexford chronicle. Wexford, 1782.
2159b. Wexford herald. Wexford, 1788-89.

2159c. Whalley's news letter. Dublin, 1714.
2160. What'd ye call it. 1724.
2160a. Whigg. W. Chetwood. 1718.
2161. Whig magazine; or, Patriot miscellany. 1779.
2162. Whipping post; a new session of oyer and terminer for the scribblers. John Dunton. 1705.
2163. Whisperer. No. 1, Oct. 11, 1709.
2165. Whiston's merchants weekly remembrancer. 1689-98. w. *Cf.* no. 1588.
2166. Whitby spy. Whitby, 1784.
2167. Whitehall courant. No. 1, May 2, 1716.
2168. Whitworth's Manchester gazette. *Continued as* Manchester magazine (from 1737). Manchester, 1730-57(?).
2169. Wife. 1756.
2170. Wilkinson's wanderer. 1795.
2171. Williamson's Liverpool advertiser. Liverpool, v. 11, 1766.
2171a. Wolverhampton chronicle. Wolverhampton, (?)-1792(?). w.
2171b. Winchester journal; or, Weekly review. Reading and Winchester, 1743-45(?).
2172. Wonder; a mercury without a lie in's mouth. No. 1, July 6, 1648.
2173. Wonderful magazine; or, Marvellous chronicle. 1764-66.
2173a. York courant. York. 1719.
2174. York courant. York, 1725+. w.
2174a. York gazetteer, with news both foreign and domestick. York, 1740(?)-45(?). w.
2174b. York herald. York, no. 79, July 2, 1791-1792(?). w.
2175. York journal. York, 1724-25.
2176. York mercury. York, 1718-40. Perhaps continued as Original York journal.
2177. Yorkshire freeholder. York, 1780.
2178. Yorkshire magazine. York, 1786.
2179. Young gentleman's and ladies' magazine. Dublin, 1760(?).
2180. Young lady. 1756. w.
2181. Youth's calendar, for 1750. 1750(?).
2182. Zion's triumph. Bristol, 1798+.

These two lists contain a total of 2426 periodicals—981 located and 1445 not located in America.

III. CHRONOLOGICAL INDEX

In this and the following index the numbers refer to the items in the two preceding lists. In the Chronological Index *italics* are used to indicate that no issues of the periodical in question for the year under which the number occurs are known to exist in America. Conversely, the absence of *italics* means that some—not necessarily all—issues for the year are available in one or more of the libraries which have reported their holdings.

1620. *1153.*
1621. 133, *1152, 1153, 1154, 1155, 1749.*
1622. *134, 1154, 1156, 1157.*
1623. 134, *1154.*
1624. *134,* 962, *1154.*
1625. *134, 1144, 1154.*
1626. *134, 1144, 1154.*
1627. *134, 1154.*
1628. *134, 1154.*
1629. *134, 1154.*
1630. *134, 1154, 1939.*
1631. *134, 1154.*
1632. *134,* 847, *1154.*
1633. 847.
1634. 847.
1635. 847.
1636. 749.
1637. 749.
1638. 1a, *659,* 749.
1639. 659.
1640. 126, 624.
1641. 295a, *1274, 2108.*
1642. 18, 99, *123,* 124, 125, 126a, 159, 175a, 175b, 175c, *203,* 295a, 337, 346, 427, 432, 700b, 701, 702, 703, 827a, 828, 831, 888, 889, 890, 890a, *1143, 1143a, 1143b, 1146, 1147, 1147a,* 1148, *1202, 1202a, 1291, 1291a, 1387, 1400a, 1500, 1762, 1812, 1850a, 1850b, 1850c, 1852a,* 1859, *1924, 1938a, 1941,* 2007, 2008, 2009, 2012, 2058, 2059, 2068, 2122.
1643. 76, 98, 115, 123, 124, 125, 132, 203, 238, 353, 466, 468, 472, 479, 528, 532, 664, 682, 700, 702, 703, 810, 816, 817, 831, 891, 916a, *916b,* 1069, 1184, *1445, 1482,* 1610, 1653, *1654b,* 1658, *1747,* 1834, 1835, *1852a,* 1940, 1979, 2113, *2114a,* 2156.

180 *A Census of British Newspapers and Periodicals, 1620-1800*

1644. 98, *124*, 127, 146, 173, 231, 353, 361, 409, 466, 472, 479, 489, 528, 534, *682*, 700, *704*, 705, 816, 891, 916b, *1023*, *1067*, *1099*, *1108*, *1163*, *1167*, *1292*, *1320*, *1482*, *1589*, *1597*, *1599*, *1602b*, *1651*, *1656*, *1657*, *1674*, *1813*, *1834*, *1837a*, *1858*, *1940*, *2014*, *2062*, *2138*, *2156*.

1645. *124*, 173, 227, 353, 354, 409, 460, 466, 472, 479, 557, *682*, 683, 700, 704, *704a*(?), 705, *816*, *891*, 916b, *1122*, *1346*, *1386*, *1402*, *1463*, *1486*, *1589*, *1594*, *1629*, *1662*, *1714*, *1813*, *1828a*, *1834*, *1849*, *2063*, *2145*.

1646. 122, *124*, *173*, 224, *353*, 472, 479, 557, 672, 700, 704a, 705, *816*, 916b, *1122*, *1203*, *1260*, *1352*, *1529*, *1589*, *1594*, *1611*, *1662*, *1672*, *1695*, *1813*, *1828*, *1849*, *1857*, *1872*, *2157*.

1647. *353*, 461, 463, 467, 470, 481, 482, *488*, 499, 501, 503, 505, 518, 526, 533, 557, 671, 673, 700, *704a*, *706a*, *916b*, *1029*, *1142a*, *1199*, *1200a*, *1203*, *1261*, *1529*, *1603a*, *1612*, *1624*, *1645*, *1654*, *1696*, *1706*, *1853*, *1857a*, *1861*.

1648. 299, *353*, 456a, 457, 462, 463, 464, 465, 467, 474, 477, 478, 483, 485, 486, 488, 490, 492, 494, 495, 497, 501, 502, 503a, 508, 518, 518a, 519, 520, 529, 531, 535, 556, 557, 668, 680, 681, 684, 685, 700, *706a*, 891a, 952, *1130*, *1189*, *1400*, *1401*, *1474*, *1487*, *1508b*, *1571*, *1590*, *1593*, *1599a*, *1608*, *1609*, *1637*, *1638*, *1640*, *1757*, *1837b*, *1850*, *1853*, *1857a*, *1860*, *1862*, *1955*, *2052*, *2055*, *2172*.

1649. 56, 204, 326, 352, 353, 426, 475, 488, 501, 504, 515, 518, *518a*, 524, 556, 557, 561, 699, 700, 706a, 825, *1027*, *1028*, *1149*, *1317*, *1390*, *1400*, *1483*, *1484*, *1601a*, *1613*, *1631*, *1635a*, *1638a*, *1641*, *1643*, *1659*, *1690*, *1694*, *1696a*, *1851a*, *1852b*, *1853*, *1857a*, *1863*, *1936a*, *1989*, *2072*, *2073*.

1650. 56, 426, 513, *518*, *557*, 699, 700a, 706, 706a, 825, 892, *926*, *1049*, *1104*, *1461*, *1462*, *1598*, *1627*, *1642*, *1707*, *1794*, *1848*, *1956*, *1957*, *1989*, *1993*.

1651. 493, 513, *557*, 699, *706*, 825, *926*, *1026*, *1200*, *1305*, *1334*, *1426*, *1632*, *1650*, *1655*, *1655a*, *1707a*, *1794*, *1848*, *1996b*, *2064*.

1652. 513, 557, 699, *706*, 825, *926*, *1236*, *1238*, *1305*, *1319*, *1335*, *1453*, *1501*, *1602*, *1604*, *1610a*, *1614*, *1620*, *1628*, *1635*, *1644*, *1646*, *1647*, *1663*, *1794*, *1848*, *1851b*, *2044*, *2057*, *2155*.

1653. *231a*, 513, 557, *699*, *706*, 825, *926*, *1187*, *1305*, *1319*, *1436*, *1545*, *1603b*, *1605*, *1619*, *1620*, *1648*, *1649*, *1652*, *1692*, *1697*, *1698*, *1699*, *1700*, *1750*, *1794*, *1848*, *1854*, *1996c*, *2060*.

1654. 231a, *491*, 509, 513, 557, 640, *699*, *706*, 825, *926*, *1102*, *1305*, *1543*, *1546*, *1600*, *1621*, *1633*, *1638b*, *1692*, *1794*, *1795a*, *1801*, *1848*, *1851*, *1855*, *1892*, *1894*, *2060*, *2066*, *2114*.

1655. *231a*, 491, 513, 699, 706, 763, 825, 926, 1103, 1305, *1794*, 1848.

1656. 513, 763, *1794*.

1657. 513, 763, *1794*, *1917*, *2121*.

1658. 513, 516, 763, *1636*, *1794*.

1659. 229, 484, 513, 517, *645*, 678, 687, 763, 944, *1302*, *1550*, *1603*, *1622a*, *1649a*, *1649b*, *1688*, *1689*, *1794*, *2114b*, *2115*, *2123*, *2125*, *2126*.

1660. 491a, 507, 510, 511, 513, 522, 645, 678, 687, 698, 763, 945, *1007*,

1290b, 1302, 1539, 1567, 1568, 1601, 1603, 1615, 1618, 1623, 1630, 1660, 1666, 1709, 1794, 1852, 1856, 1868, 1920, 2102, 2107.

1661. 476, 522, 678, *1485, 1622, 1794, 1990.*
1662. 522, 678, *1485, 1720, 1794.*
1663. 334, 522, 678, *1485, 1569, 1629a, 1794.*
1664. 332, 334, *1485, 1794.*
1665. 334, 665, 762, 798, *1485, 1794.*
1666. 160, 334, 665, 798, *1451, 1485, 1794, 1919.*
1667. 665, 798, 887, *1485.*
1668. 498, 665, 798, *1485, 1663a.*
1669. 401, 498, 665, 798, 917, *1303.*
1670. 93, 498, 665, 798.
1671. 93, 665, 798.
1672. 93, 665, 798.
1673. 93, 665, 674, 798.
1674. 93, 665, 798.
1675. 93, 665, 798, *1125.*
1676. 93, 665, 737, 798, *1125.*
1677. 93, 665, 736, 737, 798, *1664.*
1678. 93, 665, 670, 737, 798, *1544.*
1679. 93, 178, *179,* 206, 209, 230, 256, 459, 487, 665, 670, 713, 738, 798, 827, 943, *1265, 1281, 1617, 1936, 2069a, 2077, 2117, 2124.*
1680. 93, 94, 161, 162, 178, 179, 208, 293, 418, 459, 480, 496, 521, 665, 670, 738, 791, 798, 894, 895, *943, 1124, 1249, 1616, 2116.*
1681. 93, 112, 161, 178, 179, 180, 208, 297, 314, 458, 469, 604, 625, 627, 636, 637, 665, 670, 713, 757, 758, 798, 826, 895, 896, 922, 923, 941, 948, *1191, 1438, 1467, 1588, 1661, 1686, 1730, 1756, 1867, 1896, 2022, 2078.*
1682. 93, 112, 117, 129, 179, 180, 217, 297, 402, 417, 419, 636, 665, 670, 713, 754, 798, 895, 896, 934, 935, *1181a, 1259b, 1284a, 1523, 1693, 1730.*
1683. 93, 112, 129, *179,* 636, 665, 670, 798, 813, 934, 942, *1264a, 1469.*
1684. 93, 112, 636, 665, 798, *1580.*
1685. 93, 527, 636, 665, 798, *1168a, 1764.*
1686. 93, 304, 636, 665, 798, *1764.*
1687. 93, *560,* 636, 665, 798, 902, *1908.*
1688. 93, 205, 390, 404, 560, 563, 639(?), 657, 665, 739, 765, 798, 857, 883, 903, 936, *1050, 1416, 1822a, 2078a, 2129.*
1689. *1b,* 93, 175, 205, 390, 395, 404, 523, 560, 563, 605, 657, 665, 670, 743, 772, 790, 798, 903, *1214a, 1259a, 1371, 1390a, 1398, 1606, 2070, 2070a, 2078a, 2080, 2165.*
1690. 1b, 93, 523, *562,* 665, 735, *744,* 745, 798, *1129a, 1216, 1216a, 1460, 1607, 1830a, 1878, 2165.*

1691. 32, 93, 313, 523, 562, 665, 735, *744*, 745, 798, 965, *1133a*, *1216*, *1216b*, *1625*, *1757a*, *1830*, *1895a*, *2096*, *2147*, *2165*.

1692. 32, 93, 111, 116, 276, 523, 537, 665, *744*, 745, 746, 798, 965, *1126*, *1216*, *1524*, *1701*, *1724*, *1978*, *1986*, *2103*, *2132*, *2165*.

1693. 32, 93, 111, 116, 276, 444, *523*, 665, 744, 745, 746, 798, *1126*, *1216*, *1369*, *1476*, *1490*, *1795b*, *1904d*, *2165*.

1694. 2, 32, 93, 111, 116, 276, 312, 445, 500, *523*, 550, 665, 745, *746*, 798, *1126*, *2165*.

1695. 2, 32, 93, 111, *242*, 550, 567, 665, 741, 745, *746*, 798, *1263*, *1323*, *1327*, *1399*, *1452*, *1526*, *1528*, *1829*, *1870*, *2139*, *2165*.

1696. 2, 32, 93, 111, 242, 407, 550, 628, 665, 696, 741, 745, *746*, 756, 798, *1323*, *1519*, *1525a*, *1526*, *1528*, *1818*, *2153*, *2165*.

1697. 2, 32, 93, 111, 242, 308, 552, 628, 641, 665, 741, 745, *756*, 798, 867, *1018*, *1329*, *1526*, *1535*, *1886*, *2165*.

1698. 2, 93, 111, 242, 411, 641, 665, 741, 745, *756*, 798, *1183a*, *1188*, *1266*, *2165*.

1699. 2, 93, 111, *196*, 242, 317, 411, *506*, 665, 741, 745, 798, *1188*, *1273*, *1277*, *1323b*, *1540*.

1700. 2, 93, 111, *196*, 242, 317, 411, *506*, 530, 665, 741, 745, 798, *1134*, *1188*, *1237*, *1275*, *1276*, *1323b*, *1444*, *1540*, *1667*, *1714a*, *1752*, *2119*.

1701. 2, 93, 111, *196*, 242, 317, 443, *506*, 530, 665, 740, 741, 745, 798, *1188*, *1275*, *1276*, *1323b*, *1422*, *1444*, *1540*, *1759*, *1767*, *1768*, *1787*, *1893*, *2135*.

1702. 2, 93, 111, 164, *196*, 242, *315*, 317, *506*, 634, 665, 669, 740, 741, 745, 798, *1188*, *1275*, *1276*, *1323b*, *1540*, *1787*, *1885*, *1994*, *2148*.

1703. 2, 93, 111, 164, 196, 242, *315*, 317, 451, 576, *579*, 634, 665, 741, 745, 798, *1188*, *1215a*, *1275*, *1276*, *1323b*, *1407*, *1540*, *1787*, *1885*, *1885a*.

1704. 2, 92, 93, 164, 177, *196*, 242, *315*, 317, *355*, 573, 576, *579*, 634, 635, 665, 741, 745, 798, 947, *1035*, *1064*, *1131*, *1188*, *1215a*, *1219b*, *1275*, *1323b*, *1407*, *1540*, *1547*, *1663b*, *1758*, *1787*, *1800*, *1923*, *2051*.

1705. 2, 93, 164, 177, *194*, *196*, 242, 315, 317, *355*, 514, 576, *579*, 634, 635, 665, 741, 745, 798, 947, *1064*, *1188*, *1215a*, *1219b*, *1275*, *1323b*, *1324*, *1359*, *1529a*, *1540*, *1549*, *1702*, *1787*, *1799*, *1832a*, *1923*, *1982*, *2106*, *2162*.

1706. 2, 93, 164, 177, *194*, *196*, *222*, 242, 315, 317, 355, 525, 576, *579*, 634, 635, 665, 725, 741, 745, 798, 947, *1064*, *1166*, *1188*, *1215*, *1215a*, *1219b*, *1259d*, *1275*, *1323b*, *1324*, *1341*, *1787*, *1788*, *1799*, *1923*, *1935*.

1707. 2, 93, 164, 176, *194*, 196, 242, *315*, 317, 355, 525, 576, 579, 588, 634, 635, 638, 665, 717, 741, 745, 798, 921, 947, *1064*, *1166*, *1215*, *1215a*, *1244*, *1247*, *1275*, *1323b*, *1324*, *1341*, *1360*, *1362*, *1542*, *1639*, *1726*, *1787*, *1788*, *1923*, *2079*.

1708. 2, 60, 93, 96, 164, 194, *196*, 242, *315*, 317, 355, 588, 634, 635, 665, 717, 741, 745, 798, *921*, 947, *1049b*, *1064*, *1208b*, *1215*, *1215a*, *1217*, *1248*, *1259c*, *1275*, *1323b*, *1324*, *1341*, *1542*, *1680*, *1726*, *1787*, *1788*, *1832*, *1901*, *1923*, *1984*, *2024c*.

1709. 2, 60, 93, 96, 164, 194, *196, 222,* 236, 242, *315,* 317, 355, 568, 634, 635, 665, 741, 745, 798, 850, 910, 947, *964, 1064, 1137, 1203a, 1215, 1215a, 1217, 1248, 1323b, 1324, 1325, 1341, 1342, 1358, 1716, 1726, 1732, 1787, 1788, 1901, 1903, 1923, 1950, 2024c, 2032, 2035, 2163.*

1710. 2, 14a, 60, 73, 96, 164, *194,* 196, *222,* 225, 226, 236, 242, *315,* 317, 355, 442, 446, 558, 634, 665, 741, 745, 798, 850, 912, 947, 955, *964, 1034, 1064, 1076, 1215, 1215a, 1217, 1226, 1243, 1248, 1324, 1325, 1341, 1726, 1744, 1748, 1784, 1793a, 1901, 1923, 1930, 1997, 2024c, 2046, 2050.*

1711. 2, 60, 73, 93, 164, *194,* 196, *222,* 225, 226, 242, 253, 300, *315,* 317, 355, 428, 442, 446, *598,* 634, 665, 733, 741, 745, 759, 798, 832, 842, 850, 851, 912, 947, *964, 1064, 1076, 1190, 1215, 1215a, 1217, 1286a, 1297b, 1340, 1341, 1354, 1392, 1405, 1409, 1446, 1472, 1682, 1732a, 1748, 1792, 1874, 1901, 1923, 1948, 2001, 2024c, 2026, 2027, 2050, 2097, 2144.*

1712. 2, 73, 164, *194, 196,* 222, 225, 226, 242, 300, 315, 317, 355, 442, 446, *598,* 634, 665, 719, 733, 741, 745, 759, 798, 832, 940, 947, *964, 1064, 1065, 1076, 1177, 1215, 1215a, 1217, 1341, 1405, 1409, 1415, 1515, 1685, 1748, 1774a, 1882a, 1901, 1923, 1926, 1953, 2024c, 2097a, 2153a.*

1713. 2, 58, 72, 73, 107, 164, *194, 196,* 212, 222, 225, 226, 242, 263, 292, *315,* 355, 364, 446, 449, *598,* 665, 733, 741, 745, 798, *842a,* 898, 940, *947, 964, 1065, 1169b, 1215, 1215a, 1217, 1341, 1405, 1407d, 1710, 1781, 1882a, 1901, 1923, 1929.*

1714. 2, 72, 73, 164, *194, 196,* 212, 222, 226, 242, 303, 355, 364, 416, 446, 449, 564, *568a, 598,* 626, 665, 690, 733, 741, 745, 774, 798, 832, *842a,* 898, *928a,* 940, 964, *1020, 1041, 1065, 1150, 1215, 1215a, 1217, 1251, 1297, 1322a, 1341, 1405, 1435a, 1736, 1784a, 1798, 1901, 1923, 2103a, 2127, 2159c.*

1715. 2, 73, 95, 164, *194, 196,* 212, 222, 242, 248, 303, 355, *568a, 598,* 626, 662, 665, 690, 733, 741, 745, 798, 801, *804a, 842a,* 876, 898, 927, *928a,* 940, 946, *964, 1046c, 1062d, 1065, 1066, 1150, 1183, 1185, 1215, 1215a, 1217, 1251, 1264, 1293, 1297, 1301, 1341, 1374, 1393, 1408, 1449, 1530, 1582, 1585, 1683, 1791, 1821, 1845, 1901, 1910, 1923, 1949, 1969, 1972, 2010, 2127.*

1716. 2, 14, 73, 164, 194, 222, 242, 248, 310, *355,* 512, *598,* 642, *662,* 665, 733, 741, 745, 789, 798, 801, *804a, 842a,* 876, 898, 927, 928, 940, *946, 964, 1062d, 1065, 1066, 1080, 1109, 1117, 1215, 1215a, 1217, 1290, 1297, 1331, 1333, 1341, 1355, 1356, 1374, 1470, 1530, 1531, 1534, 1765, 1791, 1793, 1825, 1890, 1901, 1911, 1913, 1923, 1938, 1972, 1974, 2024d, 2033, 2141, 2167.*

1717. 2, 14, 95, 164, 194, 215, 222, 242, 249, 310, 355, *419a,* 446, 512, *598,* 642, *662,* 665, 733, 741, 745, 798, 801, *804a,* 819, *842a,* 898, 915, *927,* 928, 940, *964, 1049a, 1065, 1215, 1215a, 1217, 1297, 1341, 1481, 1533, 1665, 1791, 1804, 1846, 1876, 1901, 1909, 1923, 1947, 1964, 1967, 1972, 2023a, 2112, 2152.*

1718. 2, 14, 157, 164, *194,* 195, 215, 222, 242, 249, 254, 310, 320, 355, 471, 512, *598,* 642, *662,* 665, 677, 733, 741, 745, 798, 801, *804a, 842a,* 898, 927, 928, 933, 940, *957, 964, 1065, 1068, 1114, 1205, 1210, 1215, 1215a,*

1217, 1297, 1341, 1406, 1481, 1503, 1791, 1796, 1824, 1882, 1900, 1901, 1909, 1923, 1964, 1965, 1972, 2023a, 2143a, 2160a, 2176.

1719. *2*, 14, *164, 167,* 169, *194, 195,* 222, *242,* 254, 255, 310, 320, 355, *396,* 512, 559, *598,* 642, 650, 662, 663, 665, 677, 689, 723, 733, 741, 745, 798, *801,* 804a, 837, *842a,* 898, 927, 928, 933, 940, *957, 964, 1065, 1075, 1098, 1114b, 1116, 1193, 1210, 1215, 1215a, 1217, 1297, 1341, 1468, 1481, 1503, 1525, 1551, 1566, 1570, 1677, 1791, 1882, 1900, 1901, 1909, 1923, 1965, 1966, 1968, 1972, 2023a, 2045, 2110, 2128a, 2173a, 2176.*

1720. *2,* 6, 14, 21, 86, 109, *164, 166, 167,* 169, *194, 195,* 222, *242,* 254, 310, 329, *336,* 355, 396, 512, 587, *598, 629,* 662, *663,* 665, 677, 733, 741, 745, 798, 801, 804a, *842a,* 858, 898, 927, 928, *933,* 940, 957, *964, 1065, 1074,* 1098, *1111, 1114b, 1116, 1133, 1134a, 1169a, 1191a, 1193, 1201, 1210, 1215, 1215a, 1217, 1297, 1341, 1396, 1457, 1481, 1503, 1551, 1566, 1666a, 1791, 1841, 1847, 1882, 1900, 1901, 1902, 1909, 1923, 1963, 1966, 1972, 2016, 2023a, 2130, 2176.*

1721. *2,* 6, 14, *86,* 109, *164, 166, 167, 195,* 222, *242,* 254, 275, 310, 329, *336,* 355, 396, *598, 629,* 662, 665, 677, 733, 741, 745, 798, *801,* 804a, *842a,* 855, 898, 927, 928, 940, 957, *964, 1065, 1169a, 1186, 1193, 1201, 1208, 1210, 1215, 1215a, 1217, 1240a, 1294, 1297, 1341, 1457, 1481, 1513, 1566, 1703, 1778a, 1779, 1785a, 1788a, 1847, 1882, 1900, 1901, 1902, 1905, 1923, 1966, 1972, 2016, 2023a, 2133, 2176.*

1722. *2,* 49, 62, *86, 164, 166, 167, 195,* 222, *242,* 250, *284,* 310, *336,* 355, 396, *598, 629,* 662, 665, 677, 688, 733, 741, 745, 798, *801,* 802, 804a, *842a,* 898, 927, 928, 957, *964, 1040, 1065, 1169a, 1193, 1210, 1215, 1215a, 1217, 1222, 1272, 1297, 1300, 1308, 1321, 1341, 1457, 1481, 1532, 1532a, 1548, 1566, 1715, 1721, 1745a, 1882, 1900, 1901, 1902, 1923, 1966, 1972, 2023a, 2055a, 2118a, 2133, 2176.*

1723. *2,* 49, 62, 80, *86, 164, 166,* 167, *195,* 222, 242, 250, *284,* 310, *336,* 355, 396, 546, 569, *598, 629,* 662, 665, 677, 688, 733, 741, 745, 775, 798, *801,* 803, 804a, *842a,* 884, 898, 927, 928, 957, *964, 1065, 1129, 1157a, 1169a, 1193, 1210, 1215, 1215a, 1217, 1219a, 1222, 1262, 1297, 1308, 1321, 1341, 1397, 1457, 1481, 1532a, 1548, 1566, 1727, 1763, 1785b, 1882, 1900, 1901, 1902, 1923, 1966, 1972, 2023a, 2082, 2099, 2133, 2176.*

1724. *2,* 49, 62, *79a,* 80, *86,* 164, *166,* 167, *195,* 222, *242, 284,* 310, *336,* 355, 396, 546, *565,* 569, *598, 629,* 662, 665, 677, 688, 720, 733, 741, 745, 775, 798, *801,* 804a, *842a,* 884, 898, 927, 928, 957, *964, 1065, 1106, 1157a, 1169a, 1193, 1210, 1215, 1215a, 1216c, 1217, 1222, 1224, 1297, 1308, 1321, 1341, 1397, 1425, 1447, 1450, 1457, 1481, 1532a, 1566, 1741, 1797, 1882, 1900, 1902, 1906, 1907, 1923, 1966, 1972, 2023a, 2034, 2082, 2099, 2160, 2175, 2176.*

1725. *2,* 62, *79a, 86, 164, 166, 167, 186, 195,* 222, *242,* 269, *284,* 310, *336,* 355, 396, 546, *565,* 569, *598,* 612, *629,* 662, 665, 677, 720, 733, 741, 745, 798, *801,* 804a, *842a,* 898, 927, 928, 957, *964, 1012, 1059, 1065, 1081, 1107, 1157a, 1169a, 1193, 1204, 1210, 1215, 1215a, 1217, 1224, 1227, 1297, 1308,*

1313, 1341, 1394, 1397, 1457, 1481, 1562, 1566, 1786, 1882, 1902, 1907a, 1923, 1966, 1972, 2017, 2023a, 2174, 2175, 2176.

1726. *2, 62, 79a, 86,* 152, *164, 166, 167, 186, 195,* 222, *242,* 269, *284,* 310, *336,* 355, 396, 546, 565, 569, *598,* 612, *629,* 662, 665, *677,* 733, 741, 745, 79*3*, *801,* 804a, *842a, 898, 927,* 928, 957, *964, 1059,* 1100, *1114a,* 1165, *1165a, 1169a, 1193,* 1215, *1215a,* 1227, *1308, 1313, 1341, 1350, 1457, 1481, 1786, 1806, 1923, 1972, 2001a, 2023a, 2088, 2174, 2176.*

1727. *2, 62, 79a, 86,* 152, *164, 166, 167, 186,* 195, 222, *242,* 246, *284,* 310, *336,* 355, *394,* 396, 546, 569, *598,* 612, *629,* 643, *662,* 665, *677,* 733, 741, 745, 798, *801,* 804a, *842a, 898, 927,* 928, 957, *964, 1010a, 1019a, 1059, 1114a,* 1118, *1169a, 1193, 1200b,* 1215, *1215a,* 1227, *1287, 1308, 1313, 1341, 1350, 1457, 1481, 1489, 1786, 1888, 1923, 1972, 1992, 2000a, 2023a, 2030, 2137, 2174, 2176.*

1728. *2, 62, 79a, 86,* 152, *164, 166,* 167, *186, 195,* 222, *242, 284,* 310, 333, *336,* 355, 394, 396, 569, 570, *598, 629,* 662, 665, *677,* 733, 741, 745, 747, 798, *801,* 804a, *842a, 898,* 908, *927,* 928, 957, *964, 1059, 1169a, 1193,* 1215, *1215a,* 1227, *1308, 1313, 1326, 1341, 1393a, 1457, 1481, 1772a, 1786, 1837, 1923, 1972, 1996, 2023a, 2030, 2038a, 2137, 2174, 2176.*

1729. *2, 62, 79a, 86,* 152, *164, 166, 167, 186,* 191, *195, 222, 242, 245, 284,* 310, 333, *336,* 355, 394, 396, 569, 570, *598, 629,* 662, 665, *677,* 733, *741,* 745, 747, 798, *801,* 804a, *842a,* 878, *898,* 908, 927, 928, 957, *964, 1059, 1129b, 1169a, 1193,* 1215, *1218b, 1222c,* 1227, *1313, 1321a, 1323a, 1326, 1341, 1375, 1417, 1457, 1481, 1488, 1508a, 1786, 1923, 1972, 2018, 2023o, 2104, 2105, 2108c, 2137, 2174, 2176.*

1730. *2, 62, 79a, 86,* 152, *163, 164, 166, 167, 186, 191, 195,* 222, *242,* 245, *284,* 290, 305, 310, *324, 336,* 355, 376, 394, 396, 569, 570, *598, 629,* 662, 665, *677,* 733, *741,* 745, 747, 798, *801,* 804a, *842a, 898,* 908, *927,* 928, *945,* 957, *964, 1059, 1105a, 1169a, 1193,* 1215, *1222b, 1222c,* 1227, *1313, 1326, 1341, 1375, 1417, 1457, 1481, 1563, 1731, 1786, 1805, 1923, 1968a, 1972, 2011, 2023a, 2137, 2168, 2174, 2176.*

1731. 62, *79a, 86,* 152, 163, 164, 166, *167, 186, 191, 195, 242,* 245, 277, *284,* 290, 305, 310, *324, 336,* 355, 376, 394, 396, 551, 570, *598, 629, 662,* 665, *677,* 733, *741,* 745, 747, *798, 801,* 804a, *842a, 898,* 908, *927,* 928, 945, 957, *964, 1057b, 1059, 1105a, 1160, 1169a, 1193,* 1215, *1227, 1313, 1341, 1375, 1417, 1448, 1457, 1480a, 1481, 1563, 1786, 1805, 1823, 1923, 1972, 2023a, 2037, 2053, 2075a, 2137, 2168, 2174, 2176.*

1732. *47a, 79a, 86,* 112a, 152, 163, 164, *166, 167, 186, 191, 195,* 245, 257, 277, *284,* 290, 305, 310, *324, 336,* 355, 394, *396,* 398, 551, 553, 570, *598, 629, 662,* 665, 677, 733, 741, 745, 747, 798, *801,* 804a, *808, 842a, 898,* 908, 909, *927,* 928, *945,* 957, *964, 1052a, 1057b, 1105a, 1169a, 1192, 1214, 1215,* 1227, *1313, 1341, 1375, 1417, 1457, 1481, 1563, 1786, 1790a, 1805, 1923, 1960, 1972, 2075a, 2137, 2168, 2174, 2176.*

1733. 34, 43, *47a, 79a, 86,* 112a, 136, 152, 163, 164, *166,* 167, *186, 191, 195,* 245, 257, 262, 277, *284,* 290, 305, 310, 324, *336,* 355, 394, 396, 398,

437, 553, 598, 629, 646, 662, 665, 677, 733, *741*, 745, 747, 798, *801*, 804a,
808, *842a*, 898, 908, *927*, 928, 945, 953, 957, *964*, *1057b*, *1079*, *1105a*, *1169a*,
1192, *1214*, *1215*, *1227*, *1269*, *1341*, *1375*, *1417*, *1457*, *1481*, *1521a*, *1563*,
1678, *1786*, *1790a*, *1923*, *1972*, *2075a*, *2137*, *2168*, *2174*, *2176*.

1734. 34, 43, 79a, *86*, *136*, 152, 163, *164*, *166*, *167*, *186*, *191*, 195, 245, 262, 277, *284*, 290, 310, *324*, *336*, 355, 388, *393*, 394, *396*, 398, 437, 553, 598, 613, 629, *662*, 665, 733, *741*, 745, 747, 752, 798, 801, 804a, 808, *842a*, 869, 898, 908, 919, *927*, 928, 939, *945*, 957, *964*, *1057b*, *1079*, *1169a*, *1187a*, *1192*, *1214*, *1215*, *1218a*, *1223*, *1341*, *1375*, *1417*, *1457*, *1481*, *1563*, *1681*, *1780b*, *1786*, *1790a*, *1923*, *1972*, *2025*, *2036*, *2075a*, *2136*, *2137*, *2168*, *2174*, *2176*.

1735. 43, 79a, *86*, 152, 163, 164, 165, *166*, *167*, *186*, *195*, 245, 262, 277, *284*, 290, 310, *324*, *336*, 355, 379, 380, 388, *393*, 394, *396*, 398, 437, 553, *598*, *613*, 629, 651, *662*, 665, 733, 741, 745, 747, 752, 798, 801, *842a*, 869, 898, 908, 919, 920, *927*, 928, 939, 957, 964, *1057b*, *1065a*, *1168c*, *1169a*, *1192*, *1214*, *1215*, *1341*, *1375*, *1417*, *1442*, *1457*, *1481*, *1563*, *1681*, *1780b*, *1786*, *1790a*, *1808*, *1923*, *1972*, *2075a*, *2136*, *2137*, *2142*, *2168*, *2174*, *2176*.

1736. 79a, *86*, 152, 163, 165, 166, *167*, *186*, *195*, 262, 277, *284*, 290, 310, *324*, *336*, 355, 380, 393, 394, *396*, 398, 437, 553, *598*, *613*, *629*, 651, *662*, 665, 733, 745, 747, 752, 798, 801, *842a*, 869, 898, 908, *927*, 928, 939, 957, *964*, *1057b*, *1138*, *1169a*, *1192*, *1212*, *1214*, *1215*, *1235a*, *1284*, *1318*, *1341*, *1369a*, *1375*, *1417*, *1442*, *1457*, *1481*, *1541*, *1563*, *1780b*, *1786*, *1790a*, *1808*, *1923*, *1972*, *2075a*, *2137*, *2142*, *2168*, *2174*, *2176*.

1737. *3*, *45*, 63, 79a, *86*, 114, 152, 163, *165*, 166, *167*, *186*, *189*, *195*, 262, 277, *284*, 290, 310, 316, *324*, *336*, 355, 393, 394, *396*, 398, 437, 553, *598*, 613, 629, 651, 665, 733, 787, 798, 801, *842a*, 898, 908, 925, *927*, *928*, *939*, 957, *964*, *1057b*, *1169a*, *1192*, *1214*, *1215*, *1224b*, *1270*, *1341*, *1369a*, *1375*, *1417*, *1457*, *1481*, *1541*, *1560*, *1563*, *1775*, *1780b*, *1786*, *1790a*, *1923*, *1972*, *1998*, *2075a*, *2108a*, *2137*, *2168*, *2174*, *2176*.

1738. *3*, *45*, 79a, *86*, 114, 152, 163, *165*, *166*, 167, *186*, *189*, *195*, 262, 277, *284*, 310, 316, *324*, *336*, 355, 373, *393*, 394, *396*, 398, 437, 553, *598*, 613, *629*, 644, 651, 665, 733, 787, 798, 801, 805, *842a*, 898, 908, 925, *927*, *957*, *964*, *1057b*, *1070*, *1169a*, *1192*, *1193a*, *1214*, *1215*, *1224b*, *1270*, *1341*, *1369a*, *1375*, *1417*, *1433*, *1475*, *1481*, *1505*, *1541*, *1563*, *1582a*, *1775*, *1780b*, *1786*, *1790a*, *1923*, *1972*, *1996a*, *1998*, *2075a*, *2108a*, *2137*, *2168*, *2174*, *2176*.

1739. *3*, 12, 15, *45*, 71, 79a, *86*, 101, 114, 152, 163, *165*, *166*, *167*, *186*, *189*, *195*, 262, 277, *284*, 316, *324*, *336*, 355, 387, *393*, 394, *396*, 398, 437, 553, *598*, 600, *613*, *629*, 665, 733, 798, *801*, 805, 812, *842a*, 898, 908, *927*, 957, *964*, *1057b*, *1121*, *1164*, *1169a*, *1192*, *1214*, *1215*, *1270*, *1279*, *1341*, *1357*, *1375*, *1417*, *1481*, *1563*, *1780b*, *1786*, *1790a*, *1923*, *1972*, *1998*, *2000b*, *2075a*, *2093*, *2094a*, *2108a*, *2137*, *2168*, *2174*, *2176*.

1740. *3*, 12, 15, *45*, 79a, *86*, 101, 114, 152, 163, *165*, *166*, *167*, *186*, *189*, *195*, 262, 277, *284*, 316, *324*, *336*, 355, 387, *393*, *394*, *396*, 398, 437, 553, *598*, 600, *629*, 665, 692, 733, 798, *801*, 805, 812, *842a*, 908, *927*, 957, *964*, *1110*, *1112*, *1169a*, *1181*, *1192*, *1209a*, *1214*, *1215*, *1270*, *1341*, *1348a*, *1357*,

1375, 1417, 1481, 1563, 1786, 1790a, 1807, 1904, 1923, 1972, 1998, 2075a, 2108a, 2137, 2168, 2174, 2174a, 2176.

1741. *3,* 12, *27, 45,* 79a, *86,* 101, 114, 152, 163, 165, *166, 167, 186,* 189, *195, 261, 262,* 274, 277, *284,* 316, 318, *324, 336, 343,* 355, 387, 393, *394, 396,* 398, 437, *553,* 598, *600,* 629, 665, 768, 798, *801,* 805, 812, *842a,* 908, *927, 950, 957, 964, 1016, 1046, 1112, 1115a, 1167a, 1169a, 1192, 1209a, 1214, 1215, 1299, 1341, 1375, 1417, 1481, 1563,* 1769, *1772, 1779a, 1786, 1790a, 1923, 1972, 1998, 2075a,* 2120, *2168, 2174, 2174a.*

1742. *3,* 12, *27, 45,* 79a, *86,* 101, 114, 152, 163, *165, 166, 167, 186,* 189, *195, 261, 262,* 274, 277, *284,* 316, *336, 343,* 355, 387, *393,* 394, *396, 397,* 398, 437, *598, 600,* 629, 665, 789a, 798, 801, *805,* 812, *842a,* 906, 908, *927, 950, 957, 964, 1008, 1016, 1085, 1115a, 1169a, 1192, 1209a, 1214,* 1215, 1220, *1299, 1341, 1363, 1375, 1417, 1480b, 1481, 1527, 1563, 1786, 1790a, 1904c, 1923, 1972, 1998, 2075a,* 2120, *2168, 2174, 2174a.*

1743. *3,* 12, *27, 45,* 79a, *86,* 101, 106, 114, 152, 163, *165, 167, 186,* 189, *195, 261, 262,* 264, 274, 277, *284, 296,* 316, *336, 343,* 355, *393, 394, 396, 397,* 398, 437, *598, 600,* 629, 648, 665, 798, 801, *805,* 812, *842a, 903a,* 908, *927, 950, 957, 964, 1016, 1060a, 1063, 1074a, 1115a, 1169a, 1192, 1209a, 1214, 1215, 1299, 1341, 1375, 1382, 1417, 1481, 1522b, 1527, 1563, 1587, 1786, 1790a, 1815, 1923, 1972, 1998, 2075a, 2143, 2168, 2171b, 2174, 2174a.*

1744. *3,* 12, *27, 45, 53a,* 79a, *86,* 106, *152,* 163, *165,* 167, *186, 189, 195,* 235, *261, 262,* 264, 274, 277, *284, 296, 336, 343,* 355, 375, *393, 394, 396, 397,* 398, 433, 437, *598, 600,* 629, 648, 665, 726, 798, *801,* 805, 812, *842a, 903a,* 908, *927, 950, 957, 964, 1063, 1095a, 1115a, 1169a, 1192,* 1209, *1209a, 1214, 1215, 1299, 1307a, 1316a, 1322, 1341, 1353, 1375, 1417, 1481, 1493, 1522b, 1563, 1743a, 1778, 1786, 1790a, 1815, 1923, 1972, 1998, 2075a, 2143, 2168, 2171b, 2174, 2174a.*

1745. *3,* 27, *45,* 53a, *79a, 86,* 106, *152,* 163, *165, 167, 186,* 195, 235, *261,* 262, 264, 274, 277, 281, *284, 296, 336, 343,* 355, 375, *391, 393, 394, 397,* 398, 430, 547, *598, 600,* 629, 648, 665, *726,* 769, 798, 801, *805,* 812, *842a,* 893, *903a,* 908, *927, 950, 957, 964, 1014, 1015, 1063, 1072a, 1169a, 1192,* 1209, *1209a, 1214, 1215,* 1278, *1299, 1307a, 1316a, 1341, 1353, 1375, 1417, 1481, 1522b, 1563, 1743a, 1786, 1790a, 1815, 1923, 1972, 1998, 2062a, 2075a, 2158, 2168, 2171b, 2174, 2174a.*

1746. *3,* 27, *45,* 53a, 65, *79a, 86,* 106, 142, *152,* 163, *165, 167, 186,* 195, 235, *261, 262,* 274, 277, 281, *284, 296,* 336, *343,* 355, 375, 391, *393,* 394, *397,* 398, 430, 547, 589, 591, *598, 600,* 629, *648,* 665, 686, 798, 801, *805,* 812, *842a,* 846, 893, *903a,* 908, *927, 950, 957,* 958, *964, 1063,* 1096, *1169a, 1192,* 1209, *1209a, 1214, 1215, 1299, 1307a, 1316a, 1341, 1353, 1375, 1417, 1481, 1563, 1634, 1743a, 1786, 1790a, 1815, 1844, 1923, 1972, 1998, 2075a, 2083, 2168, 2174.*

1747. 3, 27, *45,* 53a, 65, 70, *79a, 86, 142, 152,* 163, *165,* 186, 195, *261,* 262, 274, 277, 281, *284,* 336, 339, *343,* 355, 375, *391, 393, 394, 397,* 398, 430, 547, 589, *598,* 599, *600,* 629, 648, 665, 798, 801, *805,* 812, *842a,* 846, 870, *903a,* 905, *927, 950, 957,* 958, *964, 1019, 1062c, 1063,* 1096, *1169a, 1192,*

1209, 1209a, 1214, 1215, 1299, 1316a, 1341, 1353, 1375, 1417, 1481, 1498, 1563, 1743a, 1786, 1790a, 1923, 1932a, 1942, 1972, 1998, 2075a, 2168, 2174.

1748. 3, 27, 45, 53a, 65, 70, 79a, 86, 142, 163, 165, 186, 195, 261, 262, 274, 277, 281, 284, 336, 339, 343, 355, 375, 393, 394, 397, 398, 430, 547, 555, 598, 599, 600, 629, 648, 658, 665, 798, 801, 805, 812, 842a, 846, 870, 903a, 905, 927, 950, 957, 958, 964, 1002, 1062c, 1063, 1096, 1169a, 1192, 1209, 1209a, 1214, 1215, 1299, 1316a, 1353, 1375, 1417, 1448a, 1481, 1563, 1743a, 1786, 1790a, 1923, 1932a, 1942, 1972, 1998, 2075a, 2168, 2174.

1749. 3, 27, 45, 53a, 65, 79a, 86, 142, 163, 186, 195, 261, 262, 274, 277, 281, 284, 336, 343, 355, 356, 375, 393, 394, 397, 398, 430, 547, 555, 580, 598, 599, 600, 629, 648, 665, 798, 801, 805, 812, 842a, 846, 903a, 905, 927, 950, 957, 958, 964, 1002, 1062c, 1063, 1065b, 1096, 1101, 1169a, 1171, 1192, 1209, 1209a, 1214, 1215, 1299, 1316a, 1353, 1375, 1417, 1481, 1522, 1563, 1743a, 1786, 1790a, 1880, 1915, 1923, 1942, 1972, 1998, 2054, 2075a, 2168, 2174.

1750. 3, 27, 44, 45, 53a, 65, 86, 142, 163, 185, 186, 195, 261, 262, 274, 277, 281, 284, 336, 343, 347, 355, 356, 384, 393, 394, 397, 398, 430, 542, 555, 580, 598, 599, 600, 629, 648, 665, 771, 796, 798, 801, 805, 812, 842a, 844, 846, 903a, 905, 927, 950, 957, 958, 964, 1002, 1065b, 1096, 1101, 1169a, 1192, 1209, 1214, 1215, 1298, 1299, 1316a, 1353, 1375, 1391, 1473, 1481, 1522, 1558, 1563, 1676a, 1743a, 1786, 1790a, 1880, 1923, 1932, 1942, 1972, 1998, 2031, 2075a, 2159, 2168, 2174, 2181.

1751. 3, 27, 45, 53a, 86, 142, 163, 181, 185, 186, 195, 261, 262, 274, 277, 281, 284, 331, 336, 343, 347, 355, 356, 393, 394, 397, 398, 422, 542, 555, 580, 598, 599, 600, 622, 629, 648, 665, 771, 796, 798, 801, 805, 812, 842a, 844, 846, 886, 903a, 905, 927, 950, 957, 958, 964, 1002, 1065b, 1096, 1169a, 1192, 1214, 1215, 1298, 1299, 1316a, 1353, 1375, 1391, 1414, 1473, 1481, 1521, 1522, 1542a, 1558, 1563, 1676a, 1742, 1743a, 1786, 1790a, 1816, 1923, 1942, 1972, 1998, 2075a, 2085, 2168, 2174.

1752. 3, 4, 27, 45, 53a, 86, 142, 148, 149, 150, 163, 185, 186, 195, 261, 262, 268, 271, 274, 277, 281, 284, 295, 336, 343, 355, 356, 393, 394, 397, 398, 422, 542, 580, 598, 599, 600, 618, 622, 629, 648, 665, 771, 784, 798, 801, 805, 812, 820, 842a, 846, 886, 905, 927, 950, 957, 958, 964, 1001, 1002, 1065b, 1096, 1169a, 1192, 1214, 1215, 1299, 1314, 1316a, 1353, 1375, 1391, 1399a, 1473, 1481, 1492, 1507d, 1521, 1563, 1743a, 1786, 1790a, 1923, 1972, 1998, 2013, 2075a, 2168, 2174.

1753. 3, 4, 27, 45, 53a, 86, 142, 150, 163, 186, 195, 261, 262, 271, 274, 277, 281, 284, 289, 336, 343, 355, 356, 367, 393, 394, 397, 398, 422, 542, 580, 598, 599, 600, 618, 622, 629, 648, 665, 666, 694, 760, 798, 801, 805, 812, 820, 833, 842a, 846, 852, 886, 905, 927, 950, 957, 958, 964, 966, 1001, 1002, 1065b, 1096, 1169a, 1192, 1214, 1215, 1218c, 1225a, 1299, 1314, 1316a, 1353, 1375, 1391, 1399a, 1419, 1473, 1481, 1521, 1563, 1705a, 1733a, 1743a, 1759a, 1786, 1790a, 1826, 1923, 1972, 1975, 1998, 2074a, 2075a, 2168, 2174.

1754. 3, 4, 27, 45, 53a, 86, 110, 119, 135, 142, 150, 163, 186, 195, 214, 220, 261, 262, 271, 274, 277, 281, 284, 289, 336, 343, 355, 365, 367, 393,

394, *397*, 398, 422, 580, *598*, 599, *600*, *618*, 622, *629*, 655, 665, 666, 715, 798, *801*, *805*, 812, 833, *842a*, *846*, 852, 899, 900, 905, *927*, 950, 957, *958*, *964*, 966, *1001*, *1002*, *1065b*, *1096*, *1169a*, *1192*, *1207*, *1214*, *1215*, *1225a*, *1299*, *1314*, *1316a*, *1346a*, *1353*, *1372b*, *1375*, *1391*, *1399a*, *1419*, *1454*, *1473*, *1481*, *1563*, *1564a*, *1743a*, *1786*, *1790a*, *1826*, *1923*, *1951*, *1972*, *1998*, *2056a*, *2073a*, *2075a*, *2168*, *2174*.

1755. *3*, 27, *45*, *53a*, 86, 119, *135*, *142*, *150*, 163, 172, *186*, *195*, 201, 220, 261, 262, 266, 270, *271*, 274, 277, *281*, *284*, 322, *336*, *343*, 355, *365*, *367*, *393*, 394, *397*, 398, 422, 424, 566, 580, *598*, 599, *600*, *618*, *622*, *629*, 649, 654, 665, *666*, 798, 801, *805*, 807, 812, *842a*, 846, 905, *927*, 950, 957, *958*, *964*, 966, *1001*, *1002*, *1043*, *1065b*, *1096*, *1157f*, *1169a*, *1182*, *1192*, *1198*, *1214*, *1215*, *1299*, *1314*, *1316a*, *1336*, *1353*, *1372b*, *1375*, *1391*, *1399a*, *1419*, *1473*, *1481*, *1563*, *1564a*, *1743a*, *1744a*, *1786*, *1790a*, *1826*, *1923*, *1951*, *1972*, *1998*, *2073a*, *2075a*, *2168*, *2174*.

1756. *3*, 27, *45*, *53a*, 86, 119, 121, *135*, *142*, *150*, 156, 163, *186*, *195*, 201, 220, 261, *262*, 266, *271*, 274, 277, *281*, *284*, 336, *343*, 355, *365*, *367*, 381, *393*, 394, *397*, 398, 422, 566, 580, *598*, 599, *600*, *618*, *622*, *629*, 649, 665, *666*, 742, 798, *805*, 807, 812, *842a*, *846*, 856, 905, *927*, 950, 957, *958*, *964*, 966, *1001*, *1002*, *1043*, *1065b*, *1080a*, *1096*, *1157f*, *1192*, *1214*, *1215*, *1218*, *1299*, *1307*, *1314*, *1316a*, *1372b*, *1375*, *1391*, *1399a*, *1419*, *1481*, *1511*, *1514*, *1563*, *1564a*, *1717*, *1744a*, *1786*, *1790a*, *1826*, *1923*, *1933*, *1972*, *1976*, *1998*, *2075a*, *2094*, *2168*, *2169*, *2174*, *2180*.

1757. *3*, 27, *45*, *53a*, 86, 97, 120, 121, *135*, *142*, 151, 156, 163, *186*, *195*, 220, *261*, 262, 266, *271*, 274, 277, *281*, *284*, 298, 323, *336*, *343*, 355, 365, *367*, 381, 385, 389, *393*, 394, *397*, 398, 422, 439, 543, 566, 580, *598*, 599, *600*, *618*, *622*, *629*, 665, *666*, 798, *805*, *807*, 812, *842a*, *846*, 856, 905, *927*, *950*, *957*, *958*, *964*, *1001*, *1002*, *1043*, *1065b*, *1096*, *1157f*, *1192*, *1214*, *1215*, *1254*, *1299*, *1311*, *1314*, *1316a*, *1372b*, *1375*, *1391*, *1399a*, *1419*, *1481*, *1511*, *1563*, *1670*, *1744a*, *1786*, *1790a*, *1826*, *1923*, *1952*, *1972*, *1976*, *1998*, *2075a*, *2128*, *2168*, *2174*.

1758. *3*, 27, *45*, *53a*, 86, *135*, *142*, 156, 163, *186*, *195*, 220, *261*, 262, 266, *271*, 274, 277, *281*, *284*, 288, 298, *336*, *343*, 355, *365*, *367*, 381, 385, 389, *393*, 394, *397*, 398, 422, 423, 439, 566, 580, *598*, 599, *600*, *618*, *622*, 623, *629*, 665, *666*, 761, 798, *805*, 807, 812, *842a*, *846*, 862, 905, *927*, 931, *950*, *957*, *958*, *964*, *1002*, *1043*, *1065b*, *1096*, *1157f*, *1192*, *1214*, *1215*, *1254*, *1299*, *1314*, *1316a*, *1372b*, *1375*, *1391*, *1399a*, *1419*, *1481*, *1521c*, *1563*, *1744a*, *1786*, *1790a*, *1826*, *1923*, *1972*, *1998*, *2075a*, *2076*, *2128*, *2174*.

1759. *3*, 16, 27, 41, *45*, *53a*, 86, *135*, *142*, 156, 163, *186*, 193, *195*, *261*, 262, 266, *271*, 274, 277, *281*, *284*, 288, *336*, *343*, 355, *365*, *367*, 385, 389, *393*, 394, *397*, 398, 422, 423, 439, 566, 580, *598*, 599, *600*, *618*, *622*, 623, *629*, 665, *666*, 761, 793, 795, 798, *805*, 807, 812, *842a*, *846*, 905, *927*, 950, *957*, *958*, *964*, *1002*, *1043*, *1086*, *1096*, *1136*, *1157f*, *1192*, *1214*, *1215*, *1254*, *1299*, *1314*, *1316a*, *1372b*, *1375*, *1391*, *1399a*, *1416a*, *1419*, *1437*, *1456*, *1481*, *1489a*, *1563*, *1679*, *1744a*, *1786*, *1790a*, *1826*, *1923*, *1972*, *1997d*, *1998*, *2075a*, *2076*, *2128*, *2174*.

1760. *3*, 16, *27*, *45*, *53a*, 69, *86*, 108, *135*, *142*, 156, 163, *186*, 193, 195, *261*, *262*, *266*, *271*, 274, 277, *281*, *284*, *288*, 328, *336*, *343*, 355, *365*, *367*, 385, 389, *393*, *394*, 397, 398, *422*, 439, 566, 580, *598*, *599*, *600*, *623*, *629*, 665, *666*, *761*, *764*, 793, *795*, 798, *805*, *807*, 812, *842a*, *846*, 905, *927*, 929, *950*, *957*, *958*, *964*, *1002*, *1043*, *1044a*, *1061*, *1096*, *1157f*, *1192*, *1211*, *1214*, *1215*, *1254*, *1299*, *1314*, *1316a*, *1337*, *1372b*, *1375*, *1391*, *1399a*, *1419*, *1481*, *1494*, *1563*, *1723*, *1738*, *1786*, *1790a*, *1826*, *1921*, *1923*, *1937*, *1972*, *1998*, *2075a*, *2076*, *2091*, *2128*, *2174*, *2179*.

1761. 1, *3*, 16, *27*, *45*, *53a*, 69, *86*, 108, *135*, *142*, 145, 156, 163, *186*, *195*, *247*, *261*, *262*, *266*, *271*, 274, 277, *284*, 328, *336*, *343*, 355, 363, *365*, *367*, 369, 385, 389, *393*, *394*, 397, 398, *422*, 439, 566, 580, *598*, *600*, *623*, *629*, 665, *666*, *712*, *761*, *764*, 794, *795*, 798, *800*, *805*, *807*, 812, 840, *842a*, *846*, 905, 927, *950*, *957*, *958*, *964*, *1002*, *1043*, *1044a*, *1061*, *1157f*, *1162*, *1192*, *1211*, *1214*, *1215*, *1254*, *1299*, *1314*, *1316a*, *1372b*, *1375*, *1391*, *1399a*, *1419*, *1481*, *1550a*, *1574*, *1785*, *1786*, *1790a*, *1826*, *1914*, *1923*, *1928*, *1972*, *1998*, *2019*, *2075a*, *2128*, *2174*.

1762. *3*, 16, *27*, 35, 37, 40, *45*, *53a*, *60a*, 69, 81, *86*, 108, *135*, *142*, 145, 156, 163, *186*, 187, *195*, 244, 258, *261*, *262*, *266*, *271*, 274, 277, *284*, 328, *336*, *343*, 355, 363, *365*, *367*, 369, 385, 389, *393*, *394*, 397, 398, *409a*, 439, 566, 580, *598*, *600*, *623*, *629*, 632, 665, *666*, 691, 727, 734, *761*, *764*, *795*, 798, *800*, *803*, *805*, *807*, 812, 840, *842a*, *846*, 880, 882, 905, 907, *950*, *957*, *958*, *964*, *1002*, *1011*, *1038*, *1043*, *1044a*, *1157f*, *1172b*, *1192*, *1208c*, *1211*, *1214*, *1215*, *1254*, *1271*, *1299*, *1314*, *1316a*, *1372b*, *1375*, *1391*, *1399a*, *1419*, *1434*, *1481*, *1517*, *1550a*, *1562b*, *1704*, *1785*, *1786*, *1790a*, *1810*, *1826*, *1923*, *1962*, *1972*, *1998*, *2075a*, *2128*, *2174*.

1763. *3*, 16, *27*, 35, *37*, 40, *45*, *53a*, *60a*, 69, 81, *86*, 100, 108, 128, *135*, 137, 142, 145, 156, 163, *186*, 187, *195*, *261*, *262*, *266*, *271*, 274, 277, *284*, *336*, *343*, 355, *365*, *367*, 385, 389, *393*, *394*, 397, 398, 420, 438, 439, 566, 580, 590, *598*, *600*, *623*, *629*, 632, 665, *666*, 721, 727, *761*, *764*, 767, *795*, 798, 800, 803, *805*, *807*, 812, 829, *840*, *842a*, *846*, 864, 905, 907, 918, *950*, *957*, *958*, *964*, *1002*, *1043*, *1044a*, *1157f*, *1172b*, *1192*, *1211*, *1214*, *1215*, *1256*, *1271*, *1296b*, *1297a*, *1299*, *1314*, *1316a*, *1372b*, *1375*, *1391*, *1399a*, *1419*, *1481*, *1517*, *1550a*, *1705*, *1785*, *1786*, *1790a*, *1826*, *1923*, *1946*, *1962*, *1972*, *1998*, *2039*, *2075a*, *2128*, *2174*.

1764. *3*, 16, *27*, *37*, *40*, *45*, *53a*, *60a*, 69, *86*, 108, *135*, *142*, 145, 156, 163, *186*, 187, 192, 195, *261*, *262*, *266*, *271*, 274, 277, *284*, *336*, *343*, 355, *365*, *367*, 385, 389, *393*, *394*, 397, 398, 438, 439, 566, 580, 590, *597*, *598*, *600*, *623*, *629*, 632, 665, *666*, *761*, *764*, 767, *795*, 798, *800*, *803*, *805*, *807*, 812, 840, *842a*, *846*, 905, 907, 918, *950*, *957*, *958*, *964*, *1002*, *1043*, *1044a*, *1053*, *1119*, *1135*, *1157c*, *1157d*, *1157f*, *1176a*, *1192*, *1211*, *1214*, *1215*, *1256*, *1271*, *1296b*, *1299*, *1314*, *1316a*, *1372b*, *1375*, *1391*, *1399a*, *1419*, *1481*, *1517*, *1785*, *1786*, *1790a*, *1809*, *1826*, *1884*, *1923*, *1972*, *1991*, *1998*, *2040*, *2041*, *2041a*, *2047*, *2075a*, *2128*, *2173*, *2174*.

1765. *3*, 16, *27*, *37*, *45*, *53a*, *60a*, 69, *86*, 90, 108, *135*, 142, 145, 147, 156, 163, *186*, 192, *195*, *261*, *262*, *266*, *271*, 274, 277, *284*, 336, 341, 343, 355, *365*,

367, 385, 389, *393*, *394*, 397, 398, 439, 566, 580, 590, *597*, *598*, *600*, *623*, *629*, 632, 665, *666*, *761*, *764*, 767, 795, 798, 800, *805*, *807*, 812, *840*, *842a*, *846*, 905, 907, 918, *950*, 957, *958*, *964*, *1002*, *1043*, *1044a*, *1053*, *1157c*, *1157f*, *1176a*, *1192*, *1211*, *1214*, *1215*, *1271*, *1290a*, *1296b*, *1299*, *1314*, *1316a*, *1372b*, *1375*, *1391*, *1419*, *1465*, *1481*, *1515a*, *1517*, *1786*, *1790a*, *1826*, *1922*, *1923*, *1972*, *1998*, *2075a*, *2089*, *2108b*, *2109a*, *2128*, *2173*, *2174*.

1766. *3*, 16, *27*, *37*, *45*, *53a*, *60a*, 69, 86, 108, *135*, *142*, 147, 156, 163, *186*, *192*, *195*, *239*, *261*, *262*, *271*, 274, 277, *284*, 286, *336*, 343, 355, *365*, *367*, 385, 389, *393*, *394*, 397, 398, 439, 548, 580, 590, *597*, *598*, *600*, *623*, *629*, 632, 665, *666*, *761*, *764*, 767, 795, 798, *800*, *805*, *807*, 812, 836, *840*, *842a*, *846*, *848*, 905, 907, 918, *950*, 957, *958*, *964*, *1002*, *1042*, *1043*, *1044a*, *1157c*, *1157f*, *1158*, *1176a*, *1192*, *1211*, *1214*, *1215*, *1221*, *1239*, *1240*, *1271*, *1296b*, *1299*, *1314*, *1316a*, *1372b*, *1375*, *1381*, *1391*, *1419*, *1465*, *1481*, *1515a*, *1517*, *1565*, *1583*, *1786*, *1790a*, *1826*, *1839*, *1923*, *1972*, *1998*, *2075a*, *2108b*, *2128*, *2171*, *2173*, *2174*.

1767. *3*, 16, *27*, *37*, *45*, *53a*, *57*, 69, 86, 108, *135*, *142*, 147, 156, 163, *186*, *192*, *195*, *239*, *261*, *262*, *271*, 274, 277, *284*, 286, *336*, 343, 355, *365*, *366*, *367*, 385, 389, 393, *394*, 397, 398, 439, 580, *597*, *598*, *600*, *623*, *629*, 632(?), 665, *666*, 730, *761*, *764*, 767, 795, 798, 800, *805*, *807*, 812, *840*, *842a*, *846*, 848, 905, 907, 918, *950*, 957, *958*, *964*, *1002*, *1042*, *1043*, *1044a*, *1157c*, *1157f*, *1176a*, *1192*, *1214*, *1215*, *1221*, *1271*, *1296b*, *1299*, *1314*, *1316a*, *1372b*, *1375*, *1391*, *1419*, *1481*, *1515a*, *1517*, *1565*, *1712*, *1729*, *1786*, *1790a*, *1826*, *1923*, *1972*, *1998*, *2108b*, *2128*, *2174*.

1768. *3*, 8, 16, *27*, *37*, *45*, *53a*, *57*, 86, *102*, *135*, *142*, 147, 156, 163, *186*, *192*, *195*, 210, 228, *239*, *261*, *262*, *271*, 274, 277, *284*, *286*, *336*, 343, *349*, 351, 355, *365*, *366*, *367*, 385, 389, 393, *394*, 397, 398, 439, 580, *597*, *598*, *600*, *629*, 632, 665, *666*, 667, 730, *761*, *764*, 767, 795, 798, 800, *805*, *807*, 812, *840*, *842a*, *846*, *848*, 905, 907, 932, *950*, 957, *958*, *964*, *1002*, *1042*, *1043*, *1044a*, *1142*, *1157c*, *1157f*, *1170*, *1176a*, *1192*, *1214*, *1215*, *1221*, *1225*, *1271*, *1296b*, *1299*, *1314*, *1316a*, *1372b*, *1375*, *1391*, *1409a*, *1419*, *1481*, *1506*, *1515a*, *1517*, *1565*, *1586*, *1684*, *1712*, *1786*, *1790a*, *1811*, *1826*, *1923*, *1972*, *1998*, *2084*, *2108b*, *2128*, *2174*.

1769. *3*, 8, 16, *27*, *37*, *45*, *53a*, *57*, 86, *102*, *135*, *142*, 147, 156, 163, *186*, 192, *195*, 228, *239*, 251, 261, *262*, *271*, 274, 277, *284*, *286*, *336*, 343, *349*, 351, 355, *365*, *366*, *367*, 383, 385, 389, 393, *394*, 397, 398, 439, 541, 580, *584*, *597*, *598*, *600*, *629*, 632, 665, *666*, 667, 679, 730, *761*, *764*, 767, 795, 798, 800, *805*, *807*, 812, *840*, *842a*, *846*, *848*, 860, 866, 874, 905, 907, 932, *950*, 957, *958*, *964*, *1002*, *1043*, *1044a*, *1142*, *1157f*, *1176*, *1176a*, *1192*, *1194*, *1207a*(?), *1214*, *1215*, *1221*, *1271*, *1296b*, *1299*, *1314*, *1316a*, *1372b*, *1375*, *1391*, *1409a*, *1419*, *1440*, *1506*, *1515a*, *1517*, *1565*, *1570a*, *1586*, *1777*, *1786*, *1790a*, *1826*, *1923*, *1972*, *1998*, *2074*, *2108b*, *2128*, *2174*.

1770. *3*, 8, 16, 24, *27*, *37*, *45*, *53a*, *57*, 86, *102*, *135*, *142*, 143, 147, 156, 163, 182, *186*, *192*, *195*, 228, *239*, 251, 261, *262*, *271*, 274, 277, *284*, *286*, *336*, 343, *349*, *351*, 355, 358, 365, *366*, *367*, 383, 385, 389, 393, 394, 397, 398, 406, 408, 439, 541, 580, *584*, *597*, *598*, *600*, *629*, 632, 665, *666*, 667,

679, 730, *761, 764, 767,* 785, *795, 798, 800, 805, 807,* 812, *840, 842a, 846,*
848, 871, 874, 905, 907, 932, *950, 956, 957, 958, 964, 1002, 1043, 1044a,*
1051, 1095b, 1138b, 1140, 1157f, 1176a, 1192, 1207a(?), *1213, 1214, 1215,*
1221, 1271, 1296b, 1299, *1314, 1316a, 1375, 1376, 1391, 1409a, 1418, 1420,*
1441, 1506, 1515a, 1517, 1565, 1570a, 1708, 1713, 1777, 1786, 1790a, 1826,
1923, 1954a, 1972, 1998, *2071, 2108b, 2128, 2174.*

1771. *3,* 16, 24, *27, 37, 45, 53a, 57,* 86, 102, *135, 142,* 143, 147, 156, 163,
186, 192, *195,* 223, *239,* 261, 262, *271,* 274, 277, *284,* 286, 301, *336, 343, 349,*
351, 355, 358, *365, 366, 367,* 383, 385, 389, *393, 394,* 397, 398, 406, 408, 439,
541, 580, *584, 597, 598, 600,* 629, 632, 665, *666,* 667, 730, *761, 764,* 767, *795,*
798, 800, *805, 807,* 812, *840, 842a, 846, 848,* 874, 905, 932, *950, 956,* 957,
958, 964, 1002, 1043, 1044a, 1051, 1095b, 1157f, 1173, 1176a, 1192, 1213,
1214, 1215, 1221, 1271, 1296b, 1299, *1314, 1316a, 1375, 1391, 1409a, 1418,*
1441, 1506, 1515a, 1517, 1565, 1570a, 1570b, 1777, 1786, 1790a, 1826, 1904a,
1918, 1923, 1943, 1972, 1987, 1998, *2000, 2021a, 2108b, 2128, 2174.*

1772. *3,* 16, 24, *27, 37, 45, 53c,* 57, 67, *86,* 102, *135, 142,* 156, 163, *186,*
192, *195,* 223, *239,* 261, 262, *271,* 274, 277, *284,* 286, *294,* 301, 311, *336,*
343, 349, *351,* 355, 358, *365, 366, 367, 383,* 385, 389, *393, 394,* 397, 398,
408, 421, 439, 541, 549, 580, *584, 586, 597, 598, 600,* 629, 665, *666,* 667, 730,
761, 764, 767, 798, 800, *805, 807,* 811, 812, *840, 842a, 846, 848,* 863, 874,
901, 905, 932, *950, 956,* 957, *958, 964,* 968, *1002, 1043, 1044a, 1051, 1095b,*
1157f, 1176a, 1192, 1214, 1215, 1221, 1271, 1296b, 1299, *1314, 1316a, 1375,*
1380, 1391, 1409a, 1506, 1515a, 1517, 1521b, 1565, 1570a, 1570b, 1777, 1786,
1790, 1790a, 1826, 1866, 1881, 1904a, 1923, 1972, 1983, 1998, *2000, 2108b,*
2128, 2174.

1773. *3,* 16, 24, *27, 37, 45,* 51, *53a, 57,* 86, 87, *102, 135, 142,* 156, 163,
186, 192, *195,* 198, 202, *239,* 261, 262, *271,* 274, 277, *284,* 286, *294,* 301, 311,
336, 343, 349, *351,* 355, 358, *365, 366, 367,* 385, 389, *393, 394,* 397, 398, 408,
421, 435, 439, 541, 574, 580, *584, 586, 597, 598, 600,* 629, 665, *666,* 667, *764,*
767, 798, 800, *805, 807,* 812, 823, *840, 842a, 846, 848,* 874, 901, 905, 932, 937,
950, 951, 957, *958, 964,* 968, *1002, 1043, 1044a, 1044b, 1051, 1062a, 1072,*
1095b, 1157f, 1172, 1173, 1176a, 1192, 1214, 1215, 1221, 1230, 1271, 1296b,
1299, *1314, 1316a, 1375, 1378, 1379, 1380, 1391, 1409a, 1410, 1502, 1506,*
1515a, 1517, 1521b, 1565, 1570a, 1570b, 1777, 1786, 1790, 1790a, 1826, 1866,
1904a, 1923, 1972, 1998, *1999, 2000, 2002, 2038, 2108b, 2128, 2174.*

1774. *3,* 16, 24, *27, 37, 45,* 51, *53a, 57,* 82, *86, 102,* 131, *135, 142,* 156,
163, *186,* 192, *195,* 198, 202, *239,* 261, 262, *271,* 272, 274, 277, *284,* 287, *294,*
301, 311, *336, 343,* 349, *351,* 355, 358, *365, 366, 367,* 385, 389, *393, 394,* 397,
398, 408, 435, 439, 541, 574, 578, 580, *584, 586, 597, 598, 600,* 614, 629, *665,*
666, 667, *764,* 767, 798, 800, 804, *805, 807,* 812, 823, *840, 842a, 846, 848,*
874, 901, 905, 932, 937, *950,* 951, 957, *958, 964,* 968, *1002, 1043, 1044a,*
1051, 1056, 1072, 1095b, 1157f, 1173, 1176a, 1192, 1214, 1215, 1230, 1258,
1271, 1296b, 1299, *1314, 1316a, 1375, 1391, 1409a, 1410, 1481a, 1506, 1515a,*
1517, 1521b, 1565, 1570a, 1570b, 1579, 1777, 1786, 1790, 1790a, 1826, 1833,
1904a, 1916, 1923, 1925, 1972, 1998, *1999, 2000, 2108b, 2128, 2174.*

1775. *3*, 16, 24, *27*, *37*, *45*, 51, *53a*, *57*, 86, *102*, 131, *135*, 142, 153, 156, 163, *186*, *192*, *195*, 198, 202, *239*, *261*, 262, *271*, 272, 274, 277, 284, 287, *294*, 301, *336*, *343*, 349, *351*, 355, 358, *365*, *366*, *367*, 385, 389, 393, *394*, 397, 398, 408, 410, 431, 435, 439, 453, 541, 574, 578, 580, *584*, *586*, *597*, 598, *600*, 614, *629*, 665, *666*, 667, 722, *764*, *767*, 780, 798, 800, *805*, *807*, 812, 823, *840*, *842a*, *846*, 848, 874, 905, 932, 937, *950*, 951, 957, *958*, *964*, 968, 1002, *1043*, *1044a*, 1051, 1056, 1072, *1095b*, *1105*, 1151, *1173*, *1176a*, *1180*, *1192*, *1214*, *1215*, *1230*, *1234*, *1271*, *1296b*, *1299*, *1314*, *1316a*, *1361*, *1375*, *1391*, *1409a*, *1410*, *1506*, *1515a*, *1517*, *1521b*, *1565*, *1570a*, *1770*, *1777*, *1786*, *1790*, *1790a*, *1826*, *1875*, *1923*, *1925*, *1972*, *1985*, *1998*, *1999*, *2000*, *2108b*, *2128*, *2174*.

1776. *3*, 9, 16, 24, *27*, *37*, *45*, 51, 53, *53a*, *57*, 86, *102*, 131, *135*, 141, *142*, 153, 155, 156, 163, *186*, *192*, *195*, 198, 202, 234, *239*, *261*, *261a*, 262, 267, *271*, 274, 277, 284, 287, *294*, 301, *336*, *343*, 349, *351*, 355, 358, *365*, *366*, *367*, *385*, *389*, 393, *394*, 397, 398, 408, 410, 413, 435, 439, 541, 580, *584*, *586*, *597*, *598*, *600*, *629*, 630, 665, *666*, 667, 722, *764*, *767*, 780, 798, 800, *805*, *807*, 812, 814, 823, *840*, *842a*, *846*, 848, 874, 905, 932, *937*, *950*, 951, 957, *958*, *964*, 968, 1002, *1043*, *1043a*, *1044a*, *1056*, *1062*, *1072*, *1092*, *1095b*, *1105*, *1157i*, *1173*, *1176a*, *1179*, *1180*, *1192*, *1214*, *1215*, *1230*, *1234*, *1271*, *1296b*, *1299*, *1306*, *1314*, *1316a*, *1375*, *1391*, *1399c*, *1409a*, *1410*, *1410a*, *1506*, *1515a*, *1517*, *1521b*, *1555*, *1565*, *1570a*, *1746*, *1755*, *1777*, *1786*, *1790a*, *1826*, *1923*, *1925*, *1972*, *1995*, *1998*, *1999*, *2000*, *2108b*, *2174*.

1777. *3*, *9a*, 16, 24, *27*, *37*, *45*, *53a*, *57*, 86, *102*, 131, *135*, 141, *142*, 155, 156, 163, *186*, *192*, *195*, 202, 234, *239*, *261*, *261a*, 262, *271*, 274, 277, 284, 287, *294*, 301, *336*, *343*, 344, *349*, *351*, 355, 358, 365, *366*, *367*, 385, 389, 393, *394*, 397, 398, 408, 410, 413, 435, 439, *541*, 580, *584*, 586, *597*, 598, *600*, *629*, 630, 665, *666*, *764*, *767*, 780, 783, 798, 799, 800, 805, *807*, 812, 823, *840*, *842a*, *846*, 848, 874, 905, 932, *937*, *950*, 951, 957, *958*, *964*, 968, 970, *1002*, *1043*, *1044a*, *1046b*, *1056*, *1072*, *1095b*, *1105*, *1157i*, *1173*, *1176a*, *1179*, *1180*, *1192*, *1214*, *1215*, *1229*, *1230*, *1234*, *1271*, *1285a*, *1296b*, *1299*, *1306*, *1314*, *1316a*, *1347*, *1367*, *1373a*, *1375*, *1391*, *1399c*, *1409a*, *1410*, *1439*, *1506*, *1515a*, *1517*, *1521b*, *1553*, *1556*, *1556a*, *1565*, *1570a*, *1733*, *1735*, *1737*, *1761*, *1777*, *1786*, *1790a*, *1826*, *1923*, *1925*, *1970*, *1972*, *1995*, *1998*, *1999*, *2000*, *2108b*, *2158b*, **2***174*.

1778. *3*, 16, 24, *27*, 28, *37*, *45*, *53a*, *57*, 86, *102*, 131, *135*, 141, *142*, 155, 156, 163, *186*, *192*, *195*, 202, 234, *239*, *261*, 261a, 262, *271*, 274, 277, 284, 287, 294, 301, *336*, *343*, 344, *349*, *351*, 355, 358, *365*, *366*, *367*, 385, 389, 393, 394, 397, 398, 408, 410, 435, 439, *541*, 580, *584*, 586, *597*, 598, *600*, *629*, 665, *666*, *764*, *767*, 780, 783, 797, 798, 799, 800, 805, *807*, 812, 815, *840*, *842a*, *846*, 848, 874, 905, 913, 932, *937*, *950*, 951, 957, *958*, *964*, 968, *1002*, *1043*, *1044a*, *1044c*, *1056*, *1072*, *1095b*, *1105*, *1127a*, *1157i*, *1157k*, *1169*, *1173*, *1176a*, *1179*, *1180*, *1192*, *1214*, *1215*, *1228*, *1229*, *1234*, *1271*, *1285a*, *1296b*, *1299*, *1314*, *1316a*, *1375*, *1377*, *1391*, *1394a*, *1399c*, *1409a*, *1410*, *1506*, *1515a*, *1517*, *1521b*, *1556*, *1565*, *1570a*, *1733*, *1777*, *1780*, *1786*, *1790a*, *1826*, *1923*, *1925*, *1970*, *1972*, *1998*, *1999*, *2000*, *2108b*, *2140*, *2174*.

1779. *3*, 13, 16, 24, *27*, 28, *37*, *45*, *53a*, *57*, 86, *102*, *135*, 141, 142, 155, 156, 158, 163, *186*, 192, *195*, 202, 204a, 211, 234, *239*, *261*, 261a, 262, *271*,

274, 277, 284, 287, *294*, 301, *336*, *340*, *343*, *349*, *351*, 355, 358, *365*, *366*, *367*, 374, 385, 389, 392, 393, 394, 397, 398, 408, 410, 435, 439, 544, 580, *584*, *586*, *597*, *598*, *600*, *629*, *665*, *666*, *764*, 767, 780, 783, 797, 798, 799, 800, 805, 807, 812, 815, *840*, *842a*, *846*, *848*, 874, 905, 932, *937*, *950*, 951, 957, *958*, *964*, *968*, *1002*, *1043*, *1044a*, *1056*, *1072*, *1078*, *1095b*, *1105*, *1127a*, *1157m*, *1173*, *1176a*, *1180*, *1192*, *1214*, *1215*, *1229*, *1245*, *1271*, *1296b*, *1299*, *1314*, *1316a*, *1328*, *1375*, *1377*, *1391*, *1394a*, *1399c*, *1409a*, *1410*, *1506*, *1515a*, *1517*, *1521b*, *1556*, *1565*, *1570a*, *1733*, *1753*, *1777*, *1780*, *1786*, *1790a*, *1826*, *1883*, *1923*, *1925*, *1970*, *1972*, *1998*, *1999*, *2000*, *2108b*, *2131*, *2161*, *2174*.

1780. *3*, 16, 24, 27, 28, *37*, *45*, *53a*, *57*, 86, *102*, *135*, 141, 142, 155, 156, 158, 163, *186*, 192, *195*, 202, *204a*, 234, *239*, *261*, 261a, *262*, 274, 277, 284, 287, *294*, 301, *336*, *340*, *343*, *349*, *351*, 355, 358, *365*, *366*, *367*, 368, 385, 389, 392, 393, 394, 397, 398, 408, 410, 435, 439, 544, 580, 584, *585*, *586*, *597*, *598*, *600*, *629*, 633, 665, *666*, 707, 729, *764*, 767, 778, 780, 783, 797, 798, 799, *800*, 805, 807, 812, *840*, *842a*, *846*, *848*, 874, 877, 905, 932, *937*, *950*, 951, 957, *958*, *964*, *968*, *1002*, *1043*, *1044*, *1044a*, *1056*, *1072*, *1095b*, *1105*, *1127a*, *1139*, *1157m*, *1173*, *1176a*, *1180*, *1192*, *1195*, *1214*, *1215*, *1229*, *1245*, *1246*, *1250*, *1271*, *1296b*, *1299*, *1314*, *1316a*, *1368*, *1375*, *1377*, *1391*, *1394a*, *1399c*, *1409a*, *1410*, *1435*, *1506*, *1515a*, *1517*, *1521b*, *1556*, *1565*, *1777*, *1780*, *1786*, *1790a*, *1826*, *1912*, *1923*, *1925*, *1970*, *1972*, *1988*, *1998*, *1999*, *2000*, *2108b*, *2134*, *2150*, *2174*, *2177*.

1781. *3*, 16, 24, 27, 28, *37*, *45*, *53a*, *57*, 86, *102*, *135*, 141, *142*, 155, 156, 163, *186*, *192*, 195, 202, *204a*, *239*, *261*, 261a, *262*, 274, 277, 284, 287, *294*, 301, *336*, *340*, *343*, *349*, *351*, 355, 358, 360, *365*, *366*, *367*, 368, 385, 389, *392*, *393*, *394*, *397*, 398, 399, 403, *408*, 435, 439, 454, 580, *584*, *585*, *586*, 595, *597*, *598*, *600*, *629*, 633, 665, *666*, 707, 729, *764*, 767, 780, 783, 797, 798, *799*, 800, 805, 807, 812, *840*, *842a*, *846*, *848*, 874, 877, 905, 932, *937*, *950*, 951, 957, *958*, *964*, *968*, *1002*, *1036*, *1043*, *1044*, *1044a*, *1056*, *1072*, *1095b*, *1105*, *1127a*, *1139*, *1173*, *1176a*, *1180*, *1192*, *1214*, *1215*, *1229*, *1246*, *1271*, *1296b*, *1299*, *1314*, *1316a*, *1375*, *1377*, *1391*, *1394a*, *1399c*, *1409a*, *1410*, *1506*, *1515a*, *1517*, *1521b*, *1556*, *1565*, *1776*, *1777*, *1786*, *1790a*, *1826*, *1912*, *1923*, *1925*, *1970*, *1972*, *1998*, *1999*, *2000*, *2099a*, *2108b*, *2134*, *2174*.

1782. *3*, 16, 24, 27, 28, *37*, *45*, *53a*, *57*, 68, 86, *102*, *135*, 141, *142*, 155, 156, 163, *186*, *192*, *195*, 202, *204a*, 218, *239*, *261*, 261a, *262*, 274, 277, 284, 287, *294*, 301, *336*, *340*, *343*, *349*, *351*, 355, 358, 360, *365*, *366*, *367*, 368, 372, 385, 389, *392*, *393*, *394*, *397*, 398, 399, *408*, 435, 439, 580, *584*, 585, *586*, 595, *597*, *598*, *600*, 602, 617, *629*, *631*, 633, 665, *666*, 729, 750, *764*, 767, 780, 783, 797, 798, *799*, 800, *805*, 807, 812, *840*, *842a*, *846*, *848*, 874, 905, 932, *937*, 949, *950*, 951, 957, *958*, *964*, *968*, *1002*, *1006*, *1043*, *1044*, *1044a*, *1056*, *1060*, *1072*, *1084a*, *1095b*, *1105*, *1127a*, *1139*, *1173*, *1176a*, *1180*, *1192*, *1214*, *1215*, *1229*, *1232a*, *1271*, *1296b*, *1299*, *1314*, *1316a*, *1349*, *1375*, *1377*, *1391*, *1394a*, *1409a*, *1410*, *1491*, *1506*, *1515a*, *1517*, *1521b*, *1556*, *1565*, *1751*, *1776*, *1777*, *1786*, *1790a*, *1826*, *1891*, *1923*, *1925*, *1945*, *1972*, *1998*, *1999*, *2000*, *2108b*, *2159a*, *2174*.

1783. *3*, 16, 24, 27, 28, *37*, *45*, *53a*, *57*, 68, 86, 102, *135*, 141, 142, 155, 156, 163, *186*, 192, *195*, 202, *204a*, 213, 218, *239*, *261*, 261a, *262*, 274, 277,

283, 284, 287, *294*, 301, *336*, *340*, *343*, *349*, *351*, 355, 358, *365*, *366*, *367*, 368, 385, 389, *393*, *394*, 397, 398, 399, *408*, 435, 439, 580, *584*, *585*, *586*, 595, *597*, *598*, *600*, 602, 617, *629*, 631, 633, 665, *666*, 729, *764*, *767*, 780, 783, 797, 798, 799, 800, *805*, *807*, 812, *840*, *842a*, *846*, 848, 874, 905, 932, *937*, *949*, *950*, 951, *957*, *958*, *964*, 968, 1002, *1043*, *1044*, *1044a*, 1056, *1060*, *1071*, *1072*, *1084a*, *1093*, *1095b*, 1105, *1127a*, *1173*, *1176a*, *1180*, 1192, *1214*, *1215*, *1229*, *1271*, *1277a*, *1280*, *1296b*, *1299*, *1314*, *1316a*, *1349*, *1373*, *1375*, *1377*, *1391*, *1394a*, *1409a*, *1410*, *1466*, *1491*, *1506*, *1515a*, *1517*, *1521b*, *1537*, *1556*, *1565*, *1766*, *1777*, *1786*, *1790a*, *1814a*, *1826*, *1923*, *1925*, *1945*, *1972*, *1998*, *1999*, *2000*, *2006*, *2024*, *2036a*, *2100*, *2101*, *2108b*, *2158a*, *2174*.

1784. *3*, 16, 24, 27, 28, *37*, *45*, *53a*, *57*, 86, 102, *135*, 141, *142*, 156, 163, *186*, 192, *195*, 202, *204a*, 213, 218, *239*, *261*, *261a*, *262*, 274, 277, 284, 287, *294*, 301, 335, *336*, *340*, *343*, *349*, *351*, 355, 358, *365*, 366, *367*, 368, 385, 389, *393*, *394*, 398, 399, *408*, 435, 439, 580, *584*, *585*, *586*, 595, *597*, *598*, *600*, 602, 617, 619, *629*, 633, 665, *666*, 729, *764*, *767*, 776, 780, 798, 800, *805*, *807*, 812, *840*, *842a*, *846*, 848, 865, 874, 905, *924*, 932, 949, *950*, 951, *957*, *958*, *960*, *964*, 968, 1002, *1043*, *1044*, *1044a*, *1047*, 1056, *1071*, *1072*, *1085a*, *1095b*, 1105, *1127a*, *1173*, *1176a*, *1180*, 1192, *1214*, *1215*, *1229*, *1271*, *1277a*, *1286*, *1296b*, *1299*, *1314*, *1316a*, *1349*, *1373*, *1375*, *1377*, *1384b*, *1391*, *1394a*, *1407a*, *1409a*, *1410*, *1491*, *1506*, *1515a*, *1517*, *1521b*, *1537*, *1554*, *1556*, *1565*, *1577*, *1676*, *1766*, *1777*, *1786*, *1790a*, *1814a*, *1826*, *1923*, *1925*, *1945*, *1972*, *1980*, *1998*, *1999*, *2000*, *2006*, *2024*, *2050a*, *2100*, *2101*, *2108b*, *2116a*, *2158a*, *2166*, *2174*.

1785. *3*, 16, 24, 27, 28, 29, 31, *37*, *45*, *48a*, *53a*, *57*, 86, 102, *135*, 141, *142*, 156, 163, *168*, *186*, 192, *195*, 199, 202, *204a*, 213, 218, *239*, *261*, *261a*, *262*, 274, 277, 284, *294*, 301, *307*, *336*, *340*, *343*, *349*, *351*, 355, 358, *365*, *366*, *367*, 368, 385, 389, *393*, *394*, 398, 399, 408, 414, 425, 435, 450, 580, *584*, *585*, *586*, 595, *597*, *598*, *600*, 602, 607, 617, *619*, *629*, 633, 665, *666*, 728, 729, *764*, *767*, 792, 798, 800, *805*, *807*, 812, *842a*, *846*, 848, 865, 874, 875, 905, *924*, 949, *950*, 951, *957*, *958*, *960*, *964*, 968, 1002, *1035a*, *1043*, *1044*, *1044a*, *1047*, 1056, *1071*, *1072*, *1084a*, *1095b*, 1105, *1127a*, *1173*, *1176a*, *1180*, 1192, *1214*, *1215*, *1229*, *1271*, *1277a*, *1296b*, *1299*, *1314*, *1316a*, *1373*, *1375*, *1377*, *1384b*, *1391*, *1394a*, *1409a*, *1410*, *1506*, *1515a*, *1517*, *1521b*, *1537*, *1556*, *1565*, *1575*, *1577*, *1745*, *1766*, *1777*, *1780a*, *1786*, *1790a*, *1802*, *1814a*, *1826*, *1923*, *1945*, *1972*, *1998*, *1999*, *2000*, *2006*, *2024*, *2050a*, *2098*, *2100*, *2108b*, *2158a*, *2174*.

1786. *3*, 16, 24, 27, 28, 29, 31, *37*, *45*, *48a*, *53a*, *57*, 86, 102, *135*, 139, 141, 142, 156, 163, *168*, 170, 171, *186*, 192, *195*, 199, 202, *204a*, 213, 218, *239*, *261*, *261a*, *262*, 274, 277, 284, *294*, 301, 307, *336*, *340*, *343*, *349*, *351*, 355, 358, *365*, *366*, *367*, 368, *385*, 389, *393*, *394*, 399, *408*, 414, 425, 435, 450, 540, 580, *584*, *585*, *586*, 595, *597*, *598*, *600*, 602, 606, 607, 609, 615, 617, *619*, *629*, 633, 665, *666*, 708, 728, 729, *764*, *767*, 792, 798, 800, *805*, *807*, 812, *842a*, *846*, 848, 865, 874, 875, 905, *924*, 949, *950*, *957*, *958*, *964*, 968, 1002, *1035a*, *1043*, *1044*, *1044a*, *1047*, 1056, *1071*, *1072*, *1084a*, *1095b*, 1105, *1127a*, *1173*, *1176a*, *1180*, 1192, *1196*, *1214*, *1215*, *1229*, *1271*, *1277a*, *1288*, *1296b*, *1299*, *1309*, *1314*, *1316a*, *1344*, *1373*, *1375*, *1377*, *1384b*, *1391*, *1409a*, *1410*, *1506*, *1515a*, *1517*, *1521b*, *1537*, *1556*, *1561*, *1565*, *1575*, *1577*,

1745, 1777, 1786, 1790a, 1814a, 1826, 1923, 1945, 1972, 1998, 1999, 2000, 2006, 2015, 2024, 2100, 2108b, 2158a, 2174, 2178.

1787. *3*, 16, 24, *27*, 28, 29, *37*, *45*, *48a*, *53a*, 54, *57*, 86, *102*, *135*, 139, 141, *142*, 156, 163, *168*, 170, 171, 184, *186*, 192, *195*, *199*, 202, *204a*, 213, 218, *239*, *261*, *261a*, *262*, 265, 274, 277, 284, *294*, 301, *336*, *340*, *343*, 348, *349*, *351*, 355, 358, *365*, *366*, *367*, 368, *385*, 389, *393*, *394*, 399, *405*, *408*, 414, *425*, 435, 540, 580, *584*, *585*, *586*, 595, *597*, *598*, *600*, 606, 607, *615*, *621*, *629*, 633, 652, 665, *666*, 708, 729, *764*, *767*, 792, 798, *800*, *805*, *807*, 812, *842a*, *846*, 848, 865, 874, 905, *924*, 949, *950*, *957*, *958*, *964*, *967*, *968*, *1002*, *1035a*, *1043*, *1044*, *1044a*, *1056*, *1071*, *1072*, *1077*, *1084a*, *1087*, *1094*, *1095b*, *1105*, *1127a*, *1173*, *1176a*, *1180*, *1192*, *1196*, *1214*, *1215*, *1229*, *1267*, *1271*, *1277a*, *1288*, *1296b*, *1299*, *1314*, *1315*, *1316a*, *1344*, *1373*, *1375*, *1377*, *1384b*, *1391*, *1409a*, *1410*, *1428*, *1431*, *1506*, *1507a*, *1507c*, *1515a*, *1517*, *1521b*, *1537*, *1556*, *1561*, *1565*, *1575*, *1577*, *1777*, *1782*, *1786*, *1790a*, *1814a*, *1826*, *1923*, *1945*, *1958*, *1972*, *1997c*, *1998*, *1999*, *2000*, *2006*, *2015*, *2024*, *2108b*, *2158a*, *2174*.

1788. *3*, 10, 16, 24, *27*, 28, 29, *37*, *45*, *53a*, 54, *57*, 86, *102*, 135, 139, *141*, *142*, 144, 156, 163, *168*, 184, *186*, *188*, 190, 192, *195*, 199, 202, 204a, 213, 218, 232, *239*, *261*, *261a*, *262*, 265, 274, 277, 284, *294*, 301, *336*, *340*, *343*, *349*, *351*, 355, 358, *365*, *366*, *367*, 308, 378, *385*, 389, *393*, *394*, 399, *405*, *408*, 415, *425*, 435, 580, 584, 585, *586*, 595, *597*, *598*, *600*, 606, 607, 621, *629*, 633, 652, 665, *666*, 709, 729, *764*, *767*, *782*, 792, 798, *800*, *805*, *807*, 812, *842a*, 843, *846*, *848*, 854, 861, 865, 874, 881, 905, *924*, *938*, *949*, *950*, *957*, *958*, *964*, *967*, *968*, *1002*, *1003*, *1035a*, *1043*, *1044*, *1044a*, *1056*, *1071*, *1072*, *1077*, *1084a*, *1095*, *1095b*, *1105*, *1120*, *1127a*, *1161*, *1168*, *1173*, *1176a*, *1180*, *1192*, *1207b*, *1214*, *1215*, *1229*, *1267*, *1271*, *1277a*, *1288*, *1296b*, *1299*, *1314*, *1316a*, *1344*, *1370*, *1373*, *1375*, *1377*, *1384a*, *1384b*, *1391*, *1409a*, *1410*, *1428*, *1478*, *1496*, *1506*, *1507b*, *1507c*, *1515a*, *1517*, *1521b*, *1537*, *1542b*, *1556*, *1561*, *1565*, *1575*, *1577*, *1735b*, *1743*, *1771*, *1777*, *1786*, *1790a*, *1814a*, *1824a*, *1826*, *1923*, *1945*, *1958*, *1959*, *1961*, *1972*, *1985a*, *1997c*, *1998*, *1999*, *2000*, *2006*, *2015*, *2021b*, *2023b*, *2024*, *2108b*, *2158a*, *2159b*, *2174*.

1789. *3*, 10, 16, 24, *26*, *27*, 28, 29, 33, *37*, *45*, 50, *53a*, 54, *57*, 84, 86, *102*, *135*, 139, *141*, *142*, 156, 163, *168*, 174, 184, *186*, *188*, 192, *195*, *199*, 202, 204a, 213, 218, 221, 232, *239*, *261*, *261a*, *262*, 265, 274, 277, 284, *294*, 301, 309, *336*, *340*, *343*, *349*, *351*, 355, 357, 358, *365*, *366*, *367*, 368, 378, *385*, 386, 389, *393*, *394*, 399, *405*, *408*, 415, 425, 435, 456, 580, 584, 585, 586, 592, 595, *597*, *598*, 606, 607, *629*, 656, 665, *666*, 709, 729, 753, *764*, *767*, *782*, 788, 792, 798, *800*, *805*, *807*, 812, *842a*, 843, *846*, 848, 854, 865, 873, 874, 881, 904, 905, *924*, *936a*, *938*, 949, *950*, *957*, *958*, *964*, *967*, *968*, *1002*, *1003*, *1009*, *1035a*, *1043*, *1044*, *1044a*, *1056*, *1071*, *1072*, *1084a*, *1088*, *1095*, *1095b*, *1105*, *1127a*, *1157h*, *1168*, *1173*, *1176a*, *1180*, *1192*, *1207b*, *1214*, *1215*, *1229*, *1271*, *1277a*, *1288*, *1296b*, *1299*, *1314*, *1316a*, *1344*, *1373*, *1375*, *1377*, *1384a*, *1384b*, *1391*, *1409a*, *1410*, *1423*, *1428*, *1506*, *1507b*, *1507c*, *1515a*, *1517*, *1521b*, *1536*, *1537*, *1556*, *1561*, *1565*, *1575*, *1577*, *1743*, *1777*, *1786*, *1790a*, *1814a*, *1826*, *1923*, *1945*, *1958*, *1961*, *1972*, *1997c*, *1998*, *1999*, *2000*, *2006*, *2015*, *2023b*, *2024*, *2086*, *2108b*, *2158a*, *2159b*, *2174*.

1790. *3*, 10, 11, 16, 24, *26*, *27*, 28, *29*, 33, *37*, 38, 42, *45*, 50, *53a*, 54, 55, *57*, 84, *86*, *102*, *135*, 139, *141*, *142*, 156, 163, 168, 174, 184, *186*, 188, 192, *195*, 199, 202, *204a*, 213, 218, *221*, *239*, 261, *261a*, *262*, 265, 274, 277, 284, *294*, 301, 309, *336*, 340, *343*, *349*, *351*, 355, 358, 362, *365*, *366*, 367, 368, 378, *385*, 386, 389, *393*, *394*, 399, *405*, *408*, 425, 435, 456, 580, *584*, 585, *586*, *592*, 595, 597, 598, 606, 607, *629*, 656, *665*, *666*, 729, *764*, *767*, *788*, 792, 798, *800*, *805*, *807*, 812, 822, 830, 835, 839, *842a*, *843*, *846*, *848*, 873, 874, *904*, *905*, *924*, *936a*, *938*, *949*, *950*, *957*, *958*, *964*, *967*, *968*, *1002*, *1003*, *1013*, *1035a*, *1043*, *1044*, *1044a*, *1056*, *1062b*, *1071*, *1072*, *1084a*, *1095*, *1095b*, *1105*, *1113*, *1127a*, *1157h*, *1168*, *1173*, *1176a*, *1180*, *1192*, *1207b*, *1214*, *1215*, *1229*, *1253*, *1271*, *1277a*, *1296b*, *1299*, *1314*, *1316a*, *1344*, *1372*, *1373*, *1375*, *1377*, *1384a*, *1384b*, *1391*, *1404*, *1409a*, *1410*, *1428*, *1504b*, *1506*, *1507*, *1507c*, *1508*, *1515a*, *1517*, *1521b*, *1536*, *1537*, *1556*, *1561*, *1565*, *1575*, *1577*, *1711*, *1739*, *1743*, *1777*, *1786*, *1790a*, *1814a*, *1826*, *1864*, *1923*, *1958*, *1961*, *1972*, *1997c*, *1998*, *1999*, *2000*, *2006*, *2015*, *2023b*, *2024*, *2086*, *2108b*, *2158a*, *2174*.

1791. *3*, 10, 11, 16, 24, *26*, *27*, 28, *29*, 33, *37*, 38, 42, *45*, 50, *53a*, 54, *57*, *86*, *102*, 118, *135*, 139, *141*, 142, 156, 163, 168, 174, 184, *186*, 188, 192, *195*, 199, 202, *204a*, 207, 213, 218, *221*, *239*, *261*, *262*, 265, 274, 277, *282*, 284, *294*, 301, 309, *336*, *340*, *343*, *349*, *351*, 355, 358, 362, *365*, *366*, 367, 368, 378, *385*, 389, *393*, *394*, 399, 405, *408*, 425, 435, 441, 572, 580, *584*, 585, *586*, *592*, 595, 597, 598, *603*, 606, 607, *629*, 656, 661, *665*, *666*, 729, *764*, *767*, *788*, 792, 798, *800*, *805*, *807*, 812, 822, 830, *842a*, *843*, *846*, *848*, 859, 873, 874, *904*, 905, *924*, *936a*, *938*, *949*, *950*, *957*, *958*, *964*, *967*, *968*, *1002*, *1003*, *1035a*, *1043*, *1044*, *1044a*, *1056*, *1057*, *1062b*, *1071*, *1072*, *1084a*, *1095b*, *1096a*, *1105*, *1113*, *1127a*, *1157h*, *1168*, *1173*, *1176a*, *1180*, *1192*, *1207b*, *1214*, *1215*, *1229*, *1253*, *1271*, *1277a*, *1296b*, *1299*, *1306a*, *1314*, *1316a*, *1343*, *1344*, *1372*, *1373*, *1375*, *1377*, *1384a*, *1384b*, *1391*, *1404*, *1409a*, *1410*, *1421*, *1428*, *1504b*, *1506*, *1507*, *1507c*, *1515a*, *1517*, *1521b*, *1536*, *1537*, *1556*, *1561*, *1565*, *1575*, *1743*, *1777*, *1786*, *1790a*, *1814a*, *1826*, *1864*, *1923*, *1958*, *1961*, *1972*, *1997c*, *1998*, *1999*, *2000*, *2006*, *2015*, *2024*, *2086*, *2108b*, *2158a*, *2174*, *2174b*.

1792. *3*, 10, 11, 16, 24, 25, *26*, *27*, 28, *29*, 33, *37*, 38, 42, *45*, 50, *53a*, 54, *57*, *86*, 91, *102*, 105, 118, 130, *135*, 138, 139, *140*, *141*, *142*, 156, 163, *168*, 174, 184, *186*, 188, 192, *195*, 199, 202, *204a*, 213, 218, *221*, *239*, 240, *261*, *262*, 265, 274, 277, *282*, 284, *294*, 301, 309, *336*, *340*, *342*, *343*, *349*, *351*, 355, 358, 362, *365*, *366*, 367, 368, 378, *385*, 389, *393*, *394*, 399, 405, *408*, 412, 425, 435, 440, 441, 572, 580, 584, 585, *586*, 592, 595, 597, 598, *603*, 606, 607, 608, 610, *629*, 656, 661, *665*, *666*, 693, 731, 732, *764*, *767*, *788*, 792, 798, *800*, *805*, *807*, 812, 822, 824, 830, 841, *842a*, *843*, 845, *846*, *848*, 868, 873, 874, 885, *904*, 905, *924*, *936a*, *938*, *949*, *950*, *957*, *958*, *964*, *967*, *968*, *1002*, *1032*, *1035a*, *1043*, *1044*, *1044a*, *1045*, *1046a*, *1056*, *1057*, *1062b*, *1071*, *1072*, *1084a*, *1089*, *1091*, *1095b*, *1105*, *1113*, *1127*, *1127a*, *1141*, *1157h*, *1168*, *1168d*, *1171a*, *1172a*, *1173*, *1176a*, *1180*, *1191b*, *1192*, *1205a*, *1207b*, *1214*, *1215*, *1229*, *1252*, *1253*, *1255*, *1257*, *1271*, *1277a*, *1296*, *1296a*, *1296b*, *1299*, *1308a*, *1314*, *1316a*, *1343*, *1344*, *1365*, *1372*, *1373*, *1375*, *1377*, *1384a*, *1384b*, *1391*, *1395*, *1407b*, *1409a*, *1410*, *1421*, *1428*, *1480c*, *1504a*, *1504b*, *1506*, *1507*, *1515a*, *1515b*, *1516a*, *1517*, *1521b*, *1536*, *1537*, *1556*, *1561*, *1562a*, *1564*, *1565*, *1575*, *1742a*,

1743, 1777, 1783, 1786, 1790a, 1814a, 1819, 1826, 1864, 1923, 1958, 1961, 1972, 1997b, 1997c, 1998, 1999, 2000, 2006, 2015, 2024, 2024a, 2086, 2095, 2108b, 2149, 2158a, 2171a, 2174, 2174b.

1793. *3*, 10, 11, 16, 17, 24, 25, *26*, *27*, 28, *29*, 38, 42, *45*, 46, *53a*, 54, *57*, 59, 61, 64, 83, *86*, 89, 91, *102*, 118, 130, *135*, 138, *140*, *142*, 154, 156, 163, 168, *174*, *184*, *186*, *188*, 192, *195*, 197, 199, 202, *204a*, 213, 218, 219, *221*, *239*, 252, *261*, *262*, 274, 277, *282*, 284, *294*, 301, 319, *336*, *340*, 342, *343*, *349*, 350, *351*, 355, 358, 362, 365, *366*, *367*, 368, 371, 378, *385*, 389, *393*, *394*, 399, 405, *408*, 412, 425, 435, 440, 441, 447, 580, 584, 585, *586*, 592, 595, 597, 598, *603*, 606, 608, *616*, *629*, *656*, 661, 665, *666*, 693, 718a, 732, 751, *764*, 767, 788, 792, 798, *800*, *805*, *807*, 812, 822, 824, 830, 841, *842a*, 843, 845, 846, *848*, 868, 874, *885*, 905, *924*, 930, *936a*, *938*, *949*, *950*, *957*, *958*, *964*, *967*, *968*, *1002*, *1024*, *1031*, *1035a*, *1043*, *1044*, *1044a*, *1045*, *1046a*, *1056*, *1057*, *1062b*, *1071*, *1072*, *1083*, *1084a*, *1091*, *1127a*, *1157g*, *1157h*, *1157l*, *1159*, *1168*, *1172a*, *1173*, *1176a*, *1180*, *1192*, *1207b*, *1214*, *1215*, *1229*, *1233*, *1252*, *1253*, *1271*, *1277a*, *1296b*, *1299*, *1314*, *1316*, *1316a*, *1343*, *1344*, *1351*, *1365*, *1373*, *1375*, *1377*, *1383*, *1384a*, *1384b*, *1391*, *1409a*, *1410*, *1428*, *1504b*, *1506*, *1507*, *1510*, *1512*, *1517*, *1521b*, *1536*, *1537*, *1556*, *1561*, *1564*, *1565*, *1575*, *1673*, *1675*, *1719*, *1743*, *1777*, *1783*, *1786*, *1790a*, *1803*, *1826*, *1864*, *1865*, *1898*, *1904b*, *1934*, *1954*, *1958*, *1961*, *1972*, *1998*, *1999*, *2000*, *2002b*, *2005*, *2006*, *2015*, *2020*, *2023c*, *2024*, *2024b*, *2108b*, *2158a*, *2174*.

1794. *3*, 7, 10, 11, 16, 17, 24, 25, *26*, *27*, 28, *29*, 38, 42, *45*, 52, *53a*, 54, *57*, 59, 61, 83, 85, *86*, 89, 91, *102*, 118, 130, *135*, *140*, 142, 156, 163, *168*, *186*, *188*, 192, *195*, 197, 199, 202, *204a*, 213, 218, 219, 221, *239*, *252*, 260, *261*, *262*, 274, 277, *282*, 284, *294*, 301, 319, *336*, *340*, *342*, *343*, *349*, 350, *351*, 355, 358, 362, 365, *366*, *367*, 368, 371, 378, *385*, 389, 393, *394*, 399, 405, *408*, 412, 425, 434, 435, 440, *441*, 447, 580, 583, 584, *585*, *586*, 592, 595, 597, 598, *603*, 606, *616*, *629*, *656*, 661, 665, *666*, 718a, 724, 732, 755, *764*, 767, 773, 779, 781, 788, 792, 798, *800*, 805, *807*, 812, 818, 822, 824, 830, 841, *842a*, 843, 845, *846*, *848*, 853, 868, 874, *885*, 905, *924*, *936a*, *938*, *949*, *950*, *957*, *958*, *964*, *967*, *968*, *1002*, *1035a*, *1043*, *1044*, *1044a*, *1045*, *1056*, *1062b*, *1071*, *1072*, *1084a*, *1127a*, *1157e*, *1157g*, *1157h*, *1159*, *1168*, *1172a*, *1173*, *1176a*, *1180*, *1192*, *1207b*, *1214*, *1215*, *1229*, *1233*, *1253*, *1271*, *1277a*, *1296b*, *1314*, *1316*, *1343*, *1344*, *1365*, *1373*, *1375*, *1377*, *1384a*, *1384b*, *1391*, *1409a*, *1410*, *1427*, *1428*, *1471*, *1504b*, *1506*, *1507*, *1510*, *1512a*, *1517*, *1521b*, *1536*, *1537*, *1544a*, *1561*, *1565*, *1575*, *1743*, *1777*, *1783*, *1786*, *1790a*, *1826*, *1842*, *1864*, *1887*, *1898*, *1958*, *1961*, *1971*, *1998*, *1999*, *2000*, *2005*, *2006*, *2015*, *2020*, *2023c*, *2024*, *2024b*, *2108b*, *2109*, *2158a*, *2174*.

1795. *3*, 10, 11, 16, 24, 25, 26, *27*, 28, 38, 45, *53a*, 54, *57*, 59, 61, 83, 85, *86*, 88, 89, 91, *102*, 130, *135*, *140*, *142*, 156, 163, *168*, *186*, *188*, 192, *195*, 197, 199, 202, 204a, 213, 218, 219, *221*, *239*, *252*, 260, *261*, *262*, 274, 277, *282*, 284, *294*, 301, 319, *336*, *340*, *342*, *343*, *349*, 350, *351*, 355, 358, 365, *366*, *367*, 368, 371, *385*, 389, *393*, *394*, 399, 405, *408*, 425, 429, 434, 435, 440, 577, 580, 583, 584, *585*, *586*, 592, 595, 597, 598, *603*, 606, *616*, *629*, 661, 665, *666*, 675, 711, 718, 718a, 724, 732, 755, *764*, 767, 773, 779, 781, 788, 792, 798, *800*, *805*, *807*, 812, 818, 822, *825*, 830, 841, *842a*, 843, 845, *846*,

848, 849, 853, 872, 874, 879, 885, 905, 924, 936a, 938, 949, 950, 957, 958, 964,
968, 1002, 1035a, 1039, 1043, 1044, 1044a, 1045, 1052, 1056, 1058, 1062b,
1071, 1072, 1084a, 1115, 1127a, 1157h, 1168, 1172a, 1173, 1176a, 1178, 1180,
1192, 1206, 1207b, 1214, 1215, 1227a, 1229, 1241, 1253, 1271, 1277a, 1296b,
1310, 1314, 1316, 1343, 1344, 1365, 1373, 1375, 1377, 1384, 1384a, 1384b,
1391, 1409a, 1410, 1427, 1428, 1497, 1504b, 1506, 1507, 1510, 1512a, 1517,
1521b, 1536, 1537, 1559, 1561, 1563a, 1565, 1575, 1743, 1760, 1777, 1783,
1786, 1790a, 1826, 1827, 1836, 1838, 1842, 1864, 1869, 1898, 1958, 1961,
1971, 1977, 1998, 1999, 2000, 2005, 2006, 2015, 2020, 2023o, 2024, 2024b,
2056, 2108b, 2109, 2158a, 2170, 2174.

1796. *3*, 10, 11, 16, 24, 25, 26, *27*, 28, 38, *45*, 47, *53a*, 54, *57*, 59, 61, *83*,
86, 88, 89, 91, *102*, 130, *135*, *140*, *142*, 156, *163*, 168, *186*, *188*, *192*, *195*, *197*,
199, 202, *204a*, 213, 218, 219, *221*, 237, *239*, 241, *252*, 260, *261*, *262*, 274,
277, 280, *282*, 284, 285, *294*, 301, 321, *336*, *340*, *343*, *349*, 351, *355*, 358, *365*,
366, *367*, 368, 371, *385*, 389, *393*, *394*, 399, 405, 408, 425, 429, 434, 435, 440,
545, 554, 575, 577, 580, 582, *583*, 584, *585*, *586*, 592, 595, *597*, 598, *603*, *616*,
629, 661, 665, *666*, 675, 695, 711, 755, *764*, *767*, 779, 781, *788*, 792, 798, *800*,
805, *807*, 812, 822, 830, 841, 842a, *843*, 845, 846, *848*, 849, *853*, *872*, 874, 879,
885, 905, 916, *924*, 936a, 949, *950*, *957*, *958*, *964*, 968, 1002, 1004, 1035a, *1043*,
1044, 1044a, 1045, 1052, 1056, 1058, 1062b, *1071*, *1072*, 1084a, 1090, 1115,
1127a, 1132, 1157h, 1168, *1172a*, *1173*, *1176a*, 1180, 1192, 1207b, *1214*, 1215,
1229, 1253, 1268, *1271*, *1277a*, *1296b*, 1310, 1314, 1316, 1339, *1343*, *1344*,
1345, *1373*, *1375*, 1377, *1384a*, *1384b*, *1391*, *1409a*, *1410*, *1427*, *1428*, *1479*,
1506, 1507, 1510, 1517, 1520, 1521b, 1536, 1537, 1552, 1561, 1565, *1578*,
1668, *1725*, *1743*, *1777*, *1783*, 1786, *1790a*, 1826, 1838, 1842, 1864, *1873*,
1889a, 1898, 1958, 1961, 1971, 1977, 1981, 1998, 1999, 2000, 2005, 2006,
2015, 2024, 2024b, 2045, 2049, 2056, 2090, 2108b, 2109, 2158a, 2174.

1797. *3*, 5, 10, 11, 16, 19, 24, 25, *27*, 28, 38, *45*, 47, 48, *53a*, 54, *57*, 59,
61, *83*, *86*, 88, 89, *102*, 104, 130, *140*, 142, 156, *163*, 168, *186*, *188*, *192*, *195*,
197, 199, 202, 204a, 218, 219, *221*, 237, *239*, 241, 252, 260, *262*, 274, 277,
282, 284, 285, *294*, 301, *336*, *340*, *343*, 345, *349*, *351*, 355, 358, *365*, *366*,
367, 368, 371, *385*, 389, *393*, *394*, 399, 405, 408, 425, 429, 434, 435, 440,
545, 554, 571, 575, 577, *580*, 581, *583*, 584, *585*, 586, 592, 595, *597*, *598*,
603, *629*, 660, 661, 665, *666*, 675, 748, 755, *764*, *767*, 770, 781, 792, 798,
800, *805*, *807*, 812, 822, 830, 838, 841, 842a, *843*, 845, *846*, *848*, *853*, *885*, 905,
914, *924*, *950*, *957*, *958*, *964*, 968, 1002, 1004, 1022, 1035a, *1043*, 1044, 1044a,
1045, 1056, *1059a*(?), 1062b, *1071*, *1072*, 1084a, 1090, 1097, 1115, *1127a*,
1138a, 1157h, 1168, *1172a*, *1173*, *1176a*, 1180, 1192, *1207b*, *1214*, 1215, 1229,
1253, 1268, *1271*, *1277a*, *1296b*, *1298a*, 1310, 1314, 1316, *1343*, *1344*, *1373*,
1375, *1384a*, *1391*, *1409a*, *1410*, *1427*, *1428*, *1480*, 1506, 1510, 1517, *1521b*,
1536, 1537, 1561, 1565, *1571a*, *1578*, *1584*, *1725*, *1743*, *1777*, *1783*, 1786,
1790a, *1822*, 1826, 1864, *1873*, 1898, *1944*, 1958, 1961, 1971, 1977, 1981,
1998, 1999, 2000, 2005, 2006, 2015, 2024, *2081*, 2108b, 2158a, 2174.

1798. *3*, 10, 11, 16, 19, 20, 22, 24, 25, *27*, 28, 38, *45*, 47, *53a*, 54, *57*, 59,
61, 75, 77, 79, *83*, *86*, 88, 89, *102*, 104, 130, *140*, 156, *163*, 168, *186*, 188,
192, *195*, *197*, 199, 200, 202, *204a*, 218, 219, *221*, 237, *239*, *252*, 260, *262*,

274, 277, 278, 282, 284, 285, *294*, 301, *336*, 338, *340*, *343*, 345, *349*, *351*, 355, 358, 359, 365, *366*, *367*, 368, 371, *385*, 389, *393*, *394*, 399, 405, 408, 425, 429, 434, 435, 440, 452, 455, 539, *545*, 554, 571, 575, 577, 580, 581, *583*, 584, *585*, *586*, 592, 595, 597, 598, *603*, 629, 647, 660, 665, *666*, 675, 714, 748, 755, *764*, *767*, 781, 792, 798, 800, 805, 806, 807, 812, 822, 830, 838, 841, *842a*, *843*, 845, *846*, *848*, 885, 905, 914, 924, *950*, *957*, *958*, *964*, *968*, *1002*, *1004*, *1022*, *1035a*, *1035b*, *1043*, *1044*, *1044a*, *1045*, *1056*, *1062b*, *1071*, *1072*, *1084a*, *1097*, *1115*, *1127a*, *1157j*, *1168*, *1172a*, *1173*, *1176a*, *1180*, *1192*, *1214*, *1215*, *1219*, *1229*, *1232*, *1253*, *1259*, *1271*, *1277a*, *1296b*, *1310*, *1314*, *1316*, *1343*, *1344*, *1348*, *1373*, *1375*, *1384a*, *1391*, *1399b*, *1409a*, *1410*, *1427*, *1428*, *1480*, *1506*, *1510*, *1516*, *1517*, *1521b*, *1536*, *1537*, *1557*, *1561*, *1565*, *1572*, *1573*, *1581*, *1718*, *1743*, *1777*, *1786*, *1790a*, *1817*, *1826*, *1864*, *1873*, *1898*, *1958*, *1961*, *1971*, *1977*, *1981*, *1998*, *1999*, *2000*, *2004*, *2005*, *2006*, *2021*, *2023*, *2024*, *2048*, *2075*, *2081*, *2108b*, *2111*, *2146*, *2158a*, *2174*, *2182*.

1799. 3, 10, 11, 16, 20, 22, 24, 25, 27, 28, 30, 38, *45*, 47, *53a*, 54, 57, 59, 61, 75, 77, 78(?), 79, 83, *86*, 88, *89*, *102*, 103, *104*, 113, 130, 140, 156, *163*, *168*, *186*, *188*, *192*, *195*, *197*, 199, 200, 202, 204a, 218, 219, *221*, 237, 239, 260, 262, 274, 277, 278, 282, 284, 285, *294*, 301, 306, *336*, 338, *340*, *343*, 345, *349*, *351*, 355, 358, 359, 365, *366*, *367*, 368, 371, 377, *385*, 389, *394*, 399, 400, 405, 408, 425, 429, 434, 435, 436, 440, 452, 455, 538, 539, *545*, 554, 571, 575, 577, 580, 581, *583*, 584, *585*, *586*, 592, 594, 595, 597, 598, *603*, 610, 611, *629*, 647, 660, 665, *666*, 675, 714, 716, 755, *764*, *767*, 777, 781, 792, 798, 800, 805, 806, 807, 812, 821, 822, 830, 838, 841, *842a*, *843*, 845, *846*, *848*, 885, 897, 905, 914, 924, *950*, *957*, *958*, *964*, *968*, 969, *1002*, *1010*, *1017*, *1021*, *1024a*, *1030a*, *1035a*, *1035b*, *1037*, *1043*, *1044*, *1044a*, *1045*, *1056*, *1062b*, *1071*, *1072*, *1084a*, *1115*, *1127a*, *1157b*, *1168*, *1172a*, *1173*, *1176a*, *1180*, *1192*, *1214*, *1215*, *1219*, *1229*, *1231*, *1242*, *1253*, *1259*, *1271*, *1277a*, *1296b*, *1298b*, *1310*, *1314*, *1343*, *1344*, *1348*, *1373*, *1375*, *1384a*, *1385*, *1391*, *1394b*, *1409a*, *1410*, *1413*, *1427*, *1428*, *1459*, *1480*, *1499*, *1506*, *1510*, *1516*, *1517*, *1521b*, *1522a*, *1536*, *1537*, *1561*, *1565*, *1573*, *1671*, *1740*, *1743*, *1754*, *1777*, *1786*, *1790a*, *1817*, *1826*, *1864*, *1873*, *1895*, *1898*, *1899*, *1958*, *1961*, *1971*, *1977*, *1981*, *1997a*, *1998*, *1999*, *2000*, *2005*, *2006*, *2024*, *2028*, *2081*, *2108b*, *2111*, *2146*, *2151*, *2158a*, *2174*, *2182*.

1800. 3, 11, 16, 20, 24, 25, 27, 28, 30, 38, *45*, 47, *53a*, 54, 57, 59, 61, 66, 75, 77, 79, 83, *86*, 88, *89*, *102*, 103, *104*, 113, 130, 140, 156, *163*, *168*, 183, *186*, *188*, *192*, *195*, *197*, 199, 200, 204a, 218, 219, *221*, 233, 237, 239, 260, 262, 274, 277, 278, 279, 282, 284, 285, *294*, 301, 306, *336*, 338, *340*, *343*, 345, *349*, *351*, 355, 358, 359, 365, *366*, *367*, 368, 371, 377, 382, *385*, 389, *394*, 399, 400, 405, 408, 425, 429, 434, 435, 436, 440, 452, 455, 538, 539, *545*, 554, 571, 575, 577, 580, 581, *583*, 584, *585*, *586*, 592, 593, 594, 595, 597, 598, *603*, 610, 611, 620, *629*, 665, *666*, 675, 714, *764*, *767*, 777, 781, 792, 798, 800, 805, 806, 807, 812, 821, 822, 830, 838, 841, *842a*, *843*, 845, *846*, *848*, 885, 897, 905, 924, *950*, *957*, *958*, *964*, *968*, 969, *1002*, *1010*, *1015a*, *1017*, *1021*, *1030*, *1030a*, *1035a*, *1035b*, *1037*, *1043*, *1044*, *1044a*, *1045*, *1056*, *1062b*, *1071*, *1072*, *1082*, *1084*, *1084a*, *1115*, *1127a*, *1128*, *1168*, *1172a*, *1173*, *1176a*, *1180*, *1192*, *1197*, *1214*, *1215*, *1219*, *1224a*, *1229*, *1231*, *1235*, *1253*,

1259, 1271, 1277a, 1285, 1296b, 1310, 1314, 1343, 1344, 1348, 1373, 1375, 1384a, 1385, 1391, 1394b, 1407c, 1409a, 1410, 1413, 1427, 1428, 1477, 1480, 1506, 1510, 1516, 1517, 1521b, 1537, 1538, 1561, 1565, 1573, 1576, 1591, 1671, 1722, 1728, 1743, 1754, 1777, 1786, 1789, 1790a, 1795, 1820, 1826, 1864, 1873, 1897, 1898, 1958, 1961, 1971, 1977, 1981, 1998, 1999, 2000, 2002a, 2003, 2005, 2006, 2024, 2042, 2081, 2108b, 2111, 2146, 2158a, 2174, 2182.

IV. GEOGRAPHICAL INDEX OF PERIODICALS PUBLISHED OUTSIDE OF LONDON

The italicized figures in this index refer to periodicals of which no issues are known to be available in American libraries.

ENGLAND

Aldstone. *1017.*

Aylesbury. *1038.*

Bath. 53a, *1043, 1043a, 1044, 1044a, 1044b, 1044c, 1045, 1046, 1046a, 1307, 1970.*

Birmingham. 27, 848, *1052a, 1053.*

Boston. *1057b, 1513.*

Brentford. 773.

Brighton. *1059a.*

Bristol. 57, 916, *1021, 1043b, 1046b, 1056, 1060, 1060a, 1061, 1062, 1062a, 1062b, 1062c, 1062d, 1063, 1064, 1065, 1065a, 1065b, 1066, 1139, 1307a, 1314, 1316a, 1711, 1972, 2182.*

Bury St. Edmunds. 11, *1084a, 2023a.*

Cambridge. 89, *1095a, 1095b, 1096, 1809.*

Canterbury. 349, 350, 351, *1365, 1480c, 1481.*

Carlisle. 806.

Chelmsford. 102, *1722.*

Chester. 3, 190, *1105, 1105a, 1106, 1107, 1345.*

Cirencester. *1115a, 1116.*

Colchester. *1284.*

Coventry. 341, 343, *1172a, 1172b, 1550a, 2089.*

Deptford. 849.

Derby. *1191b, 1192, 1193, 1193a, 1399c.*

Doncaster. *1205a.*

Durham. *1235a.*

Exeter. *1059, 1296, 1296a, 1296b, 1297, 1297a, 1297b, 1308, 1330, 1472, 1902, 1910.*

Gainsborough. 138.

Gloucester. 284, *1164, 1384a, 1384b.*

Hereford. *1072, 1407d.*

Huddersfield. 78.

Hull. *1427, 1428.*

Ipswich. 336, *1457, 1459.*

Kendal. *1015, 1480a, 1480b.*
Leeds. 365, 366, 539, *1503.*
Leicester. 367, *1504a, 1504b.*
Lewes. 846.
Lincoln. 842a, *1508a.*
Liverpool. 620, *1347, 1514, 1515, 1515a, 1515b, 1516, 1516a, 2023, 2171.*
Ludlow. *1551.*
Lynn Regis. *1181.*
Maidenhead. 48.
Maidstone. *1560, 1561, 1562.*
Manchester. 425, *1399a, 1562a, 1562b, 1563, 1563a, 1564, 1564a, 1565, 1566, 1904a, 2128a, 2168.*
Margate. *1365.*
Marlborough. *1570b.*
Middlewich. *1976.*
Newark. *1083, 1491, 1742a.*
Newcastle-upon-Tyne. 371, 383, 597, 598, 599, 600, 647, 806, *1285a, 1556a, 1583, 1743, 1743a, 1744, 1744a, 1745, 1745a, 1746, 1780a, 1780b, 1912.*
Newmarket. *1241.*
Northampton. 629, *1778a, 1779, 1779a.*
Norwich. 85, *1341, 1777, 1778, 1784a, 1785, 1785a, 1785b, 1786, 1787, 1788, 1788a, 1954a, 2133.*
Nottingham. *1790, 1790a, 1791, 1792, 1793, 1793a, 2118a.*
Oxford. 331, 386, 466, 652, 664, 665, 666, 667, 844, 855, *1052, 1161, 1827, 2026, 2039.*
Plymouth. *1881, 1882.*
Portsmouth. *1394a, 1394b, 1898, 1899.*
Preston. *1072a, 1904b, 1904c, 2062a.*
Reading. 7, 296, 775, *1826.*
St. Ives. *1963, 1964, 1965.*
Salisbury. 139, 805, *1196, 1968a, 1969.*
Scarborough. 808.
Sheffield. *1997b, 1997c.*
Sherborne. 924, 937, *1176a, 1998.*
Shrewsbury. *1971, 2000.*
Southampton. 294, *1394a, 1572.*
Stamford. 842a, *1544a.*
Stockton-on-Tees. *2020.*
Stourport. 382.

Tunbridge Wells. 898.
Whitehaven. 158, *1179, 1180*.
Whitby. *1022, 2166*.
Winchester. 294, *1395, 2171b*.
Windsor. 540.
Wolverhampton. *2171a*.
Worcester. 964, *2153a*.
York. 861, 968, *1681, 1781, 1915, 2015, 2173a, 2174, 2174a, 2174b, 2175, 2176, 2177, 2178*.

SCOTLAND

Aberdeen. 1, *1001, 1002, 1003, 1004, 1094, 1095, 1782*.
Arbroath. *1024a*.
Berwick-on-Tweed. 48a.
Dumfries. *1208, 1229, 1230*.
Dundee. *1127, 1231, 1232, 1232a, 1233, 1234, 1780, 2140*.
Edinburgh. 5, 25, 42, 70, 86, 87, 104, 106, 191, 192, 193, 194, 195, 196, 197, 198, 199, 200, 201, 202, 229, 233, 272, 280, 414, 435, 437, 476, 544, 554, 630, 631, 692, 715, 731, 787, 799, 812, 814, 815, 818, 851, 869, 914, 932, *1050, 1091, 1092, 1119, 1128, 1138, 1141, 1147, 1242, 1243, 1244, 1245, 1246, 1247, 1248, 1249, 1250, 1251, 1252, 1253, 1254, 1255, 1256, 1257, 1258, 1259, 1333, 1368, 1384, 1414, 1421, 1485, 1505, 1571a, 1603, 1665, 1685, 1748, 1761, 1784, 1799, 1803, 1832, 1842, 1904d, 1937, 1961, 1981, 1983, 1985, 1985a, 1990, 2056, 2111, 2128, 2129, 2134, 2150*.
Glasgow. 281, 282, 283, 936a, *1178, 1298, 1373, 1373a, 1374, 1375, 1376, 1377, 1378, 1379, 1380, 1381, 1382, 1802, 1895, 1980, 2049, 2098*.
Greenock. *1010*.
Kelso. *1071, 1480*.
Leith. *1655*.
Montrose. *1510*.
Perth. *1093, 1866*.

WALES

Carmarthen. *2071*.
Mold. 897.

IRELAND

Athlone. *1035a, 1035b*.
Belfast. 45, *1047, 1512, 1671, 1783, 2074a*.
Cashel. *1542b*.
Clonmel. *1407c*.
Cork. 135, 603, *1097, 1157a, 1157b, 1157c, 1157d, 1157e, 1157f, 1157g, 1157h, 1157i, 1157j, 1157k, 1157l, 1157m, 1372b, 1399b, 1409a, 1410a, 1435a, 1461, 1462, 1582a, 1725, 1996a*.

Drogheda. *1207a, 1207b.*

Dublin. 17, 22, 110, 150, 184, 185, 186, 187, 188, 189, 225, 241, 301, 322, 333, 338, 342, 372, 375, 388, 433, 453, 611, 744, 748, 761, 767, 807, 824, 875, 878, 900, 904, 920, 930, *1006b, 1019a, 1101, 1165a, 1168c, 1182, 1187a, 1197, 1200b, 1203a, 1204, 1208b, 1208c, 1209, 1209a, 1210, 1211, 1212, 1213, 1214, 1214a, 1215, 1215a, 1216, 1216a, 1216b, 1216c, 1217, 1218, 1218a, 1218b, 1218c, 1219, 1219b, 1220, 1221, 1222, 1222b, 1222c, 1223, 1224, 1224a, 1224b, 1225, 1225a, 1226, 1227, 1227a, 1228, 1259c, 1286, 1288, 1290a, 1299, 1313, 1321, 1321a, 1322, 1323a, 1323b, 1324, 1325, 1346a, 1348a, 1349, 1353, 1357, 1372, 1383, 1397, 1410, 1434, 1439, 1441, 1448a, 1499, 1520a, 1532a, 1542a, 1556, 1575, 1576, 1629a, 1675, 1676a, 1713, 1733a, 1741, 1742, 1751, 1764, 1772a, 1820, 1822, 1836, 1875, 1880, 1900, 1901, 1916, 1918, 1922, 1923, 1932a, 1946, 1954, 1958, 1966, 1997d, 2001a, 2021, 2025, 2038a, 2048, 2050a, 2056a, 2073a, 2075, 2075a, 2083, 2084, 2086, 2100, 2101, 2103, 2104, 2131, 2136, 2142, 2159c, 2179.*

Dungannon. *1235.*
Ennis. *1127a, 1277a.*
Galway. *1570a.*
Kilkenny. 239.
Limerick. 422, *1506, 1507, 1507a, 1507b, 1507c, 1507d, 1508, 1735, 2002b.*
Londonderry. *1521b.*
Loughrea. *1138a, 1138b.*
Monaghan. *1385.*
Mullingar. *2158a.*
Sligo. *2002a.*
Strabane. *1754, 2021a, 2021b.*
Tralee. *1481a.*
Waterford. *1096a, 1735b, 1997a, 2108a, 2108c, 2109, 2109a.*
Wexford. *2159a, 2159b.*

CHANNEL ISLANDS
St. Hélier. *1344, 1554.*
St. Peter Port. *1343.*

NETHERLANDS
Amsterdam. *1153, 1155.*
Haarlem. 117, 293, *1398, 1399.*
The Hague. 745, 746, *1152.*

www.ingramcontent.com/pod-product-compliance
Lightning Source LLC
Chambersburg PA
CBHW021405290426
44108CB00010B/390